MARKET

SQUARE

MARKET SQUARE

A HISTORY OF

THE MOST DEMOCRATIC

PLACE ON EARTH

SECOND EDITION

JACK NEELY

This book is printed on acid-free paper.

Cataloging-in-Publication Data

Neely, Jack. Market square: a history of the most democratic place on earth / Jack Neely.

ISBN 10: 0-57800-305-8
ISBN 13: 978-0-578-00305-4 (pbk.)

1. Knoxville (Tenn.)—History.
2. Knoxville (Tenn.)—Social conditions.
3. Knoxville (Tenn.)—Urban development.

This book is typeset in Adobe Minion Pro, an Adobe Original designed in 1990 by Robert Slimbach, and released as an Open Type font in 2000. Its design is inspired by classical, old style typefaces of the late Renaissance, a period of elegant, beautiful, and highly readable type designs.

CONTENTS

W riting this book has been a maddening privilege. A privilege just because I still haven't gotten tired of learning that so many disparate people and events could be so intimately associated with one small patch of the planet; maddening because, as becomes more obvious with each week's research, it's a story too rich and complicated ever to be told thoroughly in one book, or probably in one lifetime. Though I spent more than a year of spare weekends and evenings on this project, I never reached a point when I felt that it was done. Minutes before the final deadline for the final draft, I was still learning new things, adding surprising new details. Market Square, which today counts 37 addresses of old buildings, many or most of them replacing former buildings that had their own individual histories, has been home to more than 1,000 businesses. Each business had its own employees, sometimes dozens of them, and each had perhaps hundreds or even thousands of customers, many of whom had fond or funny memories of Market Square. In addition, countless thousands of farmers sold their produce on Market Square, either out in the open or in the long-gone Market House. That's not to mention residents—people were living on Market Square as early as the Civil War—or the 60-odd years that Market Square was the seat of city government, as well as the home of the jail, firehall, and police headquarters. Many good stories won't be told in this book.

This is not a work of nostalgia, by the way. I could easily have filled the book with memories of the Market House in its waning years, or, for that matter, of the Market Square Mall era, but this is intended to be a roughly comprehensive history of Market Square, 155 years at this writing. Because people have only in recent decades seen the value in saving and organizing information about this city, the last third, approximately, of the Square's history is much better documented than the first two-thirds. I could have included much more about recent decades, but did not want to alter the pace of the narrative to favor the well-documented era, especially if it meant sacrificing some of the stories from the earlier eras which are much less well known and, to me at least, fascinating. Those who would like to know more about Market Square after 1950 will find lots more information in the public library, in research projects like Media High's student documentaries, sponsored by the public library, and in the memories of hundreds of people still living.

I do want to thank several people and institutions without whom this book would have been impossible, or very difficult. The Knox County Public Library System, both in general and as the parent company of the wonderful Calvin McClung Historical Collection, including director Steve Cotham, whom I interviewed for this book, as well as Ted Behr, Sally Polhemus and all their able and cheerful assistants; the East Tennessee Historical Society, especially director Cherel Henderson; the Knox County Archives, specifically Doris Martinson; Metropolitan Planning Commission staffer Anne Bennett; Kim Trent, of Knox Heritage; her colleague Hollie Cook, who took the lead in researching photographs and illustrations; independent researchers like Ron Allen, Robert McGuinness, Wes Morgan, Bradley Reeves, and Louisa Trott, whose painstaking research, most of it on file at the McClung Collection, saved me hours of work and turned up some interesting details I would have been unlikely to find on my own; and the thousands of politicians and businessmen, architects and novelists, over the course of a century and a half, who, whether deliberately or not, left some record of the Square as they knew it. I also conducted interviews with several interesting witnesses of the Square in the 20th century, including Lawrence Brichetto, Joe Bell, Randy Mansfield, Kevin Niceley, and several current merchants on the Square who found a clue for me here or there. And I'd like especially to thank Theresa Pepin, one of Knoxville's most talented organists and gardeners, who volunteered as a research assistant for several weeks when the sheer volume of work seemed overwhelming, just because she thought this project served the public good; I can only hope she wasn't completely misguided about that prospect.

Various resources at McClung, too numerous to list, would include Knoxville City Directories; the McClung Collection possesses an apparently complete set of all those published from 1859 until the present day.

Much of the text, and most of the quoted material, came directly from the newspapers cited—the *Register*, the *Whig*, the *Chronicle*, the *Tribune*, the *Journal*, the *Sentinel*, the *News-Sentinel*—which are all available through the library on microfilm. A lengthy review of an index to the period from 1854 to 1890 was helpful, and turned up several details of which I was previously unaware, as was a brief history of Market Square, read into the minutes of City Council. The McClung's subject files were also helpful, as were their extensive biographical files. A bibliography for this book would have to include two books which still stand as

Two East Tennessee farm boys with their prized ox (see p. 103). McClung Historical Collection.

the old and new testaments of local history, *The French Broad – Holston Country*, Mary Utopia Rothrock, editor; and *Heart of the Valley*, Lucile Deaderick, editor. My copies of both are visibly more worn after completing this book. Concerning the Civil War, in which Market Square played an interesting part, I referred to the Civil War histories *Divided Loyalties*, by Digby Seymour, and the recent book *Lincolnites and Rebels*, by Robert Tracy McKenzie, as well as contemporary sources.

Beyond research, I'd like to thank John Craig, of the Market Square District Association, whose love of the Square and its history prompted him to buy a building on the property and, later, propose this project; Scot Danforth, director of UT Press, who offered valuable advice at every stage of preparation; and Todd Duren, the art director, with whom I once worked on a book called *The Marble City*, (as was also the case with Scot, come to think of it). Finally, I need to thank my housemates, Janet and Rebecca, for putting up with my absences, and more so my presences.

Interior of hardware store on Market Square: four clerks, ca. 1890, pose with a display of knives and scissors. McClung Historical Collection.

Market Square is a paradox, which is at the heart of its appeal, and of its complexity as a research subject. In some respects, no place in Knoxville has changed less. With the exception of a few churchyards, hardly any spot in Knoxville has served the same purpose—the sale of fresh produce, in Market Square's case—for more than 150 years. But no spot has served nearly as many purposes, either; the list of things that have happened on Market Square is much longer than the list of things that have never happened there. The two-acre rectangle pictured before the Civil War as the commercial center of a struggling town of 3,000—when citizens were arguing about whether slavery was worth going to war about, and wondering whether the railroad was ever going to arrive—still seems central and important to a 21st-century city with a metropolitan population approaching one million. And somehow, old Market Square is still a place to see new things.

CHAPTER 1

A Neat and Durable Market House....

An Antebellum Real-estate Scheme, a Farmers'
Market, and a Gunpowder Magazine

There may be no two acres in America that resist easy categorization like Knoxville's Market Square.

It's a place that has been, from its earliest origins, a magnet for country people, farmers who came to sell their products. But in its density and diversity and round-the-clock liveliness, it was often the most urban spot in East Tennessee. It was the locus of a concentration of saloons, and also the concentration of the efforts of the Women's Christian Temperance Union, who long maintained their daily vigil there. It was the most culturally diverse spot in town, offering a livelihood to heavily accented immigrants from several foreign countries, and at times, it was also the easiest place to find homespun rural white folk. The institution began before the Civil War as a canny real-estate scheme by two very young, wealthy investors, but came to be Knoxville's most public spot, a place that all citizens felt a sense of propriety, as if each man, woman, and child owned a piece of Market Square themselves.

It was a place that seemed old-fashioned for much of its history, and sometimes shabbily so, but it has always been, dependably, a place to find the new and modern, a place that introduced to Knoxville exotica like tropical fruits and pasta and carbonated soft drinks in the 1870s, and astonishing new consumer technology in the Internet age.

In its first 150 years, it has seen riots, symphony concerts, bar fights, temperance lectures, art exhibitions, seances, bear barbecues, the storage of military ammunition, and, always, the sales of honest farmers' produce.

In its earliest days, it hosted farmers, slaves, secessionists, Whigs, Irishmen, Democrats, bowlers, Union troops. Over the next century and a half, it saw more than any city block's share of prostitutes, suffragists, socialists, jazzmen, barbecue chefs, politicians, vagrants, fiddlers, poets, firemen, dobroists, prisoners, German bakers, Italian confectioners, society ladies, hoboes.

The history of Market Square is the history of America. In one way or another, its plot reflects almost all the history of the United States since 1853—albeit in a sometimes kaleidoscopic prism. In several astonishing ways, it also intersects with major figures in American history. A man who changed American journalism began his career on Market Square. A U.S. Treasury Secretary who did much to launch our nation's Federal Reserve system once spent time on Market Square—as a prisoner. A man who popularized the string band, leading the way not only for country music, but also rock'n'roll, played some of his earliest shows on Market Square. And, 20 years later, a major recording company discovered the King of Rock 'n' Roll by way of an odd incident on Market Square.

Some big cities boast that there's a particular corner or plaza where, if you stay there long enough, you'll see everybody in the world. It's not true anywhere, of course, but you could almost believe such a claim on Market Square. This writer has, merely by the serendipity of being on Market Square at the right time, met novelist Norman Mailer, aspiring governor Phil Bredesen, controversial author Jim Kunstler, "Prairie Home Companion" truckdriver Russ Ringsak. Other Knoxvilians I know have happened to meet, shopping or having a meal on the Square, performers David Byrne, Tom Waits, or Elvis Costello.

William Jennings Bryan spoke there. Duke Ellington performed there. Ingrid Bergman planted a tree there. Henri Cartier-Bresson took a notable photograph of it. Luciano Pavarotti spent a night in the small hotel there, the same place that Patricia Neal has called her Knoxville home. Ronald Reagan campaigned there. Carl Sandburg visited it often, and defended it from those who wanted to change it. Norman Mailer praised it. James Agee, Cormac McCarthy, David Madden, and others described it in rich detail, in novels.

Through it all, Market Square has served a unique, and vital, purpose in Knoxville. For much of its history, the city has been barely a city, often better described as a balkanized jumble of neighborhoods and non-neighborhoods, factories, schools, and churches, a confederacy of rivalrous urban factions. Unlike most Knoxville locations, Market Square was always familiar to the whole community, black and white, rich and poor, old and young, city and country. For long-time locals who claimed to know everybody, Market Square was the only place where they dependably encountered strangers.

If an immigrant who lived in an alley shack were looking for good deals on potatoes or an exotic spice for an Old World recipe, he'd first look on Market Square. If a Republican matron were serious about the quality of ingredients served at her debutante party, she would be obliged to visit Market Square; it offered a greater variety of fresh ingredients than any other grocery in the region.

The mixture of humanity in Market Square was perhaps more diverse than any shopping mall is today. Shopping malls require, at least, access to a car; Market Square never did. It was connected to every residence in Knoxville by sidewalks; the streetcar ran by it, on Union. People came by foot, by mule cart, by streetcar, by chauffeured automobile.

Though at its founding, its location was on an outer fringe of a suddenly growing town's business district, the city grew around Market Square as a cell grows around its nucleus. By the time it was 20 years old, Market Square was center of town, as today it still very much looks like the center of downtown Knoxville.

It's hard to imagine a Knoxville without Market Square. In some ways, it's hard to imagine an America without it. Market Square transcended its original role as a farmers' market to be a sort of cultural engine: it played a role in the development of country music, objective journalism, maybe even the American novel. Many worthy things Americans take for granted have started on Market Square, or gotten a critical boost.

The history of Market Square is the history of America as seen through a single lens.

∿

Even before Columbus, it was probably never a bad place to be, this relatively flat spot in the middle of an obscure plateau, convenient to fresh creeks but far enough back from the river bluff that any inhabitant wouldn't be seen unless he wished to be. Mosquitoes and gnats weren't as bad here as they were in lower-lying areas, and it has almost certainly never flooded.

There's no evidence that indigenous Americans ever lived precisely here, though several centuries ago, some Indians lived within a 20-minute sprint through the woods. White and black people began living near the site during the period of the Articles of Confederation, when the region was still plausibly part of North Carolina, or, more theoretically, part of an abortive state called Franklin. In 1786, a log stockade with a grist mill appeared not far to the southeast; a strong man could stand here and throw a shilling and hit the original White's Fort. The patriarch of the place was a militia officer named James White, and within five or six years, he had something to do with putting together a town of sorts that appeared, rather suddenly, as a territorial capital with a few hundred residents, all living roughly between this patch and the river bluff.

In 1796, maybe 200 yards south by southeast of this spot, the economically marginal but politically substantial town hosted a gathering of men who convened to form a new state called Tennessee.

The original layout of the new city of Knoxville did not even include this patch; the riverbluff town stretched only as far north as what's now Clinch Avenue. This section became part of "Knoxville" in 1815, when the village incorporated itself formally. One of their first orders of business was to establish a market house.

~

Knoxville was born twice. Founded during the first term of President Washington and named for his Secretary of War, the first Knoxville existed mainly as the administrative capital of the Southwestern Territory. The village, clustered near the river bluff, was more important than it ever looked. It boasted hardly any industry except for some creekside mills, tiny whiskey distilleries, and a printing shop: Tennessee's first newspaper, its first law books, and its first novels, were published in Knoxville. Though hardly more than a village in size, and with little architecture worth noticing, it was a village of attorneys, soldiers, and politicians. It was an isolated but distinguished enclave of hard-working opportunists, and despite all appearances, the capital of one of the most politically dynamic states in the new republic. All Americans who read the newspapers, as well as readers of some British and French publications, had at least heard of Knoxville. Several U.S. senators, a significant presidential contender, a couple of diplomats, and at least one cabinet member lived in Knoxville, a town that seemed to draw ambitious young men.

In 1815, the town incorporated to become a proper city, with a mayor and board of aldermen and a budget, and defined itself more expansively, taking up the entirety of the plateau, including this patch which was probably by then used as a farmer's field. In 1819, the schismatic Second Presbyterian Church set up near here, at Clinch and Prince, with an odd little brick chapel and a graveyard that stretched over to what would be Union Avenue. Its first pastor was Isaac Anderson, a progressive-minded reformer who, during his time as minister here, founded Maryville College.

The first attempt to establish a market house in Knoxville was likely the victim of awful timing. In 1816, when Knoxville was still clustered along the river bluff, the city built a market house of some sort on Main Street, a block west of the court-house. By one account, it was tiny, only 26 feet by 18 feet, and open only one day a week. During its brief existence, Knoxville languished as other cities much better situated to take advantages of the steam-driven wonders of the day, the riverboat and the railroad, thrived and outpaced Knoxville, leaving the town of hardly more than 1,000 more isolated by comparison. The town lost its state-capital status to points west, and with that, its original reason for being. In 1823, Knoxville tore down its market house, and sold its property. To cynics, the solution might have seemed fitting for the whole disappointing town.

Though Knoxville eventually gained limited access to steamboat traffic, for the next 30 years, the city languished, almost forgotten to a generation unacquainted with its heroic youth. The mid-19th century was a more practical era of industry and commerce. Still, with riverboat access, the promise of railroad projects making their way slowly through the mountains, the sad old town grew, if anemically, from just over 1,000 in 1820 to just over 2,000, 30 years later in 1850.

In the early 1850s, when the idea of Market Square was first conceived, Knoxville was a starkly different place from the political village James White had known: less powerful, maybe less famous, but a larger and an increasingly business-minded town. Calling a town of fewer than 3,000 citizens a "city" was not necessarily an exaggeration by the standards of the antebellum South, where most people lived in the raw country. Despite its ill fortunes, the town still made a regular appearance on national maps.

But by 1850, it had long been too clear that the wonders of the age, especially in transportation technology and the exciting new potentials of steam power, had left the city alone in its remote mountain-surrounded valley. Across America's dynamic new networks of steamboats and railroads, Knoxville hardly existed. Much of the year, riverboats had difficulty with the hazardous Upper Tennessee River, and despite the political encouragement and investment of progressive Knoxvillians for a quarter century, no railroad had yet made it across the mountains and valleys into the old town. Knoxville's economy had suffered for years as other, once-smaller cities better situated for steamboat or rail transportation, like Nashville, Chattanooga, and suddenly, a presumptuous new town with the exalted name of "Atlanta," leapt ahead. Knoxville did boast a small college on its outskirts—but East Tennessee College, later University, was significant only for the few who sent their sons there. The once-proud frontier capital seemed to be lapsing into economic oblivion.

Knoxville was on the brink of its rebirth, this time, perhaps less famously, but much more sustainably, as a place of commerce and industry. Market Square emerged with it, as an emblem of a reborn city.

Among the first proofs of sustainable life in the town came in 1844, when the state chose to establish a school for the deaf, also known as the Deaf and Dumb Asylum, in Knoxville. It was, in some ways, more important than the university, which at the time had no statewide status. The new school for the deaf was the only statewide institution in town. It even had a progressive national reputation, as one of only eight schools for the deaf in the United States.

When the deaf school's permanent home rose grandly in 1848, a rare and substantial-looking Greek Revival building with steep, temple-like steps and Ionic columns, at what was then the northwestern corner of Knoxville, its existence was a strong vote of confidence in the previously tenuous future of the village.

Directly between it and the business section of town were some fields, including the peculiar plot that is the subject of our story.

∼

Knoxville in 1853 seemed like the sort of place where something was about to happen, even if it hadn't quite yet, and no one could guess whether what would happen would be good or bad. It was home to future congressman and ambassador Horace Maynard, author and Attorney-General William Gibbs McAdoo, and author George Washington Harris, just beginning to be known in New York papers for his loony fictional creation, Sut Lovingood. Most conspicuous of Knoxville's many characters was "Parson" William G. Brownlow, the firebrand editor from Virginia, by way of Jonesborough. Brownlow had arrived here five years earlier, and it was here that he would become one of the most powerful, admired, influential, and despised figures in the South.

As small as it was, the city supported three newspapers, including two politically combative weeklies, the *Knoxville Register* and Brownlow's paper, the *Knoxville Whig*. Before journalism boasted any pretense of objectivity, those two papers represented the Democrats and, of course, the Whigs. The two major parties coexisted in Knoxville in an uncomfortable standoff. No blanket assumptions apply very well to the political beliefs of the average Knoxvillian of the antebellum generation. It was an almost rabidly political town, frequently visited by national political figures like occasional presidential contenders Sam Houston and John Bell, its passions stoked by Brownlow's editorial vitriol; along with his several rivals, the Parson made a vicious art of the political insult. But it's unlikely that any modern American, even one who admires the antebellum South, would find a comfortable place to sit in 1850s Knoxville. Political affiliation was much about slavery (in Tennessee, both parties were for it), fear of Catholics, fear of alcohol consumption, resentment over the dying Whig Party, and, especially, personal spite. Essays published in Knoxville papers of the 1850s can still elicit a chill or an uneasy squirm.

Still, fresh winds were blowing, and at least some of Knoxville's stubborn technological deficiencies were soon to be corrected, all at about the same time. The old capital was changing in fresh new ways few could have anticipated.

Dominated by the protestant Scots-Irish for half a century, Knoxville was diversifying. Suddenly you could hear different accents on Gay Street, as immigrants from Ireland and Switzerland and Germany arrived by the scores, many of them by boat. So many Irish had arrived to work on the railroad project that there was talk of building a Catholic church in town, a development opposed by Methodist firebrand Brownlow and some others of the national anti-immigrant Know-Nothing Party, which was in the midst of a brief, and weird, moment of dominance in Knoxville.

At times, Knoxville could already seem citylike. Because its corporate limits were defined, strictly, by the boundaries of what we now know as Downtown, all those 3,000 people counted as Knoxvillians in the mid-1850s lived downtown. Judged in terms of residents per acre, Knoxville's urban density in the 1850s was greater than it would be in the 21st century. Beyond those tight corporate boundaries, Knox County was home to about 20,000 people, and hence one of the population centers of antebellum Tennessee. In 1853 many Knox Countians who didn't live in Knoxville proper still lived so close to town they could smell the coal smoke. It was too many people for any one person to know, and every day strangers passed each other on the wooden sidewalks.

The shape of the city itself was changing. For its first 60 years, Knoxville's economic and cultural life was focused in one place, crowded along the bluff close to the river: the city's hotels, saloons, newspaper offices, and courthouse were clustered near Cumberland and Main. Even though river traffic was undependable, it was the avenue by which most freight arrived in mid-19th-century Knoxville, most of it via the Prince Street Wharf. It was hard enough to get freight up the hill; it wouldn't make sense to establish retail businesses much farther away.

Thus, until 1852, Knoxville's northern city limits had been at Vine Avenue, only two blocks north of Wall. A major northern annexation that year seemed destined to shift the center of town away from the river north, perhaps toward the area of Union and Wall. By then, businessmen knew that when the railroad arrived, it wouldn't bother to climb up to old Knoxville, up on the bluff, but would arrive more practically, on rails built along the low flood plain just to the north of the business district.

The street that would later be known as Market was called, for no memorable reason, Prince Street. The most central of the north-south streets, and the one with the best connection to the riverfront wharf, Prince was considered Knoxville's main commercial corridor. By 1850, though, it was clear that its neighbor to the east, Gay Street, already counted perhaps three times as many businesses, and had, for whatever reason, assumed the role of Knoxville's main street. In 1853, the city commenced paving both Gay and Prince, for the first time, with cobblestones.

Prince Street earned some improvements about that time, when a contractor rounded off its riverside end, which had previously been, more or less, a cliff. The urban part of town ended, though, when it got up to Union.

The area past Prince Street's dead end, just north of the Second Presbyterian's churchyard, once considered the northern outskirts of town, remained, mainly, a field. In the early 1850s, it was a field used mainly for growing corn and wheat. Late in the century, popular attorney and civic leader William Henderson would recall that, as a boy growing up in Knoxville in the 1840s and early '50s, he would hunt wild rabbits on the property.

But by the 1850s, with the new school for the deaf, suddenly the city's grandest building, on the far northwest side of town, and the railroad and new industry contemplated beyond that, it was clear that development in the empty spaces within was inevitable.

It wasn't obvious, though, that Knoxville in 1853 needed a Market Square, or a Market House, regardless of its location. Knoxville's citizens who were interested in farmers' produce already had plenty of access to it, via the farmers who parked their wagons along Gay or Prince Streets on any given weekday. Many could have bought or traded directly from their neighbors. Dozens of farms were within walking distance of every residence in Knoxville. However, perhaps like an enclosed shopping mall or a performing-arts center would be for cities of a later era, in 1850s America, a Market House was an undeniable symbol of a thriving city. All the great cities of the South—Charleston, Baltimore, New Orleans—had prominent market houses. Knoxville may have needed it, to begin with, as a symbol that the city and its population were to be taken seriously.

What happened in that odd remnant of a wheat field in the middle of town was thanks to the efforts of two ambitious young men. They were brothers in law who both sound like the sort of young men you would have noticed, when they walked into a room—and perhaps with some anxiety. Both were known for their business aspirations, their surprising energy, and their violent tempers. One would later serve in Confederate Congress, where he would be known for his propensity for fistfights with fellow legislators. The other, known for his vengeful nature and his proclivity for gunplay, would be shot to death in a bizarre showdown on Gay Street, an incident so darkly comical it gained national headlines and a sarcastic mention in a popular book by Mark Twain.

The older of the two was William Swan. He was born in 1821, but little is known about his youth. Some sources hold that he was from East Tennessee, others that he was born in Alabama, just months after that state's founding. He had graduated from East Tennessee College on the Hill when he was only 17, and quickly developed a reputation as an attorney—by the mid-1840s, he had offices on Gay Street but did business all over East Tennessee—and as a writer and editor of political and legal documents. By 1853, Swan was at work getting out a compilation of recent cases argued before the Tennessee Supreme Court. It was a subject of which Swan had some knowledge; though he was only 32, he was that year coming to the end of his term as state attorney general.

A major speculator in the burgeoning suburban residential area on the east side of town—we might call him a "developer" today—Swan lived on the promising east side, in a house overlooking a bend of First Creek, called Mayfair. Some chroniclers remarked with wonder that a man with so much Tennessee land owned no slaves. That fact would be perhaps even more remarkable considering that he committed much of his career to advocating the right to own slaves. It may have been more a matter of reputation than fact; Knox County records suggest that Swan at least occasionally owned a slave or two.

Swan was also a man of his times, in good ways and bad. He was waistcoat-deep in all the modern technology. He had an interest in the long-delayed, long frustrated project to connect Knoxville to the rest of the country by railroad—he made an ambitious proposal to enclose the railroad in Knoxville within a tunnel, which would allow for development above it. He also had an interest in natural gas. Gas street lights were the modern thing, and the word was that Knoxville would soon have them, thanks to the efforts of Swan and his partner in that project, another young, ambitious fellow, William Churchwell. Then Congressman from Tennessee's second district, Churchwell was not quite 30 years old, and was a Democrat. We can be confident that Churchwell did not guess he would be the last Democrat to hold that particular seat in U.S. Congress—until, at least, the 21st century.

Swan and Churchwell would convince city fathers to give them exclusive right to light the city with gas in 1854. The first gas streetlights illuminated the cobblestone and mud streets of Knoxville in 1856.

A few years earlier, Swan had married a young woman named Margaret Mabry, daughter of a well-established West Knox County family based near Concord. The Mabrys were an ambitious brood: one of Margaret's brothers was a state legislator. Another brother, five years Swan's junior, was a handsome, aspiring young business-man named Joseph Mabry. Mabry had recently made an advantageous marriage, himself, to Laura Churchwell, sister of the congressman.

Together, Swan and Mabry owned a great deal of land, much of it on the east side of town, and did much buying and selling of it in the 1850s. By early 1853, their joint real-estate ambitions drew them much closer in to the city itself. One of Knoxville's biggest landowners of the era was Dr. John Fouché, a prominent local physician who would soon serve as a city alderman. He owned much of the land on the northern half of town.

The only known image of William Swan (1821–1869), co-developer of Market Square. A Confederate partisan, Swan co-published a secessionist journal and served in the CSA's Congress in Richmond. Though a former mayor and a vigorous developer of Knoxville in the 1850s, Swan moved to Memphis after the war and died in his 40s. Courtesy of McClung Historical Collection.

Swan and Mabry offered Fouché $1,000 an acre for 11 acres, including the wheat field at the north end of Prince Street. On March 15, 1853, as a duo, they bought the tract, the largest part of which was between Gay Street and Walnut. The total price for the whole was $11,015.62½. (The U.S. Mint still manufactured half-cent pieces in 1853.)

As the ink on that document dried, Swan and Mabry approached the city of Knoxville, then led by Mayor George McNutt White, grandson of Knoxville's founder, with a proposition. Mabry and Swan would donate 43,750 square feet—slightly more than an acre—to the city, according to the original indenture document, "to be used and enjoyed by [the mayor and aldermen] for the purpose of constructing thereon a market house, to be used as such, and for no other use and purpose whatsoever." A final clause would keep mayors and City Council members awake at night a century later: "Upon abandonment of the ground for the uses aforesaid, the same with any tenements of buildings thereon, shall revert to the said Swan and Mabry, their heirs and assigns." Attorneys of the TV age would pore over those words carefully.

The original gift was a rectangle of land 125 feet wide, and stretching 350 feet north of Union Avenue; it didn't cover the entirety of what would later be known as Market Square, but about three-quarters of its length. About two-thirds of its width was on the Gay Street side of Prince Street.

"In consideration of said conveyance, the said Mayor and Aldermen agree on their part to erect a neat and durable Market House on said ground, of sufficient dimensions to answer fully the purpose for which it is intended, and to have the same completed and in use, under and by virtue of such market regulations as are usual and customary in towns and cities having market houses, on or before the first day of January next…."

In this donation, Swan and Mabry were hardly philanthropists. The two gave the city just the central acre of their recent eleven-acre purchase. They reckoned, correctly, that the other ten acres would gain in value due to their proximity to a successful city-built market house. Their gift stipulated that the city build an amenity for the city which would be, especially, an amenity for their adjacent property.

That property-value motive might have been behind many of Swan's initiatives of previous years. The proximity of the amenities of a modern mid-19th century city, like gas lighting, railroad connections—and a public market house—couldn't hurt the value of one's own investments.

At the time of the gift, developer Swan was only 32 years old. Mabry was 27.

~

The deed was dated 21 March 1853, the beginning of spring. Franklin Pierce, the Democrat opposed by most of Tennessee's voters, had just been inaugurated presi-

The inimitable Joseph Mabry. At age 27 the ambitious young developer co-donated a patch of his land to the city for the purpose of building a permanent market house. Mabry's fortunes fluctuated through war and recession until his sudden death, alongside his attorney son, in a bizarre gunfight on Gay Street in 1882. Courtesy of Tennessee State Museum. Portrait by local artist Samuel Shaver.

dent. Though a former senator from New Hampshire, Pierce was more committed to the perpetuation of slavery than his opponent, war hero Winfield Scott. Still, Tennessee had been one of only four states in the nation, and the southernmost of those four, whose voters had preferred Scott. Some Knoxvillians, including Parson Brownlow, were disgruntled with both candidates. Even locally, bitter analysis of the election overshadowed the scant coverage of the construction of a market house. Brownlow favored the lame-duck President Millard Fillmore, who had failed to earn the Whig nomination; just after the election, Brownlow started a local campaign to resurrect Fillmore as a candidate in '56, advertised in each issue of the *Whig*.

The city forged ahead with the business at hand. A committee composed of three particularly prominent and interesting aldermen led the Market Square effort. Among them were newspaperman James C. Moses, future mayor James C. Luttrell, and physician Benjamin R. Strong. Early Knoxvillians were better traveled than is sometimes assumed, and many had experience with successful urban amenities. Alderman Moses, for example, had spent his early adulthood in Boston, where he was surely familiar with Faneuil Hall, the famous farmers' market which became the commercial and cultural center of that city. On May 12, the city ordered construction to proceed.

The ever-practical Board of Aldermen apparently coupled the Market House project in the city budget with some road improvements, to macadamize Gay Street and Cumberland Avenue, one of the earliest known paving projects in town. All of it was more or less in the category of making the city look more modern, more substantial, more urban.

Under the headline, "Knoxville Goes Ahead," on April 2, 1853, Brownlow's *Whig* announced the plan with an effusive editorial: "Our neighbors of other towns in East Tennessee have boasted long and loud about their growing prospects.... As men of discernment, they see their towns have had their day! Not so with Knoxville. All interests are looking up here—real estate is advancing—the population is rapidly increasing—men of capital are coming here—manufacturing establishments are going up—prosperity, greatness, and glory await this ancient metropolis of East Tennessee. Knoxville is the point of all points in East Tennessee for men of business and enterprise to settle. Many sensible men are seeing this, are buying town property improved and unimproved and are thus preparing for the future.

"The corporation of our City has accepted the lot offered by Nelson, Mabry & Co., upon which to erect a Market House; and in connection with the McAdamizing [sic] of Gay & Cumberland Streets, now offer the work to contractors. It is estimated that the erection of the Market House, and the improvement of the two streets, will cost $10,000. This is a matter of great interest to our mechanics. Let contractors look to such jobs as these—let them bid, and act promptly in the matter."

The reference to "Nelson" in a spot where Swan's name should appear is puzzling, perhaps an error. It probably refers to Matthew Nelson, an occasional partner of Swan and Mabry's. A section of East Knoxville was once known as the Nelson, Swan, and Mabry Addition. One of the neighbors of the property at the time of Mabry and Swan's purchase and bequest was a Miss Ann Nelson; the family may have had an interest in the section.

Alderman Luttrell, who would soon serve a one-year term as the city's mayor, apparently led the project from the city's side, and the city contracted with the firm of Newman & Maxwell to build a brick house 100 feet long and 40 feet wide. The Newman was Jacob Newman, who had recently been in charge of building, and apparently also designing, Knoxville's single most impressive building in the 1850s, the school for the deaf. After issuing bonds to pay for the work, the city finally settled with a firm styled "Jacob Newman & Sons," perhaps suggesting that Mr. Maxwell was no longer in the picture.

Meanwhile, Mabry and Swan went immediately to work, subdividing and marketing lots in the vicinity of what they were already calling "Market Square." Except for a narrow allowance for a market house in the center, they subdivided most of the Fouche purchase into 66 parcels. By October, before there was a Market House in place, they were selling the lots; before the year was out, Mabry (records suggest he was on his own that day) presented a map of the prospective development to the city, bearing a remarkable resemblance to Market Square as it actually developed in years to come, with 17 rectangular lots facing each other across a long, narrow "MARKET PLACE" in the center.

It's a surprising drawing in more than one respect: it shows the Market Place as extending the entire length from Union to Asylum, the street which would only after the Civil War become the northern end of the public part of the Square. The map suggests that Swan & Mabry considered some land they owned, but hadn't donated, as the northern open part of the Square. Also, some research suggests that "Asylum Street"—so named because it intersected with the then-more-extensive grounds of the Deaf and Dumb Asylum—was not in common usage in the early days of the Square, when the access road on the north end was known as "Market

Right: The original schematic drawing of what was known as the Swan and Mabry Addition, including the "Market Place" in its center. Developer Joseph Mabry himself apparently delivered this map to the Board of Aldermen in 1853. The twin rows of 17 buildings each, facing each other across a common space was not fully realized until the 1870s. A savvy historian might assume it originated in a later era, but the fact that it's pasted into City Council's original minutes from 1853 seem to argue for its antebellum authenticity. Image courtesy of Knox County Archives.

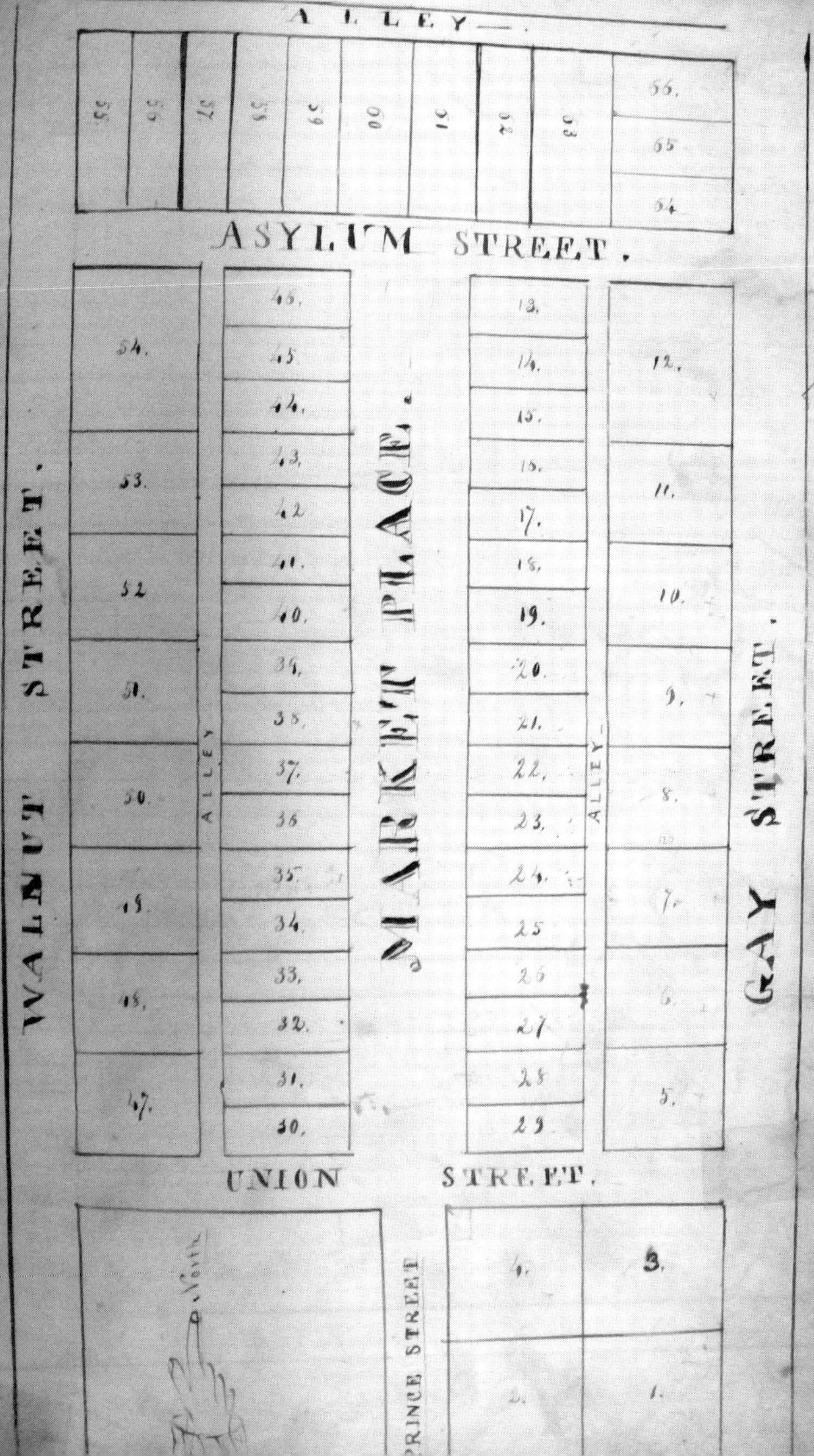

ALLEY.

ASYLUM STREET.

WALNUT STREET.

MARKET PLACE.

GAY STREET.

55 56 57 58 59 60 61 62 63 66 65 64

54 46 13

45 14 12

44 15

53 43 16 11

42 17

52 41 18

40 19 10

51 39 20

38 21 9

ALLEY

50 37 22

36 23 8

49 35 24 7

34 25

48 33 26 6

32 27

47 31 28 5

30 29

UNION STREET.

PRINCE STREET

4 3

2 1

Street." And curiously, the 1853 map indicates no Market House at all, only the twin columns of lots facing each other to form a rectangle. It looks eerily like the Market Square of the 21st century.

Predictably, empty lots near a growing city tend to attract the wrong sort of attention. A city "Ordinance to protect the Market House," passed in June 1853, and signed by Mayor James Luttrell, read that "it shall be unlawful for any person to use the Market House or its immediate vicinity as a place for obeying the calls of nature." Fines for urinating on the Market House site would be $5-20, a substantial sum. It further forbade "any person to throw or put the dead carcase of an animal, or to put or throw any other filth upon the Market House lot…"

The modest original Market House opened in January, 1854—the month U.S. Congress began considering a startling new bill to allow the expansion of slavery into the territories, even those where it had previously been banned. The Kansas-Nebraska Act would flog the issues of slavery and secession into the forefront of American politics in the middle 1850s; they were subjects many Americans had previously learned to avoid in polite conversation.

≈

The original Market House was an open-air market with tall, arched openings, a smaller, utilitarian version of other market houses of the antebellum South, some of which still exist in cities like Charleston and Baltimore. Though it was built of brick, some descriptions suggest it was part "pavilion," probably a removable tented section.

The year 1854 is a frustrating research subject, due to the fact that, though both the *Whig* and the *Register* were publishing weekly that year, few local newspapers survive. All of the January issues of Brownlow's *Whig*, however, are intact. Through those four copies, we can find discussion of the city elections the first Saturday of that year which rendered James C. Luttrell the new mayor, and reports that that day also brought the heaviest snow Knoxville had seen in years.

The local Baptist Church—Baptists were still new to Knoxville in 1854—held a fundraiser at the courthouse, which apparently constituted the city's only public auditorium: the "Swiss bellringers…52 bells of exquisite tone" gave an apparently secular concert that included "Blue Bells of Scotland," "Fisher's Hornpipe," and the "Aurora Waltzes." The *Whig* was preoccupied with politics and the new temperance movement, and ran ads for "Dr. Urban's Anti-Bacchanalian Elixir, a safe and sure remedy for the curse of Intemperance." The weekly also ran ads for some of the sorts of things you might find in a market house, like honey by the quart, and oysters by the barrel. How oysters arrived fresh that year before railroad service is not advertised.

But the opening of an actual market house on the north side of town is unmentioned. It was to open on January 31—but, without any surviving journalism from the days and weeks thereafter, we can hardly even guess about the occasion, and the public response. It's not clear that Knoxville did anything to herald the opening of the market house, the kernel of what would be Market Square. Though Knoxville was not a town of impressive buildings, the little market house still didn't compare in scale or presentation to the courthouse, or the university's buildings, or the school for the deaf, or the Methodist church.

And in January, during a winter that sounds especially fierce, there probably wasn't much in the way of produce to draw attention. In early 1854, the result of Swan and Mabry's gift was only an empty building, hardly even a curiosity yet. But the Board of Aldermen, early on, spelled out how they wanted the place to be run. The Council provided for a fine of $5 for any merchants who were found to be guilty of price-fixing, either conspiring to raise prices or preventing merchants from selling low.

What might have been Market Square's first summer also brought one of the worst epidemics ever to strike the city. Commerce staggered to a halt. In a cruel exception to Knoxville's bemoaned isolation, what hit Knoxville was apparently the worldwide cholera pandemic that had recently killed thousands in London, Moscow, Chicago. Hundreds fled Knoxville, and in the space of about six weeks, perhaps as many as 100 died, a major loss for a still-small town. In a rare moment of grim charity, Parson Brownlow buried many of the victims himself, with an Irish sextant, in the new cemetery on the north side of town known as Gray. Little was known about cholera in 1854, but some suspected it was spread via unclean fruits and vegetables. It's unlikely the new Market House played a role in the plague; it avoided suspicion thanks to its unpopularity. In any case, farmers and other country people in particular feared Knoxville, and some stopped making their regular trips into town.

～

In early 1855, William Swan was elected mayor of Knoxville. Whether gratitude for the market-house gift was a factor in his ascension is unclear. Swan was among the most ambitious of Knoxville's antebellum leaders, convinced the city had the potential to rival the great industrial centers of the north, if only its transportation options could be improved. He proposed digging a great canal on the north side of town to connect factories with the navigable mouths of the creeks, and the river. It's one of his few proposals never to be completed.

In 1855, the Catholic Church, represented by a Father Brown, bought a hilltop spot for a new church. The fact that the first Catholic Church in East Tennessee was described "north of the Market House" indicates that the Mabry-Swan gift was at least known as a landmark. At the end of that year, the city limits reached voraciously to the north, taking in the new train depot. Market Square was seeming more central all the time.

When the first railroad train arrived in Knoxville, a train from the South on the new East Tennessee and Georgia line in 1855, just a year after the completion of the Market House, Mayor Swan was there to greet it. The following year, 1856, another line would link Knoxville to Virginia and the Northeast.

One of the first known personal mentions of the market house comes in a letter written by Irish revolutionary fugitive—and future Member of British Parliament—John Mitchel, in an interesting letter describing, sometimes with understated humor, a walk around downtown Knoxville with the new mayor in March, 1855:

"Like any other town in the United States, it has a mighty future, and occupies itself much in contemplation of that good time. A railroad will in two or three years connect it with Virginia northwards and with Georgia southwards. A gas company has been founded to illuminate the place; and if I doubted it, I had only to look at the bundles of main pipes laid down here and there upon the streets; *a new market, just finished*; real estate enhancing; lots rising; Ah me! Give me a land where the lots don't rise."

In 1859, pioneer photographer Thomas H. Smiley took two rare images of his adopted city. This one, taken from the cupola of the courthouse on Main Street, shows the relatively new 1854 Market House, the one-story building with two arched openings, standing in a weedy, little-developed part of town. Smiley, a daguerrean who is believed to have studied with Samuel F. B. Morse in Philadelphia, was probably Knoxville's first professional photographer. McClung Historical Collection.

Reading Mitchel's letter, published in a book in Great Britain later in the century, you can almost hear Swan's proud exhortations in the background. Mitchel's subtle sarcasm surely suggests something about his attitude toward his young companion's municipal optimism and real-estate prospects. But over the next few months, Mitchel and Swan would form an unlikely partnership. In 1856, Mitchel built a house on the east side, near Swan's property.

Swan, suspicious of abolitionism, had separated from the Whig party to become a Democrat, eventually to become a secessionist. The Irishman Mitchel, who had only recently been exposed to slavery, became a strong advocate of it as a humane institution; he is said to have associated abolitionism with British imperialism, and secession with Irish nationalism. In Knoxville in 1856 the odd couple founded a national secessionist journal, *The Southern Citizen*, which expounded on their views. In late 1858, they chose to relocate the magazine's headquarters to Washington to obtain greater access to the halls of power, and Mitchel, who'd already spent more time in Knoxville than he expected to, went with it.

~

Soon after the opening of the Market House, one D. J. Stacks, the "town marshal," who was leading a simultaneous project to build a system of cisterns in the business district to assist in fire protection, became the first "market master." "His duties were not very onerous," joked a writer 40 years later, considering that they chiefly consisted of preventing livestock from entering the Market House.

The Market House charged farmers $3 a month for stall space—not much, maybe the equivalent of $100 a month in 21st century dollars—but certainly more than farmers had to pay if they just stopped their wagons on busier Gay Street or Cumberland Avenue. In 1856, the city, led by that year's mayor, James Cowan, banned curbside selling except at The Knoxville City Market, as it was originally called. The move would have served both the market house and his own business; Cowan had long run a Gay Street store with his brother-in-law, Massachusetts-born Perez Dickinson. (Cowan's son Perez Cowan, named for his business partner, would later become one of the few close friends of his famously reclusive cousin, the poet Emily Dickinson.)

Still, the market house was not the success its founders envisioned. Knoxville was improving in some ways, especially with the arrival of the railroad the year after the construction of the Market House, which allowed the first heavy industry to develop in the old town. A large machine shop, an iron foundry, and a steam flour mill combined to change Knoxville's sleepy economy forever, with promise of much more to come.

But disease and the dark politics of the mid-1850s, the expansion of slavery and the vilification of immigrants, especially the Irish Catholic ones, preoccupied Knoxville's citizens. As for a market, demand and supply seemed co-equally slow to arrive. Only a few farmers laid out their wares in those earliest days, and Knoxvillians, who were accustomed to other sources of produce from their own gardens or from direct trade with neighboring farmers, didn't bother with it much.

Worse, in those early winters, the Market House was even quieter—dead empty, in fact, so desolate that some city boosters worried that its vacancy might violate the terms of the Swan-Mabry deed; City Judge (and former Mayor) George White ordered his young sons Andy and Georgie to make a token show of marketing by carrying baskets full of winter vegetables around the empty Market House. Though Georgie White, who would later serve as Market Master of a very different Market Square, occasionally made a sale, his brother Andy complained that in all those winters he never sold anything at all—but some have claimed the two brothers saved the promising spot from reverting to private ownership.

The city kept paying attention to their investment. on May 26, 1856, the Board of Aldermen approved $300 in repairs to the building.

≈

In the first known photographs of Knoxville as a whole, taken from a height near the river on a sunny day in late 1859, the Market House, with its twin arches in front, is visible in the center of a broad clutter of buildings, looking surprisingly serene and free of urban adjacency, almost like a country church.

The same year, Knoxville was treated to a gushing assessment in *DeBow's Review*, a promotional series about American cities. In the long entry about Knoxville's assets, no market house is mentioned, suggesting neither the building nor the activity around it attracted much attention.

When Knoxville Postmaster George Washington Harris—better known to readers of New York humor magazines as the creator of the bizarre backwoods character Sut Lovingood—floated the idea of building the new post office on Clinch Avenue at Prince Street, one block south of the new Market House, some protested that the site was too far north. Despite the new railroad and developments on the north side, it seemed too remote from the traditional business center of town, which was still along Main and Cumberland, where the post office had always been before.

However, also in 1859, Knoxville's first city directory was published, referring to the area around the Market House, perhaps in anticipation, as the "Market Space." The term may emphasize that even in its early days, the space, not just the Market House, but the yard around it, would be important to commerce. The same directory lists a few businesses that were setting up near the Market House, apparently in freestanding buildings on the plots bought from Swan and Mabry. They were not necessarily impressive buildings, some of wood, and some of only one story, but they were the first hints that their arrangement would soon resemble a "square." (It's assumed that none of those original buildings of that era survived into the 21st century, or even the 20th. However, architectural historian Ann Bennett, of the Metropolitan Planning Commission, believes it's at least possible that a triplet of arch-windowed brick two-story buildings on the east side, at Nos. 22, 24, and 26, date from the 1855-1860 era. It would make them, by far, the oldest buildings on the Square. But appraising the age of a building is often more art than science.)

Among Market Square's first marketers was grocer Albert Hudiburg, who would later serve as a city alderman; he ran a grocery on the west side. At the same time, Patrick Tracy ran a saloon on the west side of the space "between Market and

Thomas H. Smiley's rare 1859 photograph of downtown Knoxville, supposedly from his own house on the northwest corner of the town, is the clearest image of Market Square from the Civil War era. The Market House, built five years before, is just left of center, with only a few other buildings in its surprisingly rustic vicinity. It may obscure some buildings immediately behind it. Close inspection reveals several one- and two-story buildings in its close vicinity, light-colored and built mostly of wood. The 1859 city directory already listed several businesses and residences on Market Square, or the "Market Space" as it was sometimes known. None of the buildings clearly visible in the photograph are still standing. McClung Historical Collection.

Crooked"—the description suggests there was nothing to speak of between the Market House itself and Crooked Street, later Walnut. The fact that the Square was still regarded as the fringe of the growing town in 1859 accounts for the fact that one John Jones was, for a time at least, able to run a lumber yard at the northern end of the Market Space.

The square was home to at least one resident, John Tracy, a laborer, likely kin to saloonkeeper Patrick, and likely one of the hundreds of Irish immigrants who had moved to Knoxville in the previous few years. Most Irish preferred to live near the only Catholic church in East Tennessee, and several gravitated toward Market Square, as residents and often as proprietors of saloons.

Most intriguing and surprising of those original businesses is that of Peter R. Knott (1822-1877), who ran a "Bowling Saloon" on the east side, around numbers 16–18. It might seem obvious proof that the "no other purpose" terms of the Swan-Mabry deed were not meant to extend to the buildings of the Square itself. Swan and Mabry were still prominently present to witness it—and, if they'd wished, object.

Knott's Bowling Saloon is, by the way, also the first evidence of a bowling alley in Knoxville, and a rare mention of an antebellum sport not involving betting on horses, dogs, gamecocks, or fighting bears. Bowling apparently didn't last more than a few years on Market Square, but would be a major pastime for hundreds of Knoxvillians by the end of the century.

One unsettlling question often asked about Market Square was whether the site ever served as a slave market. Slavery was legal in Tennessee during the first nine years of the original Market House's existence, and slave auctions were a feature of some other Southern marketplaces. A few slaves were auctioned in Knoxville almost up until the time of Union occupation. However, most slave auctions seemed to take place at the courthouse, or at some spot on the outskirts of town. There's no obvious record of such activity at Market Square.

~

By 1860, Market Square may still have been economically obscure, but it was, at least, easier to find from a distance. That year the Second Presbyterian Church, the nearest neighbor to Market Square, built a new chapel with a very tall steeple. The spire made the neighborhood easier to point out from the still-busier parts of town, along Main and Cumberland.

The Square's commercial importance evolved no sooner than its symbolic importance as a meeting spot. When local fire companies needed a familiar place to launch the city's first annual Fourth of July parade, they chose Market Square as the staging area. Brownlow's *Knoxville Whig* reported, "The Procession will form in Market Square at 11 O'Clock, precisely," on Monday, July 4, 1859. They were anxious times for patriotic celebrations. Within months, some of those who assembled on the Square for that first parade, including Orator of the Day John Crozier, a popular attorney and former U.S. congressman, were ready to quit the country whose birthday they helped celebrate in 1859. Crozier would be one of Knoxville's leading secessionists. When the second annual parade formed on Market Square in 1860, the Orator of the Day was James W. Humes, a Unionist who became a Confederate officer when fighting broke out.

By the 1860 census, Knoxville was suddenly much bigger than it had ever been, with 5,300 citizens, two and a half times the size it had been at the beginning of the energetic 1850s. All of the citizens lived within a space of less than two square miles, and within easy walking distance of Market Square. Beyond city boundaries, the county's population growth was accelerating, too, with almost 23,000 living in Knox County, including Knoxville. Growth would only accelerate in years to come, and Market Square grew along with the city.

It was not an ideal time for a city to finally gain some urban momentum. At election time, Market Square was the location of one of Knoxville's three polling places, suggesting that it had gained credibility as a gathering place. In the fateful election of that November, 1860, Abraham Lincoln was not on the ballot; skeptical of their chances in a slave state, the Republican Party chose not to organize in Tennessee that year. The white males over 21 who constituted all of Knoxville's legal voters favored not the Northern Democrat, Douglas, or the Southern Democrat, Breckinridge, who was popular through most of the South, but the nation's last Whig candidate, a moderate who opposed secession: Tennessee's own John Bell, a frequent visitor to Knoxville. Nationally, he came in fourth. On June 8, 1861, Tennessee, which had been on the fence about secession, held a statewide referendum on the subject of whether to leave the United States of America. Knox County voted strongly against secession, by a factor of almost three to one. That day 311 men came to Market Square to cast votes on the subject of "separation"; among those who voted were several names that would be prominent in the Square's future: B.R. Strong, Thomas Burrier, A.S. Hudiburg, and William Swan himself.

The tally for the Market Square vote is not obvious in the records, but Knoxville proper voted strongly in favor of secession, 777 to 377, reflecting the statewide margin. Parson Brownlow was convinced that the presence of the militia, which had recruits from across the state, threw off the count; he reported that the city of Knoxville, always more politically diverse than the county, had voted narrowly against secession, 372 to 325. (The seemingly low numbers, in a city of more than 5,000 citizens, are partly explained by the fact that only white male adults over 21 were permitted to vote—and some of them had already enlisted in either army and left town.)

Both Mabry and Swan were secessionists. Slavery was not central to either of their business interests. However, his journal, *The Southern Citizen*, proves that Swan was committed to the peculiar institution.

The war brought an unexpected end to the ambitious and resourceful young man's business interests in Knoxville. Swan enlisted in the Confederate army, as a private. Why a 40-year-old former mayor and former attorney general would join any army as a footsoldier isn't obvious, and may have been a symbolic gesture. In any case, another title soon superseded his rank when he was elected, in November, 1861, to Confederate Congress—beating opponent John Baxter, who had been a Unionist. By the following May, Swan had conveyed most of his Knoxville property, including some slaves, to Joseph Mabry, apparently as part of a deal whereby Mabry would supply some war materiel, perhaps the supply of Confederate uniforms for which he was later known.

As a congressman Swan proposed heavy import taxes on European nations which refused to recognize Confederate autonomy and opposed federal taxation and the arming of slaves. Swan spent most of the war in Richmond, where he lived, at least for a time, with his old publishing associate John Mitchel, who had already set up his household there as he continued to publish his Irish-Confederate diatribes. Swan was notoriously combative, even with his fellow Confederate representatives, and got in a famous fight in which he attacked well-known politician Henry Foote, the former Mississippi senator who was close to 60 at the time, with an umbrella.

Mabry was younger than Swan, 35 at the war's beginning, knew how to use a gun, and would seem to have been welcome in the Confederate army, but he did not enlist. The depth of his devotion to secessionism may not have been comparable to Swan's.

The few farmers who had used the Market House during the growing season abandoned it altogether, by some accounts, as many abandoned the dangerous and divided town of Knoxville in general. Though many Knoxvillians did remain, the old capital became more a staging ground for army operations than an economically vital town; the businesses that thrived were those that served the Confederate soldiers. By 1862, whorehouses in Knoxville reportedly outnumbered legitimate businesses.

In the early autumn of 1863, blue-uniformed troops under Union Gen. Ambrose Burnside occupied Knoxville. Captain Hiram Chamberlain of Ohio encountered a young man who introduced himself as Joseph Mabry. "I am a notorious rebel, these people will all tell you that," said Mabry. "I at one time proposed to be one of ten men to contribute $100,000 each to the Confederate Treasury. I equipped an entire company of soldiers for the Confederacy at my own expense and ran an establishment here that furnished thousands of dollars worth of clothing for the Southern soldiers. I have nothing to conceal concerning my attitude or what I have done, but I am here to tell you that whatever I have will be of use to your army, you can have it and I shall attempt to conceal nothing."

Mabry's quick confession surprised and impressed Chamberlain—who, as it turned out, returned to Knoxville after the war to found a major local industry, the Knoxville Iron Company.

General Burnside seized the Market House and requisitioned it as a barracks for troops and as an ammunition magazine.

For about two weeks in November, 1863, Union-held Knoxville was almost entirely surrounded by 15,000 Confederate forces under Gen. James Longstreet. The siege saw one of the war's eeriest scenes, memorable to the few who witnessed it. One of Burnside's most popular commanders was young, handsome, freshly promoted Gen. William Sanders, a Southerner himself. Seriously wounded during the Confederate advance on Kingston Pike, Sanders was conscious as his comrades carried him by wagon to the Lamar House on Gay Street. There, a few hours later, he died. Burnside, faced with a morale problem in the besieged city, chose not to reveal the charismatic young officer's death. The general ordered that Sanders be buried secretly, at midnight at the churchyard of Second Presbyterian, on the southwest corner of Prince and Union, a furtive whisper away from the Market House. Sanders' old comrades dug his grave there, and buried him by lantern light. Overcome with emotion, the nocturnal mourners dropped the semblance of secrecy long enough to fire a sidearm salute that must have echoed off the Market House, awakening the few who were able to sleep in the nervous neighborhood, and startling everyone else.

Sanders' death became known within a few days, whereupon Burnside chose to rename the largest Union fort, the unfinished earthworks less than a mile west of Market Square, for his fallen officer—just in time to repel the Confederate assault which punctuated the siege, and rendered the fort, for at least a week, nationally famous as the Battle of Fort Sanders.

～

The Square, and the city, spent the remaining 17 months of the war in Union hands. There may never have been a moment, day or night, that soldiers were not present on Market Square. In January, 1864, the Board of Aldermen agreed with the plea of a Market House stall renter that rents should be forgiven. At least for that month, the request was granted. The fact that there were rents to be forgiven is a little surprising; much Knoxville business had been shut down during the war, but during the Union occupation, someone was at least trying to sell produce at the Market House.

There were further complaints, that soldiers had dragged benches and stall furniture outside, where it had been ruined in the weather. And the federal magazine contained so much gunpowder that alarmed local civilians were convinced it was only a matter of time before it all blew up. According to City Council minutes, the Board of Aldermen asked Mayor Luttrell to plead with a "General Tillman" (probably Gen. Davis Tilson, U.S. commander of artillery in Knoxville) to remove ammunition from the Market House, to prevent a massive explosion in Knoxville's troubled heart. The city petitioned Union authorities to remove at least some of it so that "the disaster would not be so great."

It was on the Square itself, a few weeks after his conversation with Chamberlain in late 1863, that Joe Mabry was persuaded to take an oath to support the Union. Somewhere along the way, he had earned the honorific of "General" Mabry, a distinction generally credited to his assistance to the Confederates—though it seems remarkable that in a city dominated by Civil War veterans a non-veteran should be esteemed with the highest of military titles—but he seems to have been more pragmatic than partisan. Before the war was over, he was promoting his business by buying advertising space in Parson Brownlow's *Whig and Rebel Ventilator*. Mabry, in fact, befriended the Parson, Knoxville's most reviled Unionist.

It was clear to Mabry and most others that, after the war, Republicans would dominate business and society in Knoxville. In years to come, a slightly false rumor would spread that Mabry himself had turned Republican.

However, Mabry's old partner and brother-in-law was not as amenable to Yankee domination in the city of which he had once been mayor and proud advocate.

Ambitious, mercurial William Swan probably never witnessed his Market Square thriving as a wholly successful institution. At war's end, Swan, the unreconstructed Confederate congressman, declined to return to the city for which he'd once had such extraordinarily high hopes. By 1865, Knoxville was famously friendly to former Unionists, and the home of Parson Brownlow, Horace Maynard, William Rule, and Oliver Perry Temple, who all had regional or even national reputations as stalwart Federals, and are today counted among the earliest Southern Republicans.

Along with several old Rebel associates, Swan moved to the real, unambiguous South of Memphis, where he worked for a time as an attorney. Memphis now flew the U.S. flag, of course, but there at least, in that developing metropolis by the big river, Swan had plenty of company as a disgruntled secessionist, and didn't have to worry about Unionist favoritism in business and society. Swan lived there with his wife and two children, but didn't thrive in Memphis for long. His only son died in 1867. Two years later, Swan himself died there, of unpublished causes, at the age of 48, leaving his wife and daughter to live alone. Though his obituary reported that his body would be returned to Knoxville for burial, the co-founder of Knoxville's Market Square is buried in Memphis's historic Elmwood Cemetery.

For the time being, Swan's old partner Joe Mabry seemed to be getting along, befriending some Republicans and, despite his temper, taking the high road at least as far as the late unpleasantness was concerned. He'd suffered some business reverses—in 1865 he sold a big chunk of the property adjacent to the Market House for just $300, and his Knoxville and Kentucky Railroad project began to collapse in 1868—but Mabry lived comfortably in his unique home on Dandridge Avenue, raising a large family, including 14 children. In 1869, he bought East Tennessee's most famous newspaper, Brownlow's *Whig*, and turned it into a Democratic-leaning paper; the strange beast lasted only about a year.

Perhaps because Swan left town and left behind no local descendants to commemorate his contributions, in years to come the Market Square donation would come to be more closely associated with Mabry alone. Some 20th-century newspaper articles would remember Market Square as Joseph Mabry's gift to the city.

Mabry harbored grudges that were more complicated than the war, and he was known to go armed. His reputation would bring him trouble in the future.

CHAPTER 2

"Our Busy Little Square…."

Peter Kern, Adolph Ochs, Cholera, and the Boom Years

After Appomattox, after the reinstatement of the state of Tennessee into the Union, after the departure of the occupying troops in blue, Knoxville attempted to pick up the economic momentum it had left behind sometime just before the war, when it was a freshly minted railroad city with growing industry and the beginnings of a wholesale market. Knoxville had one particular advantage in the postwar years, in that Parson William G. Brownlow, reborn as a Republican and elected governor of Tennessee, was an unashamed Knoxville-booster. In that office he would gain better terms for Tennessee's re-admittance than any other rebellious state was allowed. When he could he also favored Knoxville, where many of his old Whig associates were turning Republican.

Progress was slow, especially at first. With its raw trenchwork, muddy streets among shot-scarred and army-abandoned buildings, postwar Knoxville could appall some visitors, who remarked that Knoxville appeared to be, "in a manner, finished." The Panic of 1867, one of the worst recessions ever to hit the region, punctuated the misery.

The Market House, hardly more than a decade old, was said to be in a "dilapidated condition"—never blown up, as some had feared, but so damaged by the soldiers who were garrisoned there that surviving city fathers like Mayor J.C. Luttrell might well have wished it had been.

A few new businesses suggested Market Square's postwar potential. One store, J.S. & N.R. Hall's store, which sold both groceries and dry goods, was originally run by James Spears Hall and his nephew, Newton. With a simplified name and a stock narrowed to clothing, Hall's would remain an institution on the Square for almost 60 years. Perhaps encouraged by such promising new businesses, in March, 1866, the city could see potential in the place. City Council voted to enlarge the square by buying a northern annex from one J.W. Griffin, stretching the Market Space north to the access road that was had been known for a few years as Market Street. Griffin had bought the property from Joseph Mabry just a year earlier. From the city of Knoxville, he got $650, more than twice what he'd paid for it.

Some research indicates that the street much later known as Wall Avenue, and previously marked on a Mabry map as "Asylum Street," was known for a time as "Market Street." At the time it didn't pass very near the Market House, which was much closer to Union. An 1867 map shows a small market house in a long rectangular yard. In the map, the Market House, set back a bit from Union but hardly longer than a quarter of the Square's total length, stretching roughly from No. 7 to No. 15, as the addresses would later be numbered. On that postwar map, the site is marked not "Market House" or "Market Space," but "Market Square."

The city invested in the uncertain future of the Square in June, 1867, when Knoxville's Board of Aldermen, which had previously met in the courthouse or whatever other building might happen to be handy, decided to move to Market Square. A committee made up of pioneer Market Square merchant Albert Hudiburg, S.B. Newman, and L.C. Shepard looked at the newly purchased section north of the Market House and planned the construction of Knoxville's first permanent City Hall. It was a simple two-story brick building, about 40 feet square, with gaping arched windows and a small belltower on top that seems undersized for the building's scale. In the only known photograph of it, City Hall looks modest and a little melancholy—but in 1868, when it was completed, it was taller than the Market House, and the most impressive building on the Square. At first it housed the offices of the mayor and city council, and the city recorder's office, a sort of pre-court for processing arrestees, and soon the police department headquarters—and a jail, popularly known as the calaboose.

City Hall bestowed something of a municipal birthright to the Square, a confidence that it would be a significant place well into the future. The Square would be the city's seat of government for almost 60 years, a time when Knoxville grew from a town of maybe 8,000 to an undeniable city of about 100,000, and city government, meeting on Market Square, made some of the most momentous decisions of the city's history.

The mortar on Market Square's City Hall had hardly dried before the building became a dramatic stage for postwar civil rights in the South.

Knoxville Mayor James Luttrell (1813–1878), the city's political leader at the time of the establishment of Market Square in 1854, and also during the entire Civil War era, when Market Square began to develop gravity as a civic gathering place. Unlike several of his associates in the 1850s, Luttrell was a Unionist during the war. He has a unique distinction among Knoxville's mayors: both of his sons, Samuel B. Luttrell and James C. Luttrell, Jr., also served as mayor. Luttrell, Senior's career as a public servant came to a forced end when he lost his bid for re-election in 1868; he at first refused to leave office, challenging the Reconstruction-era voting which had elected Marcus deLafayette Bearden. Courtesy of McClung Historical Collection.

Tennessee was the first former Confederate state to extend voting privileges to blacks, and the year 1867 saw Tennessee's first Reconstruction elections, an astonishing turnabout in which blacks, suddenly enfranchised, were voting for the first time in their lives. However, former Confederates no longer had that privilege. Though Reconstruction was not enforced by federal troops in Tennessee, as it was in most of the South, some Knoxville politicians had trouble digesting the reversal in fortunes. In that election, longtime Mayor James Churchwell Luttrell was voted out of office. He resisted the retirement, claiming the election he lost was unconstitutional. Luttrell had been one of the city's staunchest Union men in 1861, but the 54-year-old former merchant disapproved of the radical surprises of postwar politics. He had held the city's top post since 1859, longer than any mayor before him. He had done his best to keep the Square from being blown up during the war, and afterward had supervised the construction of the city's first City Hall, on Market Square. He refused to leave it without a fight.

Union veteran Marcus DeLafayette Bearden, elected mayor of Knoxville in 1867 at age 37, had to wait for a federal judge's order to take his seat in City Hall, a seat Luttrell finally relinquished on January 10, 1868. The awkward transition occurred without violence. But Luttrell, now embittered toward the Republicans, became a Democrat. (The Luttrell family may have seen it as some vindication, more than a decade later, when two of his sons successively occupied the mayor's office.)

It was just the following year, 1869, that Knoxville voters elected the city's first black official. Railroad worker Isaac Gammon became an alderman, meeting with his peers at City Hall and becoming one of the first black elected officials in the South. He was the first of at least 14 black members of City Council who would meet on Market Square over the next four decades. Among the early black aldermen was William Yardley, elected in 1872. Raised and educated before the war as a free black, Yardley was a prominent young attorney who hung his shingle near Market Square.

Part of the City Hall project, on the bottom floor, was the Fire Engine House. Right away, it accommodated a handsome steam engine, fitted with a brass Silsby motor that could pump 300 gallons of water a minute. It was named the J.C. Luttrell #1, after the recently departed mayor. The new engine was the first of its kind seen in Knoxville. In those days before an effective waterworks, a deep cistern dug on the Square's north end kept Knoxville's only firetruck supplied with water.

Later, they'd add another fire wagon, a hook-and-ladder outfit. It would also bear the name of a prominent Knoxvillian, longtime alderman Alex Allison. When it arrived in late 1878, the still-volunteer fire brigade took the fire wagon to the spot in town where its potential would be most impressive, the south end of Market Square—and shot its stream of water over the top of the steeple of Second

Presbyterian Church, then believed to be the tallest structure in town. The stunt awed children and adults alike, but the message was forceful: that no roof, and no fire, would be out of reach of the Knoxville Fire Department.

In June, 1869, the city ordered a 90-foot extension to the southern end of the Market House, perhaps a multi-story extension. An examination of the records leaves lots of questions about how the original market house evolved from a tiny square market to the fairly elaborate three-story structure it was about 20 years after the war. A full explanation of the first Market House's architectural evolution would require much architectural research and probably a good measure of speculation.

Despite all odds, Market Square began to develop a gravity of its own. Buildings, albeit not always of the highest quality, went up on either side of the Market House, facing each other and forming a long rectangle which would become known as a Square. Not much is known about the earliest ones—some may have been built of wood—but in the decade after the Civil War, Market Square assumed the shape it would keep in centuries to come: two rows of brick buildings of two to four stories each in variegated Victorian-commercial styles, facing each other across whatever market structure, or lack of such, would be in between.

By the time of the 1869 City Directory, a handful of people were living on Market Square. Among its early residents were members of the Irish Cullinan family; John Cullinan ran a grocery on the west side, and a Michael Cullinan also lived there; over the next 40 years, he would become a familiar face here.

It wasn't until the early 1870s that both sides of the Square would be built out. A detailed and generally accurate bird's eye view picture of Knoxville done by a Chicago lithographer in 1871 shows a small, one-story market house, about three times as long as it is wide, an almost cubical city hall some distance away and, on either side, buildings of only one or two stories. The west side of the Square appears to be filled in with buildings of unequal height; the east side shows a surprising empty space, perhaps four addresses wide, at the intersection with Asylum on the north end.

Much later, prominent attorney, Andrew Jackson biographer, and Knoxville Mayor Samuel Heiskell would recall that bare space on the northeast quarter of the Square as the last part of Market Square still open, with no buildings on it, in his own childhood. It was used, at least occasionally, for outdoor sales; Heiskell remembered fondly seeing his first velocipede, or primitive bicycle, there, around 1865. Repeatedly over the next century and more, many East Tennesseans would encounter astonishing new products for the first time on Market Square.

≈

Among the Square's earliest postwar merchants was an amiable fellow with a walrus mustache and a German accent who would exert the strongest positive influence on the Square for decades to come. A German cobbler from Zwingeberg, in Hesse near Heidelberg, Peter Kern had moved to America as a young man. He lived and worked for a time in New York and Charleston before settling in Georgia in 1857. When secession came, he joined his neighbors in enlisting with the Confederate infantry, and, early in the war, in the fighting near Richmond, Corporal Kern was wounded in the leg. Sent home to recuperate, with the understanding that he would rejoin the army when he was better, he kept his promise. Kern was on the train back to the front in September, 1863. But during what he expected to be a brief stay in Knoxville, a mid-way point on the main route from Georgia to Virginia, the troops in blue marched into town. Kern was arrested and jailed, but permitted to go free, with the understanding that he was not to leave Knoxville for the duration of the war. He shrugged and went into business with a German acquaintance named William Heidel who proposed mixing flour and molasses to make cookies to sell to the Union troops who arrived on the troop trains. Through trial and error the energetic young cobbler from Heidelberg learned a new trade, and the two went into business, first on State Street, at the corner of Main, what was considered the old part of town. Along the way, he met and married a local woman named Henrietta Meyer, another German immigrant who hardly spoke English.

By the end of the war, Kern gathered that Knoxville was, for him, perhaps something more than a lengthy layover. He bought out his baker colleague, and soon after the war was moving his bakery into a two-story wooden building at a particularly choice spot, at the southwestern corner of Market Square. The bakery would later be known for manufacturing bread—but in the early days, the young Kern advertised as a "Confectionary and Candy Manufacturer." Kern's sometimes claimed to be the largest candy manufacturer in East Tennessee. But they also carried what advertisements described as "Fancy Groceries": nuts, fruits, and party snacks. At various times, in years to come, he would carry everything from soft drinks to fireworks to fresh oysters to cigars. Peter Kern's defining principle seems to have been that his merchandise was all, in one way or another, fun. It was a radical new concept in a town which, even before the horrible war, had struck some visitors as a solemn, gloomy place.

Among Kern's early offerings, in season, was ice cream. The term "ice-cream saloon" has a comical ring today, but it was very much in the air in mid-19th century American retail. Kern's was not the first, even in Knoxville; the first Knoxvillian to operate an "ice cream saloon" may in fact have been a free black man in the 1850s, who advertised his Main Street business by that phrase. By some historical descriptions of the business, an ice-cream saloon was an ice-cream parlor, but fancier, often with carpets on the floor and art on the walls. Kern's was, without question, the fanciest ice-cream parlor the city has ever seen. It was no small feat to make ice cream at all, in those days before refrigeration; lake ice, insulated as well as possible by the standards of the day, came in from the North on trains.

By 1871, Kern's Ice Cream Saloon was open until midnight, at least during the warmer months when people might be craving ice cream. Women weren't welcome in those other sorts of saloons, but at Kern's, ladies were welcome, the genial proprietor advertised, "with or without escort." His ice-cream-eating rooms were "quiet and clean," and his waiters, he promised, were "attentive."

In 1874, a newspaper reported that "Peter Kern, the enterprising Market Square confectioner, used 140 dozen eggs in his business on Thursday. A pretty good day's work."

Kern's announced a rare gadget, a "neat stationary engine," a three-horsepower contraption "for the manufacture of ice cream." He didn't have to go far to find a man who would build it for him. Thomas Burrier, whose gun shop was also on the west side, was the ice-cream engine's engineer, and maybe its inventor. He apparently did a good job with it, because the machine reportedly "works like a charm." People came to Kern's just to see the thing in operation.

Market Square's long status as a venue for lively public entertainment may have begun on April 28, 1868, when the 32-year-old Kern hosted one of the Square's first recorded public parties, a Grand Ball, which served as a benefit for the Catholic Church and also promoted Kern's freshly opened Ice Cream Saloon. Kern's big party apparently went well, because the following February, he hosted another public event, a German Lutheran Festival and Fair, there in his building. Among the attractions were coffee, cakes, oysters, and a concert by the Knoxville Brass Band. From the beginning, Kern seems to have been interested in including a public hall, sometimes known as Kern's Hall, as part of his business on the Square; in a city which had few such amenities except at the hotels—the Lamar House and the Franklin House—it was a welcome addition. And in 1869, Kern announced plans to build a much-larger building on the same site.

The baker's celebrations of Catholic and Lutheran causes are interesting, in light of the fact that Kern was a Presbyterian; he was a member of Second Presbyterian Church, directly across Union from his bakery. Kern's home, business, and church, as well as City Hall, where he would play a larger and larger role in years to come, were all within a few yards of each other. Kern, who had lived in Germany and New York and the Deep South, had arrived in Knoxville without meaning to stay more than a few days. Somehow he was content to spend 40 years almost entirely on Market Square. With Kern's prodding, Market Square would come to seem more and more like a microcosm of the broad world.

≈

Peter Kern (1835–1907), the godfather of Market Square. After his accidental war-time arrival in Knoxville as an errant Confederate soldier, the German-born baker established his business on Market Square, and in 1876 built what was the grandest building on the Square, his combination bakery, "ice-cream saloon," and meeting place. He and his shop seem to have played a role in the development of several holidays in Knoxville. The popular baker, who lived just west of the Square in a nice house on Walnut, was elected the mayor of Knoxville in 1890, the last immigrant to hold the city's highest office. McClung Historical Collection.

Swan and Mabry's original Market House was not even 15 years old, and apparently rarely used to its full capacity during that period, at least as a farmers' market. In the five years after the war, it was never busier than it had been during its months as a Union barracks and ammunition magazine. But it was in such poor shape it was an eyesore, and its diminutive size began to seem inadequate for a rapidly growing city. Despite the recession, people were flowing into this fresh railroad town whose new vigor had only been stalled by the war. Many were attracted to the area's natural resources; the iron industry, represented chiefly by the Knoxville Iron Co., just a few blocks west of Market Square, was booming, and new industry, in textiles, furniture, railroad equipment, and marble, was springing up all around.

Even the 1869 addition, the Market House left a sizeable gap between itself and the new City Hall, the commercial building and the municipal one, and for several years traders made use of it as a weighing station; the robust City Scales, donated by merchant B.R. Strong, which weighed everything from horses and cattle to grain, were located right in the middle of the square.

By 1875, the people of the Square were grumbling that the city had outgrown its Market House, expanded only six years before; a newer, even bigger, better Market House was necessary to serve a city whose population was approaching 10,000. That August, a citizens' committee led by Edward S. Shepard demanded new market houses to be built elsewhere in the city, one at Gay and Main, the traditional city center, the other in budding North Knoxville. "Our city is prosperous and growing rapidly," the plea stated. "Our central market house has become too small for the accommodation of the people, and your attention is called to the urgent necessity of granting this…." The momentum would lead, for better or worse, to a major municipal project in the following decade that many would come to regret.

As Knoxville's population boomed, many of the newcomers were Unionists, attracted to what may have been the Yankee-friendliest city in the reborn South. Despite William Swan's aversion to returning, some Southerners from the deeper South were also attracted to Tennessee, because the punishments of Reconstruction rested lighter on Parson Brownlow's home state. Veterans of both sides would be conspicuous on Market Square for decades to come. In fact, both the Union veteran's group, the Grand Army of the Republic, and a Confederate veterans' society, held their meetings in second-floor halls on Market Square.

On the second floor of No. 7 was the Confederate veterans' group, the Felix Zollicoffer brigade, named for a Knoxville poet and printer of the 1830s who returned to town as a Confederate commander early in the war shortly before becoming one of the first rebel generals to die in battle. The GAR was on the east side, at

No. 2½. America had been divided by the Civil War, sure enough, but few if any cities hosted veterans' headquarters of both sides, and within view of each other. When the Market House was still a one-story amenity, the veterans had a clean shot at each other. As far as we can tell, neither group took advantage of that opportunity.

Many, perhaps most, of the entrepreneurs who built Market Square in the years after the war were veterans, and former Yankees and Rebels thrived on the Square. Most of them, even those who maintained dutiful ties to their veterans' groups, got along with their graying former enemies.

By the late 1860s, Knoxville was perhaps three times the size of the city that had built the earlier Market House. Knoxville's population was approaching 9,000 citizens, all of whom lived within walking distance of the Square. The 1860s were the city's most terrifying and destructive decade, but nonetheless Knoxville saw an unprecedented 64 percent growth rate; most of that growth was in the latter half of the decade, just after the war.

≈

War and its aftermath had delayed the construction of the federal post office and Custom House, but Horace Maynard, the Republican congressman from Knoxville who sometimes allied himself with the Civil Rights Radicals, appropriated $400,000 in federal funding to build it. Construction commenced in 1869 just one block south of Market Square. Upon arrival three years after construction began, the three-story marble building was the most solid and permanent-looking building in Knoxville, and bestowed a new gravity to this part of town. The handsome three-story marble building, a federal courthouse, custom house, and the biggest post office in East Tennessee, opened at a time when most citizens and almost all entrepreneurs had reason to visit a post office weekly, if not daily. In its earliest days, the post office was open until 7 p.m., six days a week, and for one hour on Sunday afternoon. Foot traffic on northern Prince Street was, for the first time, guaranteed. Few could view this regional communications center and doubt, as some had 15 years before, that the Market Square area was central to Knoxville business. Still, it's interesting to remember that Gay Street, parallel to Market Square, was still partly undeveloped in the early 1870s. Barely a block east of the Square, at the bottom of a weedy slope, was a former dump which by then served as a baseball field.

Of course, the problem with attracting more people is the fact of attracting more people. In early June, 1873, the *Knoxville Chronicle* ran an item titled "A Nuisance," which makes the Square sound Dickensian:

"The Market House is crowded every morning by a number of dirty, thieving boys, who throng the passageways, handle everything they can get their hands on, and doubtless slip many small articles in their pockets as they can conveniently without being noticed. Ladies cannot pass through the Market House without being jostled on every side by this class of boys…. The Market Master should put a stop to it if possible…. [P]ublic auctions are the favorite resort of this same class, who crowd around the tables where the goods are displayed, without five cents in their pockets, and thus prevent parties desiring to purchase from examining the goods, and the result is that frequently small articles are missed….."

Around the same time, Knoxville received another unwelcome diminutive guest—a small pest of the worst sort, that is, microscopic. The city's second deadly visitation of cholera came that year, part of another worldwide epidemic, and it killed hundreds. The source of the contagion was unknown at the time—cholera is usually spread through fecal contamination of drinking water—but the most common theory was that cholera could be blamed on uncooked fruit that was available on Market Square. Another theory held that overripe fruit might also cause cholera. Some medical authorities advised avoiding fruits and vegetables altogether, because they might be infected with choleric "sporads." It was not a good year for sellers of produce.

The ever-resourceful grocery known as Hudiburg's had the temerity to advertise a "Cholera Diet." "The best hams, dried beef, breakfast bacon, mackerel, cod fish, herring, rice, cheese, fresh crackers, pickles, syrup, and oranges of the best quality." Their slipping in the last item, in advertisements, when warnings about avoiding fresh fruit sometimes appeared on the same page, may suggest that Hudiburg's wasn't taking the fruit threat seriously.

Nashville got the plague first, and some newspaper editors nervously wished the best for Knoxville. "The trouble at Nashville was its extreme filth, the unusual hot weather and frequent rains after a cool summer and its poor market regulation and careless living among its poorer classes…. Knoxville is unusually well-cleaned."

Knoxville may have turned a blind eye toward some parts of the city that were not so well cleaned: the same issue includes an anonymous plea from a "CITIZEN" concerned with the Market Square area: "Wanted to know if our Mayor and City Council will take some steps immediately to clean up the stock yard and city hog pen, under the shadow of City Hall. Don't delay until the cholera comes."

The cholera did hit Knoxville that summer, and because most of those who died were poor, some of them living in shady circumstances, complacent citizens concluded that it afflicted mainly the immoral and the careless. But when the plague claimed one of Knoxville's victims, esteemed State Supreme Court Justice T.A.R. Nelson, the righteous may have reconsidered their theories.

Still, some found Market Square produce altogether too tempting. One melon shopper on Market Square appeared hesitant, at first, carefully inspecting a muskmelon with an opera glass. After some consideration, he spoke. "I'll take her," he said, "sporads or no sporads."

∽

It must have given the Square further legitimacy when Governor Brownlow's old newspaper moved there. For decades before, most newspapers were head-quartered on Gay Street, and Brownlow's was in a famously ugly old building, "Brownlow's Old Stand" near the courthouse, but at some point in the decade after the war, the paper's heir, the *Whig and Chronicle,* or just *Chronicle,* moved to Market Square, under the leadership of Brownlow associate, Union veteran William Rule. Almost all newspapers had political allegiances in those days, and the *Chronicle* was advertised as the only Republican daily in the South. Considering the potential historical interest in the precise site, in particular as it pertains to the significance of one internationally famous career that started at the postwar *Chronicle,* it's a little frustrating that the precise spot of the *Chronicle* newsroom is tough to nail down.

Records are spotty and sometimes contradictory, but by one later chronology, in a 1901 *Knoxville Journal,* during the postwar years the newspaper originally moved into a one-story brick building vacated by a bowling alley, probably Knott's, which, according to that article, was approximately at the location currently numbered 16 Market Square. In June, 1873, the *Chronicle's* own masthead lists its main address at 18 Market Square, perhaps close enough to have been the same as that bowling-alley site. An early 1875 edition of the *Chronicle* states that it moved into the second floor of No. 33 Market Square, which would seem to have been on the west side. An 1876 City Directory, the first published in several years, places it on the east side of the Square, "near Asylum." That 1901 Journal article states that the Chronicle eventually moved to 34 Market Square, likely the east side, "near Asylum" site.

It's not impossible that it was in several different locations on the Square, either at different times or with its departments divided. The *Chronicle* is locally impor-tant because it may have been Knoxville's first newspaper to hold any pretense of political objectivity. The editor was former Union Captain William Rule. Still a young man of about 30, Rule was former city editor of Brownlow's *Whig.* He had worked for partisan papers, but having seen the fury of war, knew the damage reckless words could cause. A remarkably temperate man considering his era and the company he kept, he was criticized by his Republican peers for being too lenient toward the former secessionists; later, he would show a fair-minded inter-est in socialism. The papers that he led as editor were the most even-handed and objective in the city's history.

But the *Chronicle's* significance as a crucible for genius reaches to New York and beyond.

The *Chronicle's* star apprentice, circa 1872, was an earnest, dark-eyed teenager that some of his colleagues called Mulie. Adolph Ochs, born in Cincinnati to

Bavarian-Jewish parents who had lived in Knoxville briefly before the war, had lived in Knoxville since he was about six. He grew up in a surprising family. His mother, Bertha Levy Ochs, though a Bavarian immigrant who had been involved in the revolutions of 1848, had been a fierce Confederate partisan during the American Civil War, sometimes smuggling medical supplies to the Confederates in Kentucky. His father, Julius Ochs, was an abolitionist, a Union officer, and eventually a Radical Republican politician. It was a lively household. The Ochses had been prosperous in the immediate postwar period, living in something of a chateau on the side of Sharp's Ridge, but the Panic of 1867 ruined Julius, who nonetheless commanded some respect in the community, as a civic leader, Justice of the Peace, and as co-founder of Knoxville's first synagogue, Temple Beth-El.

The Ochses moved into a shotgun-style house at the corner of Crozier (later Central) and Clinch, and all the Ochs boys went to work. Newspapers were booming, and always hiring delivery boys; three Ochs brothers got jobs as paperboys. Adolph Ochs had a few different jobs, working in a pharmacy and as an usher at the new Staub's Opera House, but concentrated on newspaper work. He eventually earned an office job. "In the capacity of a general handy boy around the office, I came in contact with the men of light and learning in the community as is only possible in a daily newspaper office in a small town," he would later recall. Though just a boy, he got to know Knoxville's gentry: mayors like Joseph Jaques and Peter Staub, judges like doomed state Supreme Court Justice T.A.R. Nelson, business tycoons like Perez Dickinson, Congressman/Ambassador Horace Maynard, and of course Parson Brownlow himself.

He advanced in the career, getting work as a "printer's devil," a typesetting apprentice, working under the *Chronicle's* printing foreman, Col. Henry Clay Collins.

The *Chronicle* was a morning paper, and Ochs's shift usually ended around midnight.

His short commute presented the boy with a dilemma. His family home was only about four blocks away from Market Square, but in between was the graveyard of First Presbyterian. It didn't require much superstition in a teenaged boy's mind to be skeptical about walking past a graveyard alone at midnight, particularly that one. The crowded churchyard had recently been closed to new burials, but one of the most recent was that of Abner Baker, a young Confederate veteran who had been lynched for the crime of murder. His monument, deliberately broken at the top, was the tallest stone in the graveyard.

At midnight, Ochs tended to tarry at the *Chronicle's* shop on Market Square. Waiting for Colonel Collins to get off his shift so he might have some company, Ochs would ask Captain Rule if he could do anything else around the office. Rule or Collins found one job after another, from sweeping up to ad copywriting, to keep the nervous teenager busy.

Ochs may have exaggerated the story, or borrowed it; his brother Milton told a similar story about himself. But a half-century later, Adolph Ochs, publisher of the *New York Times*, would credit his experiences in the wee hours on Market Square as his education in journalism. When Ochs left Knoxville in 1875—his colleagues at the Chronicle gave the 17-year-old an extravagant farewell, perhaps two, on and near Market Square. There are two stories of his sendoff, one involving an oyster supper at Nick Eifler's, which was on Asylum near Gay, one at Mike's restaurant, perhaps Mike Cullinan's saloon, on Market Square. At one or the other, they presented him with a book of poetry.

It turned out to be a false exit. After an adventure in Louisville, Kentucky, Ochs returned and worked for the *Tribune*. He moved to Chattanooga, and, not yet 20 years old, bought the failing *Chattanooga Times*, which he quickly turned into a

This section of the Beck & Pauli bird's-eye lithograph of Knoxville shows the Market Square neighborhood as it appeared in 1871. The long, double-arched building in the center is the original one-story Market House. Though it had been extended by then, it was still very small, and left plenty of open space on the Square. The almost cubical building with the cupola to its north is Knoxville's first City Hall. Note the undeveloped space in the northeast corner, which was used for open-air sales; longtime mayor Sam Heiskell recalled seeing his first bicycle there. Just to the south, the steeple nearest the Square belongs to Second Presbyterian Church, at its original site. The vacant space to the west of the Square, across Gay Street, is what was then known as "the Base Ball Grounds."

Young Adolph Ochs, son of Jewish Bavarian immigrants, lived with his family down-town. In the years after the Civil War, he began his influential career in journalism on Market Square. He later went on to own the Chattanooga Times *and later still, in 1896, the* New York Times. *The most influential publisher in that national paper's history, he invented much of the* New York Times *as we know it today, including the motto, "All the News that's Fit to Print." His name still appears in the* Times' *masthead. Collection of the author.*

major daily newspaper. In 1896, he moved north and bought another failing daily called the *New York Times*. Adolph Ochs created the *Times* as it would be known throughout the 20th century, creating many of the paper's distinctive features, including the Book Review and the Magazine. He supplied it with its famous motto, "All the News That's Fit to Print," which his cousins, the Blaufelds, claimed he had purloined from their Gay Street cigar shop: "All the Seegars Fit to Smoke."

Ochs would also change New York, founding Times Square as well as the famous New Year's Eve celebration there.

Throughout his career, Ochs kept William Rule's letter of recommendation framed in his office—of the teenager Ochs, Rule had written, in part, "He is quick to comprehend and faithful to execute whatever he may be entrusted with. He is endowed with an intellect capable of reaching the highest points in mental achievement…."—and returned to visit when he could. He came back to Knoxville to participate in a tribute to Captain Rule in 1921. In 1929, he came to visit Rule's grave at Old Gray Cemetery—the editor had died, of appendicitis, the year before, at age 89—and, when asked, declined to have his photograph taken there. He was, he claimed, superstitious about graveyards.

His name remains at the top of the *Times* masthead: "Publisher, 1896–1936." Even into the 1930s, *Times* employees at all levels were often astonished at how much the old man knew about what they were doing. It was almost as if, long ago, he'd done it all himself.

Market Square is part of the Ochs legend. In the young-adults biography, *Printer's Devil to Publisher*, by Doris Faber, published in 1963 and reprinted in a new edition in 1996, there's reference to "stepping onto the chill, dusty cobblestones of Market Square," and "an alley along one side of a faded, one-story brick building—the small, untidy home of the Knoxville *Chronicle*."

Wherever that home was, it didn't stay on the Square for long. The *Chronicle* faded and for several decades after 1880, all of Knoxville's dailies would be headquartered on Gay Street.

∼

By 1870, Market Square, after 16 years of sputtering false starts, was a Knoxville institution, busy year-round, following, finally, Swan and Mabry's antebellum plan. Businesses that lined up to face the Market House, more than 25 of them, most of them tilting toward the masculine: a blacksmith, a gunsmith, a saloon, and a couple of competing liquor and tobacco dealers. Several of these merchants, and a few others, lived on the Square, typically in second-floor apartments, often above the saloons that doubled as boarding houses. Many early businesses on the Square advertised their wares as "provisions," suggesting a still-rugged lifestyle in a town that, though almost a century old, could still almost pass for a frontier outpost.

The particular mix of businesses that lined the square sounds as rootin' tootin' as a Wild West movie set, and the theme carried into the Market House, where among the fresh meats might include a freshly slain deer, wild turkey, a bear now and then, or "long strings of wild ducks and partridges." An 1875 "Fur and Skin Market" might have appalled some moderns. There seems to have been enough of a demand for nearly every sort of hide that economic reporters were able to come up with average prices. Most in demand were bearskins, for $5, and otter skins, for $4.50. Minks were just $1.75. There was a market for the furs of raccoons, gray and red foxes, wildcats, various sorts of skunks, and even possums and house cats. The last two, it may be a relief to hear, were not much valued, at 10 to 12 ½ cents each. Only rabbit skins, at two cents, were cheaper.

If it sounds like an overheated set designer's version of Dodge City, the activities on the Square sometimes matched it. Rogue hogs sometimes roamed the Square, unsettling the horses. Saloon brawls were common. In a story remembered by an eye witness years later, without many specifics, a mob formed outside City Hall, demanding the release of an apparently popular prisoner. William Harper, one of Knoxville's early police chiefs, stepped outside and drew a line on the pavement with chalk. "Now men, the first one of you that puts a foot over this line will either be a cripple or a dead man." The laconic gesture was apparently enough to keep the crowd at bay.

It was rather easy for the public at large to greet prisoners as they waited in the calaboose, ask them why they killed the guy, and police did little to prevent such dialogues.

The round-the-clock presence of the police on Market Square during the saloon era surely influenced the fact that Market Square was one of the safest blocks in town; most other blocks downtown were associated with murders, sometimes multiple murders, sometimes spectacular murders. Murder was so rare on Market Square that research for this history failed to disclose a single one.

~

But the Square could also surprise with an unpredictable combination of people and activities that seem, at times, urban. The early Square was attractive to many immigrants, especially Germans and Irish, along with a few Swiss, Austrians, Hungarians, and others. One of the few bakers who had the temerity to compete with Peter Kern on Market Square was John Ricardi. Having moved to Knoxville with his brother almost 30 years earlier, he's remembered, if barely, as one of Knoxville's first Italians.

During the same era, two African American shoemakers hung their shingles on the Square; one had the advantage of a familiar name: Ben Franklin. Though it would be an exaggeration to suggest that life in Knoxville was fair to blacks, and racial resentments occasionally did erupt into violence, blacks and whites tended to get along on Market Square. More black-owned businesses, and black residents, were just around the corner on Union.

A pre-election rally one summer evening in 1876, brought out the pro-civil-rights Radical Republicans to Market Square, where they assembled just outside of the Market House. "The Market Square crowd was a mixed assemblage," according to the *Daily Tribune*, "though the colored element strongly dominated. A cohort of over a hundred, of whom probably less than one-fifth were white, marched in from the 12th district," the Mechanicsville neighborhood. They heard several speakers, among them editor William Rule and future Republican Congressman Leonidas Houk.

Knoxville's best-known black citizen of the Reconstruction era—perhaps even Tennessee's best-known black politician of that strange era—was attorney William Yardley. Some thought the mutton-chopped politician, born a free black in 1844 and educated by whites, looked like Frederick Douglass. Before the age of 30, he'd been elected to represent his district in both city and county government. And in 1876, he ran a surprising third-party campaign for governor.

Yardley seemed to favor the Market Square neighborhood as a location for his law offices; at the time of his run for governor, his office was on Asylum, near the Square; later on, he kept his offices above a saloon on Union Avenue, just across from the market. In 1873, Yardley, a justice of the peace, led the committee to oversee municipal business on the Square.

An incident on the Square that August might have provoked his surprising run for statewide office. "Last night the Republicans had a sort of jollification on Market Square, where several oil barrels lit the scene with a lurid glare" reported the drily Democratic *Tribune* concerning a poll-watching party for a county election. Yardley, invited to speak on behalf of outgoing Sheriff M.D. Swan, mounted the platform, only to be interrupted, almost immediately, by black hecklers. "You shall not speak, sir, so get down," one said. As Yardley, renowned even by enemies for his eloquence, began a polite response, another black man pulled him down. The throng devolved into a shoving match that fell not far short of riot, a fracas "disgraceful in the extreme," according to the *Tribune*, which blamed it on "a crowd of Negroes and a few ill-disposed white rowdies." The conservative Democratic paper ascribed widespread local hostility toward Yardley to racism. Curiously, white Republican civil-rights supporters and black activists seemed to resent Yardley.

Perhaps emboldened by the weird incident, two weeks later Yardley surprised the state by becoming an 11th-hour candidate for governor of Tennessee, and the first black to campaign for that office. Running as an "independent Republican," he had little local support—even the local black Republicans, professing to believe he was a "traitor" operating on behalf of Democrats to split the Republican vote, denounced him. During the nine weeks of his campaign, he stumped statewide, especially in Memphis. He came in third in November, earning more than 2,000 votes statewide—but, if we can believe the papers, only six of them were in Knoxville. Still, his campaign earned national attention; some big-city papers hailed him as "the coming man."

Reconstruction politics were complicated; the Democratic Party was still strong, and associated with former Confederates. There were two Republican parties: the party of Lincoln, the mainstream GOP— and the Radical Republican Party, which took an uncompromising stand on civil rights. Each of the three parties had adherents in Knoxville, and each was characterized by internecine conflict, mixed motives, and corruption. Yardley got out of politics after that gubernatorial adventure, but continued to argue some important civil-rights cases. In the late 1870s served as an assistant fire chief, based in the firehall on the square's north end.

The stricter segregation of the South's Jim Crow era was yet to come. Even those years would never thoroughly homogenize Market Square.

$\sim$

Some of Market Square's advertised offerings sound like those of a New Age herbalist. Ginseng root went for a consistently reported price of $1.60 in 1875, probably per pound.

By the mid-1870s, Market Square cultivated a reputation as a place where you could find nearly "Anything you'd ever want to eat, drink, or wear," as one advertisement had it. One of the Square's pioneer merchants was among its most liberal. If you'd walked into Hudiburg's, "The Market Square Grocer" and obviously successful in that role, you'd have found a choice of at least a couple of different kinds of pasta— macaroni and vermicelli, in one advertisement—plus Swiss and Limburger cheeses, sauerkraut, tapioca, sago palm starch, oatmeal imported from both Scotland and Ireland, cranberries, "cocoanuts," currants, dates, figs, citrons, and other exotica that we might not habitually associate with Reconstruction-era Tennessee. Occasionally, Hudiburg's also offered dried buffalo tongue, apparently an import from the real Wild West. Market Square was where Knoxvillians went to be surprised.

By then, more than a decade after Swan and Churchwell had installed gaslights on Gay Street, the city finally saw fit to install gaslights on the Square. It was a great amenity, even if there were only two of them. The butchers who came in before dawn to wield their blades on raw meat were particularly grateful. The following year, the city installed a brick floor in the Market House.

The improvements weren't impressive for long, and Knoxvillians are always happy to complain about something. No working market house is likely to seem pleasant to everybody. The *Knoxville Press & Herald* had the temerity to complain about one of the Square's chief draws. "It is generally agreed by all parties visiting the Market House," went a November, 1871, editorial, "that the number of hogs in the institution is not very agreeable or pleasant to visitors."

The city finally passed an anti-hog ordinance in 1875, but it wasn't immediately effective. At least as of January, 1876, hogs were "still walking the streets with impunity."

～

Another modern innovation was to arrive in the 1870s, one which would last for a very long time, much longer than gaslights. Some Market Square businesses began to offer numbers as a help in locating them. Knoxville had not been big enough to require street numbering until about the time of the Civil War. The name of a street was all that was necessary, or perhaps mention of a nearby street corner. Until the mid-19th century, patrons generally picked up their mail, by name, at the post office, anyway. By the 1870s, postal delivery to an address was routine.

When door-numbering started, all city addresses were numbered in a casual 1-2-3 manner, without regard to cross streets or blocks or the relative width of properties, or respecting any common point of origin. There were no "North" or "South" addresses in town, but, to its originators it made sense to start with the lower numbers nearest the older part of town, by the river. Hence, on all north-south streets, the lowest numbers indicated the southernmost end of a street; the number climbed as one went north. Knoxville streets weren't very long, and most addresses required only one or two digits.

Market Square was slower to number itself than some of the longer streets, like Gay. In the early days, most businesses on the intimate Square were content to describe themselves as being on the "east side" or the "west side," perhaps adding, "near Union" or "near Asylum." When some Market Square addresses started using numbers, they followed the city's antebellum pattern of ascending south to north, with odd numbers on the west, even on the east. By the 1880s, all Market Square addresses had numbers, a slightly lopsided 1 through 37; the west side, because of variations in architecture, has one more numbered address than the east.

Around 1890, the city standardized its numbering system, giving all buildings addresses of three, four, or eventually five numerals, based on their position in a given block, and each block numbered by its distance north or south of Jackson Avenue, or east or west of Central Avenue. The corner of Jackson and Central is therefore Ground Zero for Knoxville and Knox County addresses, even into the 21st century. Today, the only exception downtown, and the only part of Knoxville that still goes by its one and two-digit Reconstruction-era numbering system, is Market Square. Contrary to its neighborhood, in which all numbers rise as they go south, Market Square's numbers rise as they go north, by the old, pre-1890 system.

It may have been no mere oversight. Peter Kern, who also happened to be the mayor of Knoxville at the time of the citywide renumbering, retained for his business the perhaps prestigious address of No. 1 Market Square. He may have liked the old system, as it pertained to his favorite block of town—and he was mayor.

~

Kern didn't have a monopoly on selling good cheer to Knoxvillians. Another immigrant-run establishment, Spiro Brothers, from Hungary, did good business in confections and ice cream over on Gay Street. In 1875, they advertised "Their hall is the largest and coolest of their kind in the city…" They might as well have said they were larger and cooler than Kern's.

Soon after that, though, in July, 1875, Kern announced the construction of a whole new building, which the *Daily Herald* described as "a handsome three-story brick building on the southwest corner of Market Square…. The structure to be erected will be an important addition to the appearance of the Square, and be the handsomest of its buildings."

Few professionally trained architects lived in 1875 Knoxville, but Kern seems to have been confident in the skills of one young man, Joseph F. Baumann.

Born at Tellico Plains to German parents who had previously lived in New York, Baumann was a bright young man who would have a great influence over the look of the square over the next century or so. His father had been a carpenter, and just six years earlier, Joseph seemed to be following in his dad's footsteps. But by 1872, Baumann had begun advertising himself as an "architect." In Knoxville he built houses for the rich, each seemingly more elaborate than the last. And in 1875 he designed the much-anticipated new Kern building.

The Kern Building, or Oddfellows Hall, as it would sometimes be known, was one of the most impressive commercial buildings in town. Fifty-one feet wide and 120 feet deep, it stretched halfway to Walnut, and would accommodate all of Kern's operations, including his bakery and candy factory.

Its first floor would hold Kern's retail component, and confectionary; its second floor, his "Ice Cream Hall" of three rooms, the finest of them finished in black walnut and ash; and its third would be "elegantly fitted out and furnished by the Oddfellows" to serve the Knoxville branch of that fraternal organization. "Mr. Kern is one of our representative men," the *Herald* boasted. He had "risen to an enviable position among the wide-awake and progressive citizens of the East Tennessee metropolis."

Near the end of construction, the project suffered a horrific setback. On November 8, 1875, a small crew of specialists was applying galvanized iron cornices to the almost-finished building. Just after returning to work after lunch, two were on a scaffold about 40 feet above the ground, waiting for three others to arrive. Enos Warters, a young man from Shieldstown, was reaching out to grasp a piece of iron cornice a co-worker attempted to hand to him just before climbing aboard the scaffold when one of the iron supports broke loose, sending Warters plummeting to the pavement. He landed on his head, crushing his skull. His colleague, Mike Burchell, fell too, but somehow grabbed some of the scaffolding rope; he saved his own life, but slid "with such rapidity that the rope took all the flesh from his hands, laying the bones bare."

A doctor lived within sight of the accident and arrived immediately, but Warters died on the scene 20 minutes after the fall. "The cause of the accident cannot be explained, nor can any reason be given why the iron should give way…had the rod but held but a few minutes longer, five men would have precipitated down instead of one."

Over the next few months, the building was finished by degrees, the tragedy all but forgotten. By spring, hundreds of people had already had a good look at the interior of the building, and raved about it; earlier in the spring, fraternal groups from the Oddfellows to the Daughters of Rebekah had already held grand banquets in the building's complex honeycomb of halls—from the second floor one had to go downstairs to get to the two or more halls on the third floor. On April 26, celebrating the 55th anniversary of the Independent Order of Odd Fellows, the local chapters, comprising about 300 members, convened for a "grand procession" which commenced at the Kern building at noon, "rigged up in their regalia, with banners afloat, and headed by a band of music." After a parade through Knoxville, the Odd Fellows reconvened at Kern's at 3:00 for a formal dedication of the hall. Employers were apparently forgiving about the time off on a Wednesday afternoon.

Hardly any business opening in Knoxville history has seen the sort of grand opening that Kern's main retail business did, on May 11, 1876, just in time for the height of ice-cream season. Kern painstakingly carted in his equipment, and fitted out the new, updated version of his ice-cream saloon in a grand style befitting the Gilded Age. He had installed an elevator and oscillating fans, both of them steam-powered, in those days before Knoxville was wired for electricity.

Only after he bought some original art, obtained at an auction, for the walls of the ice-cream saloon, did he pronounce it ready. It was, according to the *Chronicle*, "beautiful." Disregarding conflict of interest, the newspaper admitted that its night crew of editors and printers had accepted "a bountiful supply of splendid cake and ice cream."

The building was "a monument to the enterprise of our worthy citizen Mr. Peter Kern, and one of the finest and largest brick buildings in the city.…everything in arrangement about it showing the good taste of Mr. Kern.... The saloon is large and well ventilated, and will prove a delightful retreat from the scorching sun of the day, and a pleasant place to pass an hour at night."

The building at 1 Market Square would be a major institution, not only on the Square but in Knoxville, and famous throughout East Tennessee. Even Chattanooga papers wrote admiring and perhaps envious stories about Kern's. Kern would advertise that his ice cream would be "served at all hours by polite waiters."

You don't make many enemies selling candy, even if you're a foreign-born former Confederate soldier in a Union town, and Kern may have been the most popular Knoxvillian of his era.

The original, two-story Kern building was used, at least temporarily, by Knoxville's fledgling YMCA. The same night that the new Kern's opened, the reformist Christian society held a sociable amidst works of painting and sculpture, as an "Italian string band...discoursed sweet music on the balcony. A melodeon had also been provided, and good singing was also a part of the programme."

∾

At age 25, Market Square was, without question, an institution. In March, 1878, an unsigned editorial in the *Daily Chronicle* noted, "Our busy little Square is rapidly attaining no little importance as a trade center in our city, and it is more noticeable every day. We now have every branch of trade in the city represented, almost, and all seems to do a healthy business, considering the times. [The Panic of 1878 was a significant recession that touched several corners of American business.] Of a solid row of business houses on each side of the Square, there is only one vacant room at this time. This is a striking contrast with other portions of the city. There has been a marked and noticeable improvement in this respect in the past year or two. Prior to that time, the Square had a reputation only for marketing purposes, the sale of groceries, etc, and was only visited for that purpose, with rare exceptions. But now, see the contrast. We can boast of some establishments who keep just as fashionable stocks of dry goods, ladies furnishing goods, etc., etc., as are to be found anywhere, and it is a noticeable fact that the fashionable bon-ton trade of the city is being more attracted to the Square daily...."

That upscale, cosmopolitan trend would dominate the Square for about 40 years, at least as an ideal.

∾

Kern became one of Knoxville's earliest and best-known purveyors of soft drinks. It may be that when the first Coca Cola was sold in Knoxville in the 1880s, it came from a Kern's tap in the Ice Cream Saloon.

But he had impressive competition, right on the Square. Another contender for that speculative honor is George Washington Albers, the Cincinnati-born son of a German immigrant. Trained in the Cincinnati College of Pharmacy, he was known in his own day as a prominent Knoxville pharmacist—though he's not as well remembered as his younger brother, Andrew Jackson Albers, the Union veteran who founded a major pharmaceutical company that thrived for more than a century. G.W. Albers, who came to Knoxville a few years after the Civil War to help with A.J. Albers' early firm, Sanford, Chamberlain, and Albers, split off on his own sometime in the 1870s to open a single-storefront retail drugstore on the east side of the Square. It was a small but not necessarily a modest place. The elaborate tiara-like pediment of his building at 14 Market Square—it once also included an oversized mortar and pestle—still sets it apart from its neighbors, and contemporary descriptions of the place make it sound like a standout: "one of the neatest and most attractive establishments in this trade…a large and handsome store, which is tastefully fitted up…." Albers was a college-educated pharmacist, of course, known to be "thoroughly skilled, scientific and practical" and much respected by medical doctors as a trustworthy pharmacist—but he may have been most famous for his extravagant soda fountain, which was a wonder to behold, whether one was thirsty or not.

G.W. Albers, who lived just a few doors to the north of the Square, was the more politically active of the two brothers, serving prominently on the Board of Aldermen for about 15 years in the 1870s and '80s. He continued to run his drugstore through the end of the century.

~

Several Oddfellows fraternal organizations thrived in Knoxville in the years after the Civil War; one of them was reserved for women. They all met in the Kern Building's hall, on different nights. That fraternal organization may have had a hand in the investment, in cooperation with Kern, because even Kern's address was sometimes given as Oddfellows Hall. Oddfellows and other of Knoxville's several secret organizations would use the building for evening meetings on a weekly or biweekly basis, entering from the Union Avenue side.

In the late 19th century, many other fraternal organizations met on the Square, usually in a second- or third-floor chamber. So many converged there that in any given month, the Square saw more evenings with a lodge meeting than without. The added after-dark foot traffic of middle-class men (and at least that one chapter of female Oddfellows) enhanced the Square's round-the-clock reputation. Perhaps because of the habit of regimentation and trauma of war, the postwar years have never been matched, before or since, as a time for men to join fraternal groups.

One of the more earnest and less secretive of all the fraternal organizations was the Young Men's Christian Association. The Knoxville YMCA had been one of the nation's first when it was first founded in the early 1850s. When it was re-founded after the war, it met occasionally in places like Kern's, but later located in the upper

The earliest known photograph of Peter Kern's 1876 building, advertised as "P. KERN'S CONFECTIONERY" At the top it says "Oddfellows Hall"; the building's upper floors headquartered male and female chapters of that fraternity. The tree visible to the left apparently stood in the graveyard of Second Presbyterian Church. McClung Historical Collection.

floors of the Borches Building, just across Asylum Avenue, at the north end of the Square. The Y was an activist organization, preaching against alcohol consumption and racial injustice. It also formed some of the region's first football and basketball teams.

∾

By 1876, when a new City Directory came out, the Square comprised 37 businesses, not counting the Market House merchants. Among them was a liquor store on the northwestern corner run by a fiercely partisan former Confederate artillery

The elegant interior of Peter Kern's Ice Cream Saloon, from a photograph taken around 1900. The "saloon" boasted several cosmopolitan amenities: chandeliers, art on the walls, white-jacketed waiters, and late-night hours. It was reportedly a scene of much flirtation. McClung Historical Collection.

sergeant named John F. Horne. Without the burden of a family of his own, he became one of East Tennessee's most vigorous Confederate veterans, helping to organize several reunions. He wasn't yet 20 when he'd been captured by Union forces at Cumberland Gap, whereupon spent the balance of the war in a prison camp near Chicago, but in Knoxville he was known, apparently without irony, as "General Horne."

Nearby was Thomas Burrier, the gunsmith; and by then, Market Square boasted at least two saloons. The Square kept its rough-edged frontier flavor, but the block was diversifying. It hosted a physician, Dr. Levi Woods; a "millinery and fancy goods" store; a dress maker's shop; a jeweler.

An easy mix of immigrants and locals is suggested in some of the grocery partnerships: Fanz and Jones, Grocers. Chapman & Bolli, Grocers. But rarer than these immigrant shopkeepers in the 1870s were women who owned prosperous businesses. In 1876 the Square hosted a boarding house run by a Mrs. Lavincy Hall, perhaps a widow. If she was not the first female entrepreneur to establish a permanent presence on Market Square, she was certainly one of the first. Another, Mrs. B.F. Story, ran another boarding house around the corner on "Union nr. Mkt. Sqr."

These no-frill dormitories were popular among the urban single people of all ages, who might stay for days or years. Knoxville also offered hotels, which tended to be more expensive.

Many more boarding houses would follow; most of the women who ran legitimate businesses downtown in the 19th century were mistresses of boarding houses. Women's management of these early hostelries is a neglected chapter in the history of women in business, and of business in general. Boarding-house management was a rare industry that rewarded familiarity with domestic skills women might have learned through their families, like cooking and laundry. Boarding houses would be an institution on the Square for 70 years—the Market Square area, including adjacent blocks, especially those of Union and Prince just to the South, constituted one of the city's highest concentrations of boarding houses. Thanks to the fact that there were always at least a few dozen people living, or staying, on the Square—tenants stepping out for a smoke, windows glowing with the lantern light of a late-night reader—the place never seemed empty.

The *Whig's* progeny, the *Chronicle*, would move to Gay Street before spawning into another Republican paper, the *Knoxville Journal*, in 1885. Parson Brownlow had died in the spring of 1877, at the age of 72, a perhaps surprisingly old age, given his health complaints and well-armed enemies. Still, it seemed the end of an era, as Knoxville was more and more putting the Civil War, and the passions that inspired it, behind.

After Brownlow's death, Joseph Mabry, who was becoming better known for his depth of personal spite than any of his business fortunes, including Market Square, began casting aspersions about the possibility that the late Parson Brownlow had, while he was governor, received bribes in a complicated railroad-bond scheme. Mabry's story sounded bizarre in some of its particulars, especially when he matter-of-factly brought his own consultations with a "New York spiritualist" into the equation.

For his new paper, the *Chattanooga Times*, a remarkably mature 21-year-old Adolph Ochs wrote an appropriately ambivalent appreciation for this man he had known on Market Square: "Brownlow was a harsh man; a reliable hater; not particular to be politically consistent; eager to carry any point he set his head or heart on; endowed with a violent temper and a vindictive nature...." but he was not dishonest. "Mabry cannot harm Brownlow," Ochs concluded. "He is too thoroughly known throughout the South. He left a photograph of himself, a moral and political picture, which will pass into history with all its lights and shades in strong relief. Detraction cannot hurt him nor praise help him."

A Musical Crucible

I n the 21st century, Market Square traffics even more in music than in fresh produce, and it's one of Market Square's main draws, on a daily basis. Since the 1980s, small nightclub-style bars on the Square have brought in jazz, bluegrass, punk, and folk acts. And for the last decade, Knoxvillians have grown accustomed to witnessing big festival-style events like the Sundown in the City series, which have brought Aaron Neville, George Thorogood, Steve Winwood, and many other major international acts, witnessed by crowds estimated upwards of 10,000 people. Even on a quiet Friday night, buskers playing guitar, fiddle, cello, or accordions appear, either singly or forming pick-up bands. No one has ever come to Market Square seeking silence. Nearly everything else is available on the Square in some form, but silence is a rarity.

Music and the Square go way back. Knoxville played a role in the development of several forms of American popular music, and Market Square often turned out to be its main stage, if, in many cases, an accidental one. Some country and blues figures, and even some jazz legends, played the Square early in their careers.

We're often reminded that country music is named for the country, and many of its original heroes did hail from remote hills and farms, areas much more sparsely populated than Knoxville, an industrial city with a major university. However, by the late 19th century, downtown Knoxville offered the largest daily concentration of country people in East Tennessee, and that demographic anomaly accounts for much of Market Square's early reputation for music. Here, between sales, farmers sawed on a fiddle or plucked a banjo or perhaps encountered exotic new instruments, like a steel guitar or a dobro or a Spanish guitar, for the first time.

It's impossible to know when live music first drew a crowd in Market Square, but it was probably before Peter Kern's cultural events at his bakery in 1868 and 1869, which were accompanied by brass-band performances.

An 1869 description of the state of musical entertainment in Reconstruction-era Knoxville notes "Kern's Hall, Ramsey's Hall, the Hall in the new buildings on Market Square, and Turner Hall, are all neat and pleasant places...but entirely too small for the needs of our citizens." Apparently Knoxvillians witnessed some musical events, likely of a classical sort, at Kern's, the new City Hall assembly room, and elsewhere before the construction of Staub's Opera House on Gay Street in 1872.

Folk music and marketplaces have always gone together, and it's more than possible that the first farmers who sold on the Square played a little fiddle to while away the time or to attract customers. The first musical concert or band show outside on the Square is probably unrecorded. It may have been a snake-oil huckster or one of the small brass bands that formed in the wake of the Civil War, or a fiddler who took advantage of the modest farm-produce crowds even before the war.

Around the 1870s or early '80s—we know this by one old-timer's memory, recounted in a column published in the 20th century—an "Indian doctor" who went by the name of Dr. Lighthall appeared regularly on the square with a Mexican band. "Dr. Lighthall performed seemingly remarkable feats in the way of teeth extraction, and sold his panacea after his really fine band had given a concert to attract an audience."

Market Square had the city jail, and a generation of Knoxvillians grew accustomed to the fact that they'd be serenaded, whether they liked it or not, by inmates. A tongue-in-cheek item in the Knoxville Chronicle of May 28, 1874 noted, "One of the Brummett boys entertained the citizens of Market Square yesterday evening, with songs from his cell in the calaboose. He had been drunk, and wanted to stab a colored man."

The following day came another item which, again, doesn't tell the whole story, but does serve to suggest a scene: "One of the inhabitants of the 'Market Square Institution' aroused the neighborhood yesterday evening with cornfield songs. He was taking it easy."

Historians sometimes run across vague allusions to fiddling contests on the Square in the late 19th century, but contemporary accounts of them seem hard to come by. A fiddling contest held at Staub's Opera House as a novelty in 1883, as part of a classical-music festival, may have led to successors in the more-natural location of Market Square.

By 1886, one particular group was known as the Market House Fiddlers. The quartet included some affluent, college-educated professionals, and may have chosen the name as an arch reference to the country people who sold their wares in the Market House; it may also imply that the Market House was associated with fiddling.

The quartet included Dr. Dave DeArmond, Shed Armstrong, Bartley Griffin, and its celebrity, Robert Taylor. That last member, a fiddle virtuoso from Carter County in Upper East Tennessee, was also an author, a motivational speaker, and a Democratic politician. In a race that gained national headlines, he ran against his Republican brother Alf for the governorship of Tennessee. Celebrated as the War of the Roses, and sometimes presented symbolically as if it were a fiddling championship, the election rendered "Fiddlin' Bob" Taylor the governor; almost always depicted with his fiddle, he was perhaps the most popular governor in the state's history. (Until Roy Acuff, he was probably also the most popular fiddler.)

Though mainly a politician, Taylor was also arguably the best-known musician in post-Civil War East Tennessee, and is sometimes credited as the original popularizer of country music.

The Market Hall, upon its completion in 1897—the dedication ceremonies were accompanied by live music by the Legion Band too-vaguely described in the newspaper as "splendid"—supplied Knoxville with a second-floor public space which served as a public auditorium. Though it sounds like most of the attractions at the auditorium around the turn of the century were speeches, musical events were also common, much of it religious or patriotic in nature.

By 1900, street musicians who played for change, or sometimes sold billets— or cards with lyrics on them—were afoot in downtown Knoxville, and tended to gravitate toward where the largest numbers of people were, including Market Square. Many, perhaps most, of the early hat-out street musicians were blind or otherwise disabled, and played because it was their only way to make a living. Among them were vision-impaired musicians Charlie Oaks and George Reneau, who would much later travel to New York to make some of the first recordings in country-music history. Blues singer and guitarist Brownie McGhee and his brother, Stick McGhee also did some busking in downtown Knoxville, and likely gave Market Square a try.

At least one Market Square music store catered to local musicians albeit probably of a different stripe. Though a Union County native, J.V. Ledgerwood had lived in Illinois and traveled out West as a piano salesman before returning to settle in Knoxville in 1911, when he opened his piano store at the corner of Wall and Market. Ledgerwood, who with his brother Shirley also carried organs and phonographs, moved a few doors west, to 417 Wall Avenue, in 1921, where the store would remain for 40 years. Later, a third Ledgerwood brother, Frank, would operate a dance studio in the Kern building, specializing in tap and ballroom dancing, but also offering piano and vocal lessons.

Market Square became, for a while, a musical marketplace. Around the time of World War I, Wilhite Pianos and Starr Pianos competed next door to each other on the 500 block of Market, near the Arnstein Building. The Starr Pianos building, at 515 Market, offered teaching studio space to several music professionals above its showroom, as well as Cable Hall, apparently a small second-floor auditorium suitable for recitals. The best known of the musical tenants who taught in the rooms upstairs was one Ole Bull Jones, Knoxville's best-known concert violinist of the early 20th century. Named for the legendary Norwegian violinist Ole (pronounced "Oley") Bull, Jones tried to live up to his namesake. Raised in Monroe County, Jones came from a family known both for its musical talent as well as for their involvement in a multi-generational feud. Several of the Joneses died young, violently, and sometimes mysteriously. Ole Bull Jones may have come to Knoxville both to further his musical career and to escape the family fate. By one account, in 1907 the colorful prodigy opened the Ole Bull Theatre on Union near Market Square, in a time when that name still resounded with high culture. That venture apparently didn't last long, but Jones maintained his reputation as a performer, especially on the concert stages of the South, with the help of his famously valuable Cremona violin. He was a familiar figure on Market Square.

Almost as much talked about as his violin technique was his unconventional relationship with an older unmarried woman, Pattie Boyd, the Knoxville Journal *society columnist who's remembered as one of Tennessee's first female working journalists. Jones lived openly with the eccentric Miss Boyd on her estate just east of town, and the two were often seen riding together in her surrey around downtown, but Jones kept his studio on the third floor of the Starr building from 1915 until his sudden death of appendicitis in 1928, at the age of 49.*

≈

Whether Jones ever inspired country fiddlers is unrecorded, but classical and country music cross-pollinated in Knoxville more than most would suppose.

Fiddling contests, held every year in the Market House auditorium, were well in place by the 1920s, though they may have started much earlier. Newspaperman Burt Vincent arrived in Knoxville in 1928. The best-known local newspaper columnist of his time, Vincent had a particular affection for Market Square and the talented characters it attracted. In years to come he would remember the "Old Fiddlers' Conventions" once held on the Square. "Fiddlers came from the cities and the towns, from mountain coves and hollows. They sat upon that stage, and they sawed and sawed, and patted their big muddy shoes on the floor, keeping time to the tunes."

"Seem to recall," Vincent recalls, "that a fellow named Murphy was in charge." A "Squire Murphy" pops up in some memories as a sort of impresario of the fiddling contest, but records don't offer much further detail. A county judge described as a "ruddy-faced lawyer and jurist," Frank Murphy served as Justice of the Peace from 1911 to 1919, and for many years lived at 605 Prince, just about a block from Market Square. He's listed as a Knoxville resident through 1938.

Knoxville's association with the popularization of country music, much of it via live radio shows like the "Tennessee Barn Dance" and, most famously, the "Mid-Day Merry-Go-Round," which happened mainly at Gay Street locations, are well remembered, and their heyday from the mid-1930s to the mid-1950s is legendary for its associations to many major Nashville careers. WNOX's signature lunchtime show "Mid-Day Merry-Go-Round," which drew crowds every weekday, did take place in the Market Square auditorium for a few months around 1936, after the sometimes rowdy show had been evicted from the Andrew Johnson Hotel, but before WNOX's new permanent auditorium was ready for it. It was, in one sense, a return of a party that may have started there.

Some old-timers remember an older, longer-lived but now almost forgotten Market Square institution, the Tennessee Jamboree, as the origin of the live-audience radio show in Knoxville. The weekly show—it arrived every Saturday night—was thriving in the mid-1920s, hosted in the old Market Hall by a now-obscure figure named Horace Hunnicutt. He's hard to trace in local records—a 1932 City Directory does list Hunnicutt as a "studio manager" for WNOX, later, briefly, in "radio promotions" for the News Sentinel. He disappears altogether before World War II. Still, an older generation remembered him as a forgotten hero of country music, perhaps the originator of the live-audience broadcast in Knoxville at a time when country music was enjoying its first wave of popularity.

In the press, country musicians and country-music events were taken for granted, only occasionally mentioned in news stories, and then condescendingly. In that era, classical musicians were described in detail in news stories, even when they were second-rate, and even if they came to Knoxville only once, for a single performance. Performances by local folk musicians rarely got any press attention, and in library files there's very little biographical information handy about local musicians before 1930. We know they were on the Square from the few occasions when a reporter did mention them, usually in describing something else. In her 1929 essay about the strange ways of Market Square's country people in the New York Times, *Rosa Naomi Scott describes street musicians as part of the scene in any visit to the place. "There are minstrels in quaint old Market Square. All day a blind mountaineer with flaxen hair and a guitar walks slowly down the market sidewalk, keeping close to the walls of the stores. He sings wistful hymns, or occasionally an old English ballad that has gained a novel twist by centuries in the Appalachians. He is not incongruous in the welter of flowers and vegetables and bargaining. He is of and with his kind.*

"Another minstrel, a little boy in a khaki suit, with a moving childish voice tramps the pavement, too. A brother, hardly older, moves along beside to give aid if necessary. As the little blind boy walks bravely forward, in his utter blackness, lifting his small clear song, the women in the marketplace are swept with an electric impulse of giving."

The reputation for fiddling contests may have had something to do with why the Square attracted a national record label's recording crew in the fall of 1929.

≈

Though Knoxville has bred many groundbreaking musicians, and owns a rich heritage of musical performance, both in concert and on live radio, it was never a major recording center. In 1929-30, though, Knoxville enjoyed a fascinating, if brief, era as a regional recording mecca.

The St. James Hotel was a six-story place on Wall, just barely offset from the Square. Though outwardly built in the graceful styles of its turn-of-the-century era, it was constructed mostly of concrete, and still advertised itself as "Fireproof." The St. James had been built not long after the great fire of 1897, which began in a hotel on the block of Gay Street parallel to Market Square.

Radio station WNOX, established in 1921 and the first radio station in East Tennessee, usually broadcast from a studio around the corner on Gay Street, but had previously kept its main studio at the St. James. Apparently there was enough of it left to make it easy to set up a soundproof room there.

Up through the mid-1920s, almost all recordings, even those of folk and country musicians, were made at studios in New York. Several Knoxvillians had made the trip north to make their first records. A few big-time record labels had come south to make field recordings of country musicians in the region before, most famously in Bristol in 1927; Columbia had tried Johnson City in 1928. Not to be outdone, in 1929 Brunswick/Vocalion decided to try Knoxville.

When a crew of four unloaded almost a ton of audio equipment at the St. James, the guy giving the orders was one Richard Voynow. A pianist himself, Dick Voynow was a minor star in jazz circles. One of the few musicians who had ever collaborated with near-mythical cornetist Bix Beiderbeck, Voynow had later co-authored, with Hoagy Carmichael, the '20s pop hit "Riverboat Shuffle." In Knoxville, Voynow led an apparently open-minded series of recording sessions—two extended series of sessions, in late 1929 and early 1930—that made recordings of dozens of local musicians in open auditions.

Most of those who showed up were country acts, including the Tennessee Ramblers, with its rare female guitarist, Willie Seivers, perhaps the first woman to take such a prominent role in a popular country band. Nashville had no reputation as a recording center at the time, and a few musicians came over from Middle Tennessee, including Uncle Dave Macon, the iconic banjoist, who recorded some sides at the St. James, on March 31, 1930. (He probably knew Market Square already. In a song he cut in the early 1920s in New York, he made a cryptic reference to being "Here at the Windsor Hotel, in Knoxville, Tennessee." The only Windsor Hotel in Knoxville history was back in the late 1890s, when Macon was a young man—on Asylum Avenue, adjacent to Market Square.)

Country music was a lucrative, and fairly new industry, and may be what Brunswick came for. But in fact musicians from several other genres appeared at the St. James to play into the same microphones. Among them were cafeteria-worker Leola Manning, a spirited hard-blues singer who lived in East Knoxville; though

The St. James Hotel, on Wall Avenue, ca. 1925. Built mostly of concrete as Knoxville's first "fireproof" hotel, it had a small radio studio in its lobby which hosted a series of recordings for the Brunswick label in 1929–30, featuring Uncle Dave Macon, the original Tennesee Chocolate Drops, the Tennessee Ramblers, and Maynard Baird's jazz orchestra, the Southern Serenaders. It remained in business as a hotel until shortly before it was torn down for TVA's new headquarters in the 1970s. Courtesy of Mark Heinz.

the only recordings she ever made were at the St. James, she has a bit of a cult following today. One of her St. James recordings which appears in some modern collections is called "The Arcade Building Moan." A bluesy dirge about a fatal fire in a Union Avenue apartment building, it was, remarkably, recorded just days after the tragedy itself. One line goes, "Listen, listen how the bell did ring / When the Arcade Building burned down." It's almost certainly a reference to the bell in City Hall, which tolled such tragedies.

Another act was the black uptempo jazz-for-strings group known as the Tennessee Chocolate Drops, featuring guitarist Carl Martin and violinist/mandolinist Howard Armstrong, who later reunited as the trio Martin, Bogan, and Armstrong. Under that name they made several records in the 1970s, when they were campus favorites. Maybe the largest band to record at the St. James was an early horn-based jazz orchestra called Maynard Baird and his Southland Serenaders, a popular local band who had a following up and down the East Coast. They were also among the most success-ful, both in their own time and in posterity, albeit modestly: a St. James recording, "Postage Stomp," appears on jazz compilations released in the 1990s.

The Depression hit right in the middle of the recording session, and nothing much became of the St. James sessions in a commercial way. Some participants were bitter about the disappointment.

A few years after Voynow and his crew wrapped up, the young Duke Ellington and his jazz orchestra played a show at the Market Hall in 1934. Descriptions of it are elusive; we know about it only because Ellington himself mentioned it in an interview many years later. Cutting-edge jazz in the old Market Hall was probably the excep-tion; more and more, in the '20s and '30s, the music heard on Market Square was the indigenous music of the country people who had come to dominate the Square after World War I.

Columnist Vincent would later claim, "Why, country music, as public entertain-ment, was born in that Market Hall. It was there that Roy Acuff started sawing his fiddle for pay, and Lowell Blanchard gave birth to the 'Merry-Go-Round' and the 'Tennessee Barn Dance.'" Originally Blanchard was the popular disk jockey and MC for WNOX; the "Tennessee Barn Dance" was a Saturday-evening radio show on WNOX, which eventually moved into the much-larger Lyric Theatre on Gay Street.

Vincent knew Acuff, who joined the Grand Ole Opry in the late 1930s and became country music's first nationwide superstar, and a major influence on musicians of the era, especially the young Hank Williams, who imitated his nasally lonesome singing style. Acuff's early fame was based partly on a song he'd learned from other Knoxville street musicians, called "The Great Speckled Bird." If Vincent's claim that Acuff began his career as a professional musician on Market Square was true, as it likely is, it's another major distinction for the Square. Acuff would be one of the most influential musicians of the 20th century, for popularizing country music as a national phenomenon—but also for popularizing the small string band, which in *the latter half of the century had become the basis for most pop music. Acuff is often mentioned even in rock'n'roll histories.*

Who knows what effects the musical Square might have had on a couple of teenage brothers who regularly accompanied their father driving all the way from northeastern Alabama to sell sorghum on Knoxville's Market Square. Ira and Charlie Loudermilk, as they were then known, would be better known as the Louvin Brothers when they became famous for their guitar and mandolin work and especially their close harmonies, earning membership in the Grand Old Opry. Along the way they lived in Knoxville, briefly, to broadcast on WROL, but it was probably coincidental that one of their most successful recordings was a weird old ballad called "Knoxville Girl."

Major novelist Cormac McCarthy mentions music on Market Square in two of his books: In The Orchard Keeper, *set around 1940, an accordion player works in conjunction with a singing evangelist. "[H]e turned left and went up to Market Square. On the corner a man was screaming incoherently and brandishing a tattered Bible. Next him stood an old woman strapped into an accordion, mute and patient as a draft horse…. The man stopped screaming and the accordion began and they sang, the two voices hoarse and high-pitched rising in a sad quaver to the calliope-like creaking of the instrument."*

In Suttree, *set in the early 1950s, another musician takes a turn as the Square's street musician. "Suttree went on through the markethouse and out the double doors to Wall Avenue. A blind black man was fretting a dobro with a broken bottleneck and picking out an old blues run." The fisherman had just sold a catfish for $1.04. "Suttree let the four pennies into the tin cup taped to the box. Get em, Walter, he said."*

(Walter's choice of instument may call for a footnote: the dobro was little known before the late 1930s, when Roy Acuff's band, the Crazy Tennesseans, introduced the obscure instrument, designed to capitalize on the Hawaiian-music craze of the 1920s but never successfully. Some music historians credit Acuff and Knoxville with popularizing the previously unusual sound, which became part of country's fabled twang.)

Neither of McCarthy's Market Square musicians plays a role in the book; they're just there, part of the scene, and impossible to ignore.

Market Square's musical reputation may have been the main reason an RCA *scout named Brad McKuen made a stop at one particular record shop a regular feature of each of his mid-century trips to Tennessee. He had a theory about this shop, and Market Square in general.*

Sam Morrison was a merchant on the east side, at 22½ Market Square, who ran a store called Bell Sales Company. Morrison had started it as a general store in Mechanicsville a few years earlier, but by the time he got to Market Square, Bell was mainly a record store. Country music was hot in 1954, and on his trips South, McKuen made a point of stopping in at Bell Sales to see what was selling. Morrison attracted an unusual combination of both city and country customers. McKuen's theory was that anything that sold well at Bell Sales on Market Square had the potential to go nationwide. That summer, he happened to pop in at the front end of a phenomenon.

Just a few weeks earlier, Morrison had gotten a new disk from the small independent Memphis R&B record company, Sun. "There's something very interesting happening here," he told McKuen. "It's really weird." He claimed he was selling a box a day, and had sold perhaps as many as 5,000 copies, just that summer. Just to show McKuen what he meant, he put a 78 on the turntable, and played it on the outside speakers. Immediately, a middle-aged white farmer came in. "By Granny, I want that record," he said.

RCA's McKuen had never heard of the recording artist, a teenager with the unlikely name of Elvis Presley. He bought a copy to send back to the studio boss at RCA in New York, and a copy to keep for himself. Though Elvis hardly visited Knoxville early in his career, the big-time recording industry first encountered his music on Market Square.

Though Market Square did draw some musical performances in the 1960s and '70s, often in association with the Dogwood Arts Festival, the Mall era was not necessarily a high point for music on the Square. It did at least host an excellent record store in the form of Tucker's, an appealingly cluttered place on the west side which was maybe the most encyclopedically stocked record store in town at the time.

Sam Morrison, in his record store at 22½ Market Square. In the early 1950s, RCA scout Brad McKuen considered Morrison's shop, Bell Sales Co., a bellweather, so to speak, of the potential for regional recording artists to go national. RCA first became aware of Elvis Presley by way of his phenomenal popularity at Bell Sales in the summer of 1954, when the singer was still unknown in most of the country. Courtesy of Mary Linda Schwarzbart.

In the early 1980s, small nightclubs like the Hang Up occasionally hosted live music, usually a rock or jazz band just on a weekend; in the middle part of the decade, jazz recording artist Lee Miles Stone ran a club on the east side known as the Milestone which brought a suave touch of urbanity to the Square, otherwise almost vacant in the evenings—but it was short-lived.

The Square remained mostly quiet at night until 1992, when young music promoter Kevin Niceley opened a place at No. 28, in one of Fikret Gencay's unimproved buildings, called the Mercury Theatre. Just a long, spare room without much in the way of seating and a minimal beer bar to one side, the Mercury served a market disappointed by the closing of the groundbreaking Old City nightclub Ella Guru's, which was one of very few nightclubs of its era which featured live performers almost every night. The Mercury brought in numerous big-time acts from counterculture troubadour Jonathan Richman to rising pop-radio band Cake. The Mercury's most memorable attractions trended toward the loud and the startling. With well-connected music maven Benny Smith doing the booking, the Mercury would be a stage for lots of cutting-edge bands of the era, including Yo La Tengo, the Old '97s, the Donnas, the Deftones, and rock-jazz innovators Medeski, Martin, and Wood. Fans remember a particular show by Atlanta band / psycho-burlesque troupe Impotent Sea Snakes, which featured, among other attractions, a cross-dresser breathing fire while walking on stilts.

Maybe more significantly, the Mercury and its hundreds of habitues nurtured local bands. The Mercury Theatre served as the the cradle of several emerging groups, notably alt-pop band Superdrag, which, with its national radio hit "Sucked Out (the Feelin')", was Knoxville's most successful musical group of the late 20th century—and the V-Roys, a.k.a. the Viceroys, another nationally known rock 'n' roll band who sometimes appeared on the Mercury stage with their mentor/producer, major Texas alt-country songwriter Steve Earle.

For a time in the early '90s, Market Square regulars nurtured an edgy reputation, connecting mainly its few businesses that kept evening hours: the dependably surprising Tomato Head, which occasionally featured unusual and even avant-garde live bands late at night; the Snakesnatch, which might be described as an alternative bar—though it was much smaller than the Mercury, it also attracted crowds to see occasional live bands; the Printer's Mark bookstore, which specialized in radical literature and sometimes hosted readings and unusual films. Market Square devotees liked to juxtapose their neighborhood's vibe with that of the Old City, barely four blocks away, which was in the '90s considered more staid, quaint, expensive, and more likely to appeal to older, more settled customers from the suburbs. Even in its quieter times, the Square retained some of its capacity for serendipitous encounters. Eugene Johnson, who became a locally prominent promoter of eastern music and offbeat jazz, was working at the Soup Kitchen in the old Kern Building when he unexpectedly met an inspiration: Indian sitar legend Ravi Shankar came in for lunch.

The Mercury was often the only business open on the Square after 9:00 or so, but it closed in 1999.

Meanwhile, AC Entertainment, the booking agency on its way to launching a new rock-festival institution called Bonnaroo, moved into the top floor of the Arnstein Building, which offered an excellent view of the Square, and with the city's sponsorship, began hosting a series of live shows on the Market Square stage called Sundown in the City. Its early years offered only a handful of performances by mostly local musicians like R.B. Morris, but those shows drew crowds. When a 1999 V-Roys show drew a crowd of about 3,000 to Market Square, even downtown's 9-5 businessmen were impressed. In years to come, names got bigger, and shows got bigger. In the early 2000s, Sundown was a regular every-Thursday event in the spring and early summer, augmented for a couple of years by a similar show in the Autumn, and the free shows became a routine attraction for Knoxville's youth, and some others not so young.

In 2003, enterprising retailers Scott and Bernadette West (Scott West was guitarist for the popular rock band Boy Genius, himself) opened the Preservation Pub in the old Mercury space. Remodeled to look much warmer, more like a traditional bar, with a wait staff and actual seating, it was hardly recognizable to old Mercury fans; still, the Preservation Pub would draw live bands from around the country, many of them touring groups of eclectic styles, leaning toward jazz and folk, liberally defined—generally a quieter vibe than the space's Mercury Theater days. They developed a relationship with maverick public radio station WDVX, which promoted many of their shows. Bands would come from the Northeast or the West Coast for the package of playing live on WDVX and, later, a gig at the Preservation Pub. It would prove to be a durable attraction.

In 2005, the World Grotto, a fancifully decorated basement bar with a quartz bar, a steaming fountain, and faux-cave walls, offered a unique attraction. Originally conceived to have a purely international theme, it honored that with some consistency, bringing in musical groups from Africa and Asia, but in its early years, it would host everyone from '60s-'70s folk star Janis Ian to keyboard great Leon Russell, to, perhaps most surprising of all, considering the venue, bluegrass legend Ralph Stanley.

Still, the most surprising visitor of the early 21st century might have been a fellow who was obvious on the Square in the 19th century: the street musician, the busker. Sometimes resented and run off the Square in the latter 20th century, he returned with more clearly expressed permission from city government. Almost nightly, cellists, pipers, fiddlers, drummers, guitarists, accordion players are audible on the Square, drawn as their forebears were 150 years earlier to the open public space. Some seem to make a living at it, others just come out with an instrument expecting to find an old-time band to play with. They all bring life to the Square, or, rather, honor the life that's always been lurking here.

CHAPTER 3

"A House for All"

*Southern Chivalry, Watermelon Row, and
"The Elegant New Market House"*

Market Square and its host city boomed in the 1880s. Knoxville, claiming that it was adding 1,000 new residents every month, boasted it would soon be the largest city in the South. A walk around Market Square might have made hyperbole easy to believe. Descriptions of the Square, and the people and businesses listed in the City Directory, make it sound still a little like the Wild West, with its saloons and gunsmiths and harness-makers—but perhaps a little more like a brisk neighborhood in a larger city of the Gilded Age, even, perhaps, New York's East Side.

The Square itself hosted an ever-more urban mix of businesses and services: import shops, dentists, cigar stores, and more boarding houses, with fraternal societies and trade unions using upstairs floors in the evenings, as the Market House was more crowded with vendors than ever. In 1882, the Board of Aldermen ordered some repair to the old market building and also responded to pleas for expanding it. They commissioned a 101-foot extension to the northern end. McLemore, Cody & Co. got the contract, and were paid a reasonable-sounding $769.50 for the job, which was more practical than architectural.

Knoxville was becoming a different city, a much-larger city of European immigrants, ambitious young Northerners, and many thousands of others, including

Tennesseans, whose memories of the city did not reach back as far as the Civil War. The city never had much of a sense of its own narrative, anyway: It may be safe to assume that most Knoxvillians in 1882 had never heard of William G. Swan, the progressive young civic booster who a long generation earlier had given the city gaslights—by the 1880s, people were already talking about electric lights, anyway— and co-donated the land for Market Square.

The same oblivion wasn't true of Swan's old partner, Joe Mabry, who remained a conspicuous and recognizable figure in town. Now in his mid-50s, Mabry had experienced a mercurial career as a businessman, litigant, and combatant. In those days, it was typical for men of a certain standing in the community to be called "Colonel" or sometimes "Major" or "Captain." Mabry, in middle age, was known as "General" Mabry. Most sources attribute it, rather vaguely, to the fact that he had contributed uniforms to Confederate troops during the war. But even the hardest-core former Unionists, including Parson Brownlow, also called him General.

As if to compensate for his lack of military service, Mabry got in several "shooting affrays" in the postwar years. Known to carry a derringer, he reportedly drew a gun in anger at a political convention in Nashville. In 1870, in front of the Lamar House barber shop on Gay Street, Mabry actually shot and wounded attorney John Baxter, a political enemy whom Swan had defeated for Confederate Congress, and who had insulted Mabry in a series of letters published in the *Chronicle*.

Mabry's fortunes fluctuated, often downward; his fondest project was a railroad project which foundered in the 1870s. Through it all, he was always able to supply for his family in their fine home on Dandridge Avenue, a mile east of downtown. At the Custom House just south of his Square in May, 1881, his "blooded horses" were auctioned off.

His sons seemed to take after him, in some ways. One was killed in a saloon fight on Gay Street, just this side of the Southern station, in late 1881. The elder Mabry may never have gotten over that.

On Tuesday morning, October 19, 1882, the sounds of several loud gunshots muted by the morning rain, startled shoppers on the Square. Banker Thomas O'Conner, Joseph Mabry, and his son, Joseph Mabry III, all lay dead in front of the Mechanics Bank & Trust building, on the 600 block of Gay Street.

O'Conner, the president of the bank, seems to have fired the first shots at the elder Mabry, from a shotgun in the doorway to his bank, before the younger Mabry returned fire, as he was killed himself. Several bystanders were wounded. The reason a wealthy, middleaged bank president should have ambushed and shot an aging businessman to death, regardless of the man's reputation as a gunfighter, has been a matter of speculation for more than a century. It was rumored to have had something to do with Mabry's suspicions and threats concerning the murder of his son almost a year earlier.

Mark Twain, then finishing his memoir, *Life On the Mississippi*, couldn't resist citing, in a lengthy footnote in Chapter 40, the sudden death of three armed men in downtown as an illustrative example of modern "Southern chivalry."

Mabry and his son were both buried in Old Gray, on the same day as Thomas O'Conner was buried a few hundred feet away in the same graveyard. The Mabrys' modest obelisk is not far from the massive obelisk of Parson Brownlow and the stones of Thomas Humes, Oliver Perry Temple, William Rule, and many other prominent old Unionists.

≈

With both the police station and the fire department keeping a daily vigil on the north end, Market Square may have been safer than the rest of town from some sorts of disasters. However, there seems to have been a major fire on the west side of the Square, probably in the early 1880s. News accounts are hard to come by; our main evidence of it is that in an 1884 Sanborn fire-insurance map of the Square, there's a gap in the middle of the west side, at addresses 15, 17, and 19, between a cluster of three saloons and a grocery. In the gap is the simple phrase "RUINS OF FIRE." Some of the original buildings were constructed of wood, and these may have been among them. Demand was such on the Square that they were quickly replaced, this time with brick.

Peter Kern's elaborate bakery still ruled Market Square. According to an 1884 assessment of business in Knoxville, Kern's "breads, rolls, and cakes are simply unequalled in lightness, freshness, and delicacy." The store sold "every variety of sweet-meats and bon-bons imaginable, of the purest and most wholesome manufacture. Mr. Kern makes all his own kiss-candies, taffy sticks, and fancy candy," with the help of 14 assistants. "Mr. Kern also deals extensively in foreign fruits, fireworks, etc., ice cream, and fresh oysters in season."

Kern's place was a palace of polished wood and marble, paintings and engravings, cut-glass chandeliers whose "brilliant jets of light reflect every color of the rainbow," according to one admirer, who added a particular reputation of Kern's: "Around white marble tables scattered all over the great hall, youth and beauty meet.... It has been said that Cupid has done more effective work within this enclosure than [in] any other place in the land." For a couple of generations, Kern's was the safest place in town to take a date.

Kern apparently dealt with the Albers soda-fountain threat by installing one of "solid onyx" which was advertised to be equally good for hot beverages in the winter and cold beverages in the summer.

Kern was one of the most popular guys in Knoxville, once elected alderman, and it wasn't too surprising, in 1890, when voters elected the German confectioner mayor of Knoxville. He would be the last of several foreign-born politicians to hold that office.

However, from an economic point of view, the Square's most impressive business of the early 1880s was the one at 24 Market Square. Col. Benjamin Rush Strong was responsible for establishing the fountain in the middle of the square for watering livestock. He also had a store, from which he sold dry goods, boots, and shoes. The B.R. Strong & Co. employed 14 assistants—both male and, significantly for the times, female. Strong's did more than $200,000 worth of business a year—several million, in modern dollars—with regular customers in four states. Part of what made it impressive was its architecture, or at least one feature that made it a wonder to behold.

Kerns' locally famous soda fountain, ca. 1890. Note the unusual standing fans. It was just part of the complex attraction of Peter Kern's landmark store, which also included a bakery, an ice-cream parlor, a candy shop, and a toy store, but on a hot summer day the large fountain, made of marble with brightly polished brass fixtures, was Kern's chief draw. The complicated machine dispensed more than a dozen beverages. High on the fountain is the famous logo of Coca-Cola. Many Knoxvillians first encountered the surprising new beverage from Atlanta in this room. The place was so popular it's a safe bet this photograph was taken before it opened for the day. McClung Historical Collection.

Strong's store combined two buildings, one facing Gay Street, the other facing Market Square, back to back, "from street to street, with *an arcade over the alley*, making their store-room the largest in the city, over 250 feet in length," according to an 1884 guide to Knoxville business. "It is generally conceded to be the most extensive and admirably arranged...in the city." Benjamin Rush Strong and A.W. Strong were "live business men, conducting their affairs on the most elevated plain of commercial honor and integrity, and are deservedly esteemed among the best business men of East Tennessee, and the city has every reason to feel proud of the possession of so reliable and enterprising a firm."

Strong left his name on the Square in one lasting way; the intact alley between Market Square and Gay Street, and perhaps the best-preserved alley in town, is the one B.R. Strong's arcade somehow traversed. Although the arcade/bridge over the alley vanished probably more than a century ago, it's still sometimes known as Strong Alley. (It's also sometimes known as Armstrong Alley, likely a nod to the clothing store of that name located at No. 34 in the early 20th-century.)

If Kern's soda jerks were all men, it appears his candy clerks were women. Kern's candies, manufactured in the same building, are stacked cannonball-style in these display cases. Kern's also sold toys and holiday accessories. McClung Historical Collection.

Another lasting name on Market Square was that of Jacob Borches, an in-law of Strong's. Described as both a "charitable and public-minded citizen," but also "one of the most conservative businessmen in the city…a businessman of the old type," Borches had a grocery business at 32 Market Square; he eventually built a large edifice on Prince, immediately north of the Square, known as the Borches Building. It would house his own business, but its third and fourth floors would be devoted to the 19th-century YMCA, during the height of its era as a Christian reformist organization.

An elaborately detailed bird's-eye view of the city and its buildings, illustrated with apparently exacting precision by Milwaukee lithographers Beck & Pauli in 1886, is just a drawing, but is also our only clear image of Market Square of that era. In it, the Market House is represented as a long, low, simple building with a double-arched front, very similar to the building that appears in 1859 photographs. The two-story City Hall building is still separate, an almost cubical building on the north, the dot above the Market House's *i*. Most of the buildings of the Square are taller than the Market House, two-story buildings with arched-window facades.

This circa 1890 interior shows, on close inspection, 10 clerks waiting to answer customers' needs for baking supplies, among them yeast, Purina Health Flower, and, most prominently, Kennedy's Biscuit, a well-known Chicago firm. We may not think of Tennesseans as relying on Chicago for biscuits, but the company's product apparently enjoyed a vogue on Market Square. McClung Historical Collection.

The Kern building stands out as much taller than anything else, and appears to be the most elaborate building on the Square.

Most of the buildings of Market Square, however, were simple, for the times; some sported unusual cornicework or cast-iron construction, but they were mainly brick, built with little or no foundation. Fancy facades not only added to cost, but on Market Square, they were unlikely to impress; the large and ever-growing Market House, by the end of the century, blocked any frontal vantage point more distant than 50 feet or so. That fact in itself may have muted any motive for elaborate facades.

A picture of the west side of Market Square, taken circa 1928. Signs for Mrs. L.E. Banks, a boarding-house matron, and grocer Louis Licht are visible. The elaborate tall building at center, with its variegated arches and bay window, was an oddity among its mostly stoic neighbors on the Square. It's unclear why its unknown builder constructed a taller, showier and more expensive building than those near it. This building at No. 19 served many purposes over the years, including a harnessmaker's shop, a boarding house and a movie theater. It vanished with little comment around 1960, replaced with a simple two-story cinderblock building. McClung Historical Collection.

The era did offer some exceptions, besides Kern's, one of which remains an architectural mystery. On the west side of the Square, at No. 19, was an especially elaborate three-story building which appears in old photographs rising sharply above its neighbors with a big gable that broke free from the conservative horizontal lines of the west side; by the 1890s it was easily the more ornate building on the Square. The mystery is why is was so elaborate; it appears to have served mostly modest purposes, first a harnessmaker's shop, then a stove shop, with, at least intermittently, boarding on the floors above.

It's possible that its location is the key; before the Market House joined with City Hall and blocked views entirely, a few of the middle addresses, including No. 19, might have been visible from the other side of the Square, and offered a motive to impress from that vantage.

Unfortunately, it's one of the few buildings from its era that no longer exists. It was torn down, apparently without fanfare or general regret, around 1960. A business built over the site without bothering to clear all the rubble that fell into the basement, with a much-shorter two-story building of plain cinderblock.

Market Square was generally the domain of merchants, in the 19th century, not necessarily artists. But as with every rule proposed for Market Square, there are exceptions. Probably the first true artisans who ever hung a shingle on Market Square were at No. 33, home of W.B. Fenton's Monumental Marble Works. Originally from New York, Fenton set up his shop on the Square around 1872, employing a team of six sculptors. Among Knoxville's first full-time professional artists, they worked daily on gravestones. The late Victorian era was an all-time high point in funereal statuary, and many of the statues and intricate carvings people would admire for more than a century to come in grand old cemeteries like Old Gray were carved right here at Fenton's. The stone-carving business was advertised to be "the most extensive of its kind in East Tennessee," delivering its works to customers throughout the South. Knoxville was just then developing its reputation as the Marble City, for its natural supply of several grades of marble and limestone.

Some fine artists occasionally appeared on the Square, too, if ephemerally. Late 19th century Knoxville saw a flowering of interest in oil painting, mostly among hobbyists, inspired by the successes of a couple of local professionals. Some artists had the luxury to study technique and express their talents, and one of the best of them was named Adelia Lutz. Wife of a prosperous insurance man who lived on Kingston Pike, she had studied art formally at the Corcoran Gallery and the Pennsylvania Academy of Fine Arts, and would eventually be central to an ambitious organization called the Nicholson Art League, which would nurture some of Tennessee's first and best efforts in impressionism. By 1888, the young artist and her friend Sally Thomas were working out of a studio in the Kern's building, offering "lessons in painting, drawing, and embroidery."

~

Business along the sides of the Square was diverse and dynamic. Complaints about the condition of the Market House itself, though, were almost as old as the oldest bricks in its hulk, and in 1886, City Council approved still another extension, to add still more square footage for the vendors. But by the mid-1880s, some were

This shot, looking north on Prince Street (later Market) toward the Square from Clinch around 1900, shows the block known as Watermelon Row. During high-volume weekends in the summertime, it was regarded as an extension of Market Square. On the right, on the location of the present Krutch Park, are a dense cluster of businesses, including watchmakers, grocers, sewing machine merchants, and druggists. The sign shaped like a boot indicates Hackworth's cobbler shop. Next to it is McCallie Brothers Dentists' office. And the fancifully striped front is apparently the shop of barber Nathan Ostfeld. McClung Historical Collection.

complaining that the Square itself was "too small" to serve a city the size of Knoxville. The space wasn't always big enough for the crowds and vendors that jammed it during the growing season, and sometimes overflowed beyond the boundaries of the Square. On heavy days, wagons jammed Asylum Street from the Square to Gay Street. Meanwhile, another block to the south became an institution, of sorts, for its ability to accommodate the spillover.

Between Market Square and the Custom House, the 500 block of Market Street, then still known as Prince, already had some Market Square-type permanent businesses on it: a couple of grocers and fruitsellers, and W.F. Robinson's Restaurant, when restaurants—as opposed to boarding houses or saloons that also served food—were still a novelty. All those businesses were on the east side of Prince; the west side was still occupied by the godfather of the neighborhood, the old Second Presbyterian Church and its graveyard. (The arrangement of that block, with dense buildings on the east side, and green open space, with trees, on the west, was exactly opposite of what it would be in the 21st century.)

By 1881, especially at the height of the summer melon season, farmers who didn't get to the Square in time to claim a space began spilling toward the south, effectively making the city block an unofficial annex to Market Square. One East Tennessee product was particularly bulky, and tended to swell in supply—and demand—during the middle of the summer. Each August, it was not unusual for 80 to 100 cartloads of watermelons to try to jam into the Square. The 500 block of Prince became known as Watermelon Row. Few complained about that particular manifestation of the Square's problem with overcrowding. Less crowded, smelly, and noisy than the Market House itself, and often cooler, in the shade of the trees of Second Presbyterian's old graveyard, it would become an icon, in years to come: an afternoon of lemonade and shopping for melons would be the picture of a Knoxville summer.

～

In June, 1883, an editor for the *Knoxville Daily Tribune* wrote, "Yesterday morning we had the pleasure of a stroll though the market, and we found that we were amply repaid for our time and trouble. It is, indeed, a pleasure to see the variety and amount of good things…. Strangers coming to the city should always be taken to the market. There is nothing that would more convince them of our agricultural resources…. Men who know pronounce Knoxville['s] vegetable market to be the finest in the South!"

In years to come, others would describe Market Square as an essential Knoxville experience for reasons having less to do with its variety of produce than its particular mixture of humanity.

The Square seems always to have been partly residential, but it's hard to tell for certain how many people lived there in the late 1800s. The City Directories list some of them, but other sources often suggest there were more residents than those counted under the "Market Square" category. Some lived alone; some saloonkeepers lived upstairs, sometimes with large families. Only occasionally, and usually when it's something remarkable, do newspapers ever offer a glimpse inside someone's home.

In 1883, a tinworker named Joseph Fraser was apparently able to afford to live in a rather large apartment upstairs at 36 Market Square. One night he sponsored an unusual guest, A.F. Ackerly, spiritualist, and invited the public to attend his séance, charging a substantial admission, for the time, of a half dollar, perhaps comparable to a $10 or $15 cover charge today. Ackerly's reputation

A rare perspective by a photographer who may have been standing in the graveyard of Second Presbyterian Church, along with parked wagons along what was known as "Watermelon Row." The graveyard, established before the Civil War, coexisted with the Market House for only a short time, before 1905, when the church sold and moved to another location at Walnut and Church; the graves of the old churchyard were moved to various locations before the construction of the Arnstein Building. The Haynes House was a small hotel on what's now Krutch Park. Courtesy of Mark Heinz.

was such that about 30 paying customers showed up. With a complex series of curtains, and a woman playing the organ, which was believed to help the spirits get past their inhibitions, Ackerly presented several objects, including a guitar, some bones, and a tambourine, on a table. According to a witness, "Soon after the music commenced, something began to rap on the table." The tambourine jingled. Later, "the spirit began to scratch across the strings of the guitar, knock the bones, and 'do about' generally, taking the tambourine up on a cane and twirling it about in view of the crowd."

When one customer peeked behind the curtain, Ackerly, perhaps like the Wizard of Oz, got upset. "The spirits had been so disturbed by this interference that they could not be induced to act again," he explained. The audience left, arguing about what they'd seen.

~

Maybe it was an occult version of the noisier sort of come-ons that customers on the outside were getting used to.

By the 1880s, the narrow streets and limited space proved inadequate for large, slow-moving animals, and the livestock scales were moved out of the Square to the east side of town. The resulting gap was, at least sometimes, interesting to watch. By way of a 20th-century columnist, we have a vague description of one particular salesman who made the space useful. A Dr. Lighthall was known as "the Indian Doctor." Whether he was an Indian, or a doctor, isn't clear, but his most impressive talents were apparently in dentistry. He performed "remarkable feats of teeth extraction" while selling his "panacea," some sort of patent medicine from which he made his living. Most interesting, perhaps, was that to draw attention to his show, he employed the services of a "Mexican band" which drew a crowd on the Square, ca. 1880. What sort of music they played isn't described; it's interesting that this scant reference is roughly coincidental with the earliest development of the mariachi band, several hundred miles to the southwest in Mexico. Whatever it was, Knoxvillians may have found the music appealing enough to put up with the rest of Dr. Lighthall's show.

It's interesting that one of the earliest references to street musicians in Knoxville is also one of the earliest references to Mexicans. Naturally, both are on Market Square.

~

The Knoxville public-library movement, after some false starts before the Civil War, had gained momentum in the 1870s. Originally concentrated around a modest "Reading Room" located in the Franklin House on Main Street, it had to move before that antebellum hotel could be torn down to build the present Knox County Courthouse. In 1883, Knoxville's public library, with all of 5,000 books, not counting periodicals, moved to the second floor of the Swann Building, at the southeast corner of the Square. Occupying the entire floor, apparently a much larger space than it had ever known before, the library was open to the public though supported entirely by private contributions. In charge as librarian was former New Yorker Miss E.T. Hill. At its location on the Square, it received about 400 visits per week. Some might have come in to have a look at Mark Twain's latest, *Life on the Mississippi*, to see if it was true that he had the gall to repeat details of the Mabry-O'Conner triple slaying in a humorous context.

It was never intended to be a permanent location; while the library was located on the Square, the library board organized and built Knoxville's first permanent public library, the original Lawson McGhee Library, which opened a few blocks away at Gay Street and Vine in 1886. Many of the leaders of the library movement were older men like Thomas Humes, the former journalist and Episcopal priest, freshly resigned as UT's president after losing a power struggle on the Hill, for whom a public library in Knoxville had been a long defered dream. Among these honchos was industrialist Charles McClung McGhee, who wished to memorialize his daughter, Lawson McGhee. However, the president of the library board at the time was a 24-year-old lawyer named Samuel Heiskell, who prodded the board to "see the library permanently quartered in a handsome and substantial building of its own."

Another fledgling institution, the YMCA, had been attracted to the Square for years. For a time, the Y was apparently adjacent to the library, in "elegant parlors" at 4 Market Square; they remained there for about two years, before moving into a larger space on Gay Street. Later still, they'd move to the third floor of the new Borches Building, the four-story building completed around 1889 across Asylum Avenue from the Square, shortly before moving into a long-term home in an old hotel down on State Street.

Market Square emerged as a natural incubator for progressive institutions. Perhaps because so many working people came to the Square on a daily basis, several trade unions located their local headquarters there, where they could be a visible daily presence.

By 1890, the Knights of Labor, a reformist group, a sort of hybrid fraternal organization and radical labor union, and certainly among the first of its kind in East Tennessee, established their Knoxville headquarters at 11 Market Square. They opposed child labor, demanded equal wages for women, and promoted a graduated income tax. It was a bold gesture for one of America's most radical groups to locate their local chapter in such a public place; it was during the time when their conservative enemies were trying to link them to Chicago's deadly Haymarket Square bombings and riots of 1886.

Journalism also returned to the Square in a small way in the early 1890s, when an apparently short-lived weekly called the *Sunday Sun* opened its headquarters at 16½ Market Square.

Hotels and some saloons had always served meals to customers, but one of Knoxville's first "restaurants" as such opened around 1888, in the elaborate building at 19 Market Square, formerly Isaac Gore's Saloon. The proprietor was W.G. Wilson, and already he had competition: the Women's Christian Temperance Union operated its own luncheonette within the Market House, within spitting distance of saloons. Near the entrance to the Market House, Sol Hyman ran a billiard and pool room at 6 Market Square; it was, of course, also a saloon.

The saloon industry grew, and the best known and most durable of Market Square's saloons over the years was Michael Cullinan's—sometimes known as Red Mike's, likely in reference to the Irish saloonkeeper's hair. His pub at No. 15 was a Market Square institution for more than 25 years. Cullinan, who may have been a resident on Market Square since the 1860s, lived upstairs from his saloon with his wife and five children. At least two of his sons eventually worked downstairs as bartenders.

Among Cullinan's rivals was John T. Burke, who began his Jersey Lily Saloon around the corner on Union, and reopened at 5 Market Square around 1889, sort of on the model of the old-fashioned tavern: His wife, Maggie, ran a boarding house upstairs, perhaps for those patrons who were in no shape to go home.

At the time, another saloon, Houser & Mournan's, was immediately next door, at No. 7. There seemed to be plenty of business to go around.

~

Beyond the usual Christmas pickpockets and the occasional brawl, there was little serious crime on Market Square during the saloon era. The constant vigilance of the police station, with its attached "calaboose" as an ever-present reminder of the wages of sin, seems to have put a damper on the sorts of flamboyant gunfights that broke out elsewhere in town. Each of several different blocks of Gay Street have a well-told story of The Gunfight, each based on some truth. Some blocks of Central were known to see two or more murders in the same week. Not Market Square.

Bar fights did break out on Market Square, but tended not to be as frequent or as deadly as those three blocks to the east, where Crozier Street was earning the nickname "the Bowery."

Murder on the Square was, at least, quieter. In the early 20th century, a clothier at the north end of the Square, just barely around the Wall Avenue corner, named Augustus Swindoll—maybe not a propitious name for a man in retail—was excavating to expand his business in the back when he discovered a skeleton, crammed into an old cistern. Judging by the skeleton's out-of-fashion clothing, police agreed, he looked like he belonged back in the middle 1880s. The unfortunate was assumed to be a murder victim, but memories were short in the ever-changing city, and they didn't have adequate records to figure much more about it. It was a cold case before it was even opened.

Despite the salutary presence of cops, Market Square did witness an occasional murder attempt. The late summer of 1885 witnessed one of the Square's stranger altercations. An acrobat named Professor W.H. Davidson had been performing on a tightrope over Union Avenue, near the Square, and in the evening walked into Bearden's store, at Prince and Union just in front of the Market House, to get a cigar. A man he didn't recognize attacked him with a heavy object, striking him in the head and knocking him down. "I will kill you!" shouted the man, whose name is recorded as Bowyer, as he pummeled Davidson. The professor broke free and ran into Kern's confectionary, jumping behind the counter when Bowyer pursued him. Davidson sought help from John Kern, Peter Kern's son, who tried to break up the fight. A policeman appeared, then another, and took the men separately to city hall. It was assumed that Bowyer was incensed because Davidson had used his brother Charlie in his tightrope act, carrying the boy partway across the street. Davidson, angry at the assault, made a public challenge to Bowyer to meet him outside of city limits for a bout of fisticuffs, strictly governed by Marquis of Queensbury rules. Whether that score was ever settled is unrecorded.

In October, 1892, police brought in teenager Francis Baker, who had just killed his father, to the calaboose. The story of the "parricide" in Mechanicsville captured the public's attention, and people around Market Square crowded the jailhouse just to look at the prisoner, which was easy to do, both inside and outside the walls. Late that night, the prisoner obligingly answered questions from the public. He wasn't proud of what he'd done, he told them, but his father had been drunk and abusive, and he had no other choice. The boy was visibly upset about it all. "It was one of those sad scenes that the nighthawks of journalism so frequently run across, while the guileless world turns on a couch and sleeps," wrote a reporter. "Homeless, friendless, in the eyes of the law he sat like a statue and told his story to the *Tribune* reporter." As it turned out, the boy wasn't completely friendless in the eyes of the law; three days later, he was exonerated, and freed.

One Christmas season a few years later, a fad among children was to buy one particular brand of toy cap gun—which, Knoxville boys quickly learned, could be loaded with a real .22 bullet and fired. The phenomenon had been blamed on one death, a kid who, in play, had shot his friend to death. Noticing that several children on the Square were playing with the toy guns, the Market Master, "Daddy" White, confiscated a toy gun from a kid. ("Daddy" White was likely the same person as Georgie White, the kid who 40 years earlier had been one of the brothers who kept the new Market House by carrying vegetable baskets to the empty stalls in the winter.) One of the other officers in the station house on the Square looked at the gun, and was skeptical of whether it would actually cause any damage. "Try it," Daddy White said. Lt. George McIntyre aimed it vaguely toward a wall, and fired. The pistol exploded, injuring McIntyre and damaging the wall. McIntyre, recovering, assessed the event: "We will consider that we had a most narrow escape."

~

A cluster of saloons also seemed to thrive on Union between the Square and Gay Street. And that short block also hosted the offices of a couple of especially interesting attorneys; one was young Lewis Hopkins Spilman, future attorney for the U.S. Supreme Court, as well as, under a pseudonym, a national-magazine sportswriter. Another was well-known black attorney William F. Yardley, the former

A view of old City Hall, on the north end of Market Square, around 1890. McClung Historical Collection.

gubernatorial candidate, who kept his office for years on that short block, above a saloon. Another saloon near Market Square on Union, Henry Jones' place, catered to blacks. However, by the 1880s, black proprietors seem to have departed from Market Square itself. Black businesses and a few black residents would hang on in this little block of Union adjacent to the Square, but only into the middle 1890s, when one black barber shop, Bauman & Taylor's, remained.

Though blacks would always be present on the Square as customers, Knoxville lapsed toward segregation in the late 19th century, in the early days of Jim Crow, imitating the rest of the South, in fact most of the rest of the country.

~

The Market House seemed to be in worse shape all the time. Though nothing about it was very old, by 1887 citizens were calling for it to be demolished and replaced. In the 1887 City Directory, the Market House is curiously unmentioned among a listing of the city's 25 "Halls and Public Buildings"—perhaps it was an oversight, or maybe, considering the complaints, city fathers were hoping people wouldn't go look at it. In 1889, the city approved one last "extension"—by then, the Market House had connected all the way to City Hall; there was no room to extend any farther.

It was about that time that the city, under the administration of Mayor Martin Condon, chose to build a new, bigger City Hall to replace the sad, plain old two-story brick structure on the north end of the Square, which had served its purpose since shortly after the Civil War.

One fact about Condon probably seems more remarkable today than it did when he was elected in 1888. The son of an Irish immigrant, he was Catholic. The fact that Knoxville ever had a Catholic mayor might surprise moderns (he was, in fact, the first of three) but in the 1880s, when St. Patrick's Day was often the occasion for a big parade down Gay Street, Catholics wielded considerable power. Though New York and Boston had only recently elected their first Catholic mayors, religion seems not to have been an issue in Condon's successful campaign in Knoxville. Condon led the effort to build a new City Hall, which would stand on Market Square for more than 70 years.

The Board of Aldermen held their first meeting in the new building on March 29, 1889. It was a fine building, and came with a belltower and a relatively new bell, a 2,600-pound beauty manufactured by the McShane Bell Foundry in Baltimore, embossed with the date "1883," presumably its date of manufacture. Where it spent the intervening six years isn't completely clear, but it seems likely that it wasn't cast expressly for the new city hall. Perhaps it had hung in the previous building, or perhaps the thrifty government may have gotten a deal on a bell that had hung elsewhere, in some financially ill-fated project. For 30 years or so, the bell served as a public alarm, its sound audible for miles around, offering the first alert of emergencies and disasters; Knoxville would offer several occasions for its use. Some of the worst disasters in the city's history occurred during the bell's tenure in City Hall.

The worst personal disaster in city-government history, and perhaps the first time the bell tolled with any urgency, followed in August of that year. A whole delegation of aldermen, past and present, and other city boosters had departed on a ceremonial trip on the new Knoxville & Cumberland Gap Railroad. The trip was sponsored by one Alexander Arthur, the well-heeled, English-born Knoxville industrialist who had just built a new city called Middlesborough, Kentucky. To get to what he planned to be a sort of industrial utopia, he built a new railroad. Prominent Knoxvillians were excited about the prospect and went along on the maiden trip. Only the railroad wasn't quite finished. Just 23 miles out of town, over Flat Creek, the new railroad bridge buckled under the weight of the trainload of dignitaries, a car derailed and tumbled down the bank, and several city officials were seriously injured. Peter Kern was among the injured, but not too seriously. Among the dead were the Knox County sheriff, the chairman of the Board of Public Works, a judge, and a particularly popular alderman, cigarmaker Frederick Hockenjos, the German immigrant from Baden-Baden who'd been meeting with his colleagues here on the Square for six years.

≈

The Market House was a hothouse for young businesses; several longstanding businesses got their starts in the Market House during this era, including the venerable florist Baum's, which began as a flower stall in 1889. H.T. Hackney, which would become a major wholesale grocery firm with offices downtown into the 21st century, started with a stall on Market Square.

Many years later, columnist Lucy Templeton would remember Market Square as it was in the late 19th century. Shoppers would pick what they wanted, then leave the groceries in baskets on the curb. The grocers would then have them delivered to their homes.

She remembered several individuals in intimate detail. Grocer Tom Caldwell was "the largest and fattest man I ever knew. He was enormous, well over six feet tall, and broad in proportion…. Mr. and Mrs. Caldwell had three sons, George, Hugh, and Tom Jr." One of those kids who grew up running around Market Square, Hugh Caldwell, not nearly as big as his father, would grow up to become the flamboyant mayor of 1920s Seattle, and an early promoter of professional hockey.

"Nobody could have looked less like the popular image of a grocer than Jim Anderson," whose store was at 4 Market Square, wrote Templeton, recalling that he rode the dummy line—the old steam trolley from Fountain City—into town every day. "He was thin, delicate-looking, and bore a strong resemblance to the portraits of Charles I of England."

Another Templeton memory illustrates the Square's early cosmopolitan nature. "Once when a British-born visitor at our house was boasting about how many delicacies he had introduced to gastronomically ignorant Knoxville, he mentioned orange marmalade. I was just a child, but I announced firmly, 'We have had waffles and orange marmalade for breakfast every Sunday morning since I can remember.'" Templeton's family bought the English delicacy from T.E. Burns at the north end of the Square, which advertised "fancy groceries" and stocked many imports.

The large Burns building, whose twin arches are conspicuous in many photographs of the Square, sat just across Asylum/Wall Avenue from the Square's eastern corridor. (It remained there until torn down for the new TVA headquarters in the 1970s.)

By the end of the century, Market Square retail had a motto: "Anything that man could desire to eat, drink, and wear."

~

The Square saw a remarkable concentration of certain sorts of businesses, especially butchers. Of Knoxville's 25 meat markets in 1887, 18 of them were on Market Square—as were both of the city's sausage manufacturers. The Square hosted many sausageers over the years, and most appear to be German immigrants. Many years later, a famous barbecue chef of Mechanicsville known as Brother Jack would claim that he owed part of his famous taste to a secret he'd learned from a German butcher on Market Square.

The most legible evidence of history on the Square may be one word, high on the west-side facade above No. 9. In a block of marble in the mostly brick ca. 1880 two-story building is the word "ZIEGLER." As was the fashion in the 1880s, the single word ends with a period. The building has served many purposes over the years, and even in its earliest years, the second floor hosted residences, as well as the dress shop of a Mrs. S. L. Fitzgerald.

But a generation or so of Knoxvillians knew the street level as the meat market of Anton Metler, Adolph Ziegler, and Ignaz Fanz, three German-speaking immigrants who specialized in making sausages. They had three locations on the Square; their building itself, plus two market stalls at opposite ends of the Market House.

Why Ziegler's name should proclaim itself alone there is unclear. In surviving records, he's the least well known of the three, but may have been the one who financed the construction of the building.

Ignaz Fanz (1842-1927), a Union veteran of the Civil War originally of Steinbach, Germany, was the most recognizable of the trio. By 1879, he had established a large sausage factory, a "porkery," in North Knoxville, and had also been one of the Square's early tenants, operating two shops, one on the east, and one on the west side. Economic pressures may have forced him to downsize and form a partnership with Metler and Ziegler. In the 1890s, Fanz attained elective office, serving a term as city alderman at a crucial moment in the history of the Square.

Anton Metler, a former dairyman originally from Switzerland who had lived in the countryside before moving in to Knoxville in the early 1870s, formed a partnership with Ziegler, and the two ran the Metler & Ziegler slaughterhouses and pork-packing plant just north of town, near Sharp's Gap, until that facility was destroyed by fire in 1887.

Older than his colleagues, Metler died at age 66 in 1893. For a short time after his death, the business was known as Ziegler & Fanz.

Ziegler, who was apparently Metler's son-in-law, lived nearby, at 428 Walnut; he could have commuted to work without even crossing a street. But he disappears from the records after 1894. Ignaz Fanz would remain in the building into the early 20th century, when he re-established a larger sausage factory on Jackson Avenue, while still selling at a stall in the Market House. In the late 1890s, Fanz's astonishingly beautiful dark-haired daughter Emma would pose with another woman's baby as the Biblical Mary in a nationally famous photograph that would be known as the Knaffl Madonna. Even in the 21st century, it's still being used, apparently without permission, for Hallmark Christmas cards.

Within the Market House, the Waltz Brothers sold meats, while William Bowman, on the north end, was, to a generation or two, the Square's best-known fishmonger.

One butcher may have outdone Fanz in extravagant sausagery. Paul Huray, who eventually made a second career in soda pop, had a stall in the Market House and was known for the creative shapes he was able to sculpt with sausage and creative use of pigs' intestines. By the 1890s, he was creating whole Christmas trees, constructed entirely of multiple varieties of sausage.

Butchers added to the round-the-clock nature of the Square. Saloons tended to stay open very late; butchers arrived very early. Some cops were in their office on the Square's north end all night long. The Square spawned some surprising rivalries. James S. and Newton R. Hall, the partners who opened one of the first new stores after the Civil War, had split, with J.S. Hall running the original dry-goods store on the Square's east side, specializing in men's clothing, and using "On the Square" as its motto. But his nephew Newton R. Hall opened a "Gents' Furnishings" store on the opposite side. The two Halls coexisted, perhaps peacefully, in a cross-Hall rivalry, for 25 years.

The variety of professionals who hung a shingle on Market Square continued to diversify. Joe Harris, whose office was at 18 Market Square, was a former state legislator who, according to a display ad which included a portrait of his mustachioed face, "is a humorist of rare talents, and is recognized as the greatest living Real Estate Auctioneer in America."

Another prominent real-estate man based on Market Square was an ambitious Pennsylvanian with the enviable name of Barnabas Braine. One of the early developers of the booming residential section near the still-extant Civil War ruin Fort Sanders, a neighborhood then known as West End, Braine was building a house of his own on Forest Avenue. But he kept his office at No. 28 Market Square.

(Along with Mr. Braine's, some other proper names associated with Market Square in the late 19th century can catch your eye. The Market Master in 1899, an employee of the Police Department, was one Lycurgus Peltier. A man listed as a Market House "huckster" bore the lordly moniker of Pendleton Shropshire.)

At the time Braine was established there in the 1880s, he was involved in an ambitious effort to bring a "street railway"—a streetcar line—to the Fort Sanders vicinity. Braine was president of a small streetcar line that had routes to both Fort Sanders proper and "the Circle"—Circle Park, in what would be known as UT; the routes originated one block south of Market Square, at the Custom House.

Streetcars existed in Knoxville even before the introduction of electric streetcars in 1890. As is characteristic of the time, a number of private companies competed to serve the burgeoning demand for transportation in a rapidly expanding city with mule-drawn streetcars. Some of the lines were very small, and at least one of them had Market Square as its terminus. The Market Square and Mechanicsville Streetcar Co., formed in 1884, connected its two namesakes via rails along Asylum Avenue.

∾

Around 1888, Market Square had competition from a rival almost entirely forgotten today. Since at least 1875, some had proposed that the city was big enough for two or more market squares, and far too big for this particular one.

By 1885, there were renewed calls for a "North Knoxville Market," which would both alleviate crowding on Market Square and better serve the northern parts of the city, which was seeing major residential development. In May, 1888, the City Council, meeting in old Market Square, accepted a gift of land, about two-thirds of a mile north of Market Square, at the northernmost end of newly lengthened Gay Street.

There, in 1888 and '89, another market house rose, with room around it for farmers' wagons. In the late 19th century, the old Central Market was a significant entity, a long, two-story wood-frame building, bent to fit its odd space, greeting both

Broad Street and Crozier, soon to be known as Central Avenue, perpendicularly. Within was room for 33 stalls. It offered several advantages; one was that farmers, especially those coming in from fruitful Union, Anderson, and Grainger Counties, would not have to negotiate city traffic, the narrow, twisted streets of downtown Knoxville, the streetcars that spooked the mules, the traffic jams that sometimes lasted for hours, the smoke and urban muck.

A greater motive was apparently to put a well-stocked food market closer to where so many of the affluent middle class seemed to be building new houses, in what was then incorporated as North Knoxville. Confidence in the Central Market encouraged developers to build around it, just like they had in Market Square, around that older Market House. A few merchants moved from Market Square to the Central Market, and the city established a new Market Master just to govern business over there.

If it represented real competition for the old Square, some merchants may have been relieved. Crowds were so dense that some of their favorite customers—middle-class "ladies" in Victorian clothes—had difficulty even getting to the vendors. Police were called in to break up packs of loiterers. Merchants may have complained most about the "Negro idlers," though there seem to have been plenty of both races.

Knoxville and Chattanooga were in the thick of an interurban rivalry. Chattanooga may have had certain advantages, like much better river navigation, but as certain Knoxvillians were happy to point out, it had no big market house. For a while, Knoxville was able to boast that it had two.

The Central Market might be seen as an early experiment in suburban retail, of moving stores closer to the new residential streetcar-accessible neighborhoods of houses and yards. Some details of its fate are obscure, but clues suggest that it was a spectacular failure.

As Judge Henry H. Ingersoll, dean of UT's law school, would remark in an 1897 speech: "[W]itness the vacant indenture on the north side, that curious invitation to the people there to trade at home. None came. The plan was presented as a furtive scheme to divide our city, to destroy our unity, to abridge the right of peaceable popular assembly; and so the Central Market became a desert."

It's interesting that Ingersoll seems to suggest that it's important to democracy itself that there be only one Market Square, a place where everybody came, and saw everybody else, on a regular basis.

And shoppers may have agreed; in any case, they rode or walked past the Central Market, insisting on coming all the way in to town, through the traffic, to dirty, crowded, outdated Market Square.

By the turn of the century, the Central Market was converted to warehouse use. Sometime thereafter, it apparently burned. Around 1904, it was converted into

Emory Park. Lined with two-story Victorian buildings and looking something like a bent version of Market Square, it's known today as Emory Place.

~

The street at the north end of Market Square seems always to have been an awkward proposition. It had been called Asylum Avenue since the 1860s, even though its connection to the Deaf and Dumb "Asylum"—the future Tennessee School for the Deaf—was a twisty and tortured affair through uncooperative blocks to the west. Around 1890, the section from Gay to Walnut, on either side of Market Square, was renamed Wall—though after what wall is unclear. Likely it was merely an homage to the street of the same name in Manhattan, which seemed to be doing pretty well. At the time, several parts of Knoxville were trying hard to seem like New York.

On the other end of the Square, the only institution that had been in the neighborhood longer than the Square itself, the Second Presbyterian Church, was thriving under the leadership of pastor Nathan Bachman and later his brother Robert Bachman, and growing. The old chapel, despite its impressive spire, was beginning to seem not quite up to the task of holding a congregation of 300 every Sunday.

It may have been never more evident than one Sunday in 1894, when the congregation welcomed a guest speaker, Julia Ward Howe, the 75-year-old abolitionist, feminist, and author of the old Yankee anthem, "Battle Hymn of the Republic." She would have to be included on any list of the unlikely personages one would encounter, if one were only able to sit on Market Square forever.

~

In future centuries, Market Square would be famously local, one of the few places in town where locally owned businesses thrive without much competition from chains. But maybe, given the Square's reputation of introducing the New—whether the New is welcome or not—it shouldn't be surprising that national-chain retail first landed in Knoxville in, or very near, Market Square. In early 1896, the Great Atlantic & Pacific Tea Co., a well-known New York-based chain, opened a store at 322 Union Avenue, barely around the corner from the Square, under the management of H.V. Campbell, a company man from Richmond. Soon it would relocate to 8 Market Square. During its early years on the Square, the company sold coffee, tea, and imported exotica like Asian cookware.

It would later be better known, of course, as A&P. After 1912, A&P broadened its specialty to general groceries, and in decades to come, supermarkets like A&P would alter Americans' grocery-shopping habits, and along with other chain groceries, undermine the original idea of the Market Square. But when it opened in 1896, this cosmopolitan, eccentric-seeming importer was another of the many worldly novelties of which Market Square seemed to have no end.

∾

The most ancient part of the Market House was only about 40 years old, and apparently had received some heroic face-changing improvements in that time, now with a three-story front with some tower-like structures on it that, in the few images of it that exist, look plausibly impressive. But to critics, it was a cramped, creaky, potential death trap.

In early 1896, the *Knoxville Daily Journal* gave it a poor review: "Everybody knows that Knoxville has the best market in the South—some go so far as to say it is the best in the United States. However that may be, the present market house is wholly inadequate for the business of the market. It is too small. It is

A Market Square scene of a decrepit Market House, ca. 1896, just before the construction of the new one. It's unclear whether any of the older market house survived as part of the 1897 structure. The steeple of the 1886 Immaculate Conception Catholic Church is visible in the background, to the left, as it is today. The stone mortar and pestle which crowned G.W. Albers' drugstore is visible at right. McClung Historical Collection.

an eyesore. It is liable, it is said, to tumble down someday and hurt someone." City Council, under the leadership of a young new mayor, began considering improvements.

Citizens had complained for years that Knoxville needed a new market house, like they complained about the weather. People had been complaining that Knoxville had no public parks for longer, and nothing had ever happened. Despite the city's growth, city government remained fiscally conservative, and aldermen were re-luctant to sponsor anything that called for raising taxes.

It took a vigorous new administration to take on the willful chaos that was city government in Knoxville, and to make the Market House happen. Samuel Gordon Heiskell, the former library-board leader, was just 37 when he was elected to the first of several terms as mayor of Knoxville. Already a former city attorney, Knox County representative in the state legislature, and Democratic Party chairman, Heiskell had a progressive, inclusive reputation and, departing from Tennessee Democratic policy, a reputation of racial liberality. His term in the state legislature was a single year, but in those few months he drafted the successful bill to insure that the mental institution at Lyons View would have accommodations for blacks. Also a historian, he would later write a landmark two-volume biography of his fellow Democrat, Andrew Jackson.

In 1896, however, he was chiefly concerned with building a new, modern Market House, one fit to the needs of a rapidly growing city, one that would still be ad-equate in the future, as the city grew to a metropolis of 100,000. As mayor, Heiskell worked on the Square every day, of course—but his association with the Square was more personal. When he had moved to Knoxville from Monroe County with his parents in the 1860s, he had thought Market Square a wonderful place. It was there, in an open spot on the east side of the Square that he first saw, for sale, an inspired new invention: a bicycle.

On October 2, 1896, Heiskell formally recommended the construction of a new market house. The current one was the Pride of the City, he said, perhaps out of politeness to his elders who may have had a hand it making it what it was. And rents were bringing the city $5,000 a year in revenue. But it had lapsed into a "dangerous" condition.

Heiskell and City Council, which then included, among others, Market Square sausage merchant and Alderman Ignaz Fanz, passed an improvement bond of $50,000 to build a new market house.

Knoxville was still not a city of architects. The city's best-known architect was George Barber, who had a national business in designing single-family homes, mostly for the new suburban market. He was never known for large public buildings.

They turned to the most dynamic firm of the day, Baumann Brothers. Joseph F. Baumann had designed the much-admired Market Square institution, the Kern

Knoxville's first mayor who grew up with Market Square—he saw his first bicycle here, just after the Civil War—lawyer-historian-politician Sam Heiskell (1858–1923) was the most durable mayor of his day, and oversaw the construction of the new Market House in 1897. McClung Historical Collection.

Block, 20 years earlier, and later the Church of the Immaculate Conception, always visible to the north. Now joined by his much-younger brother, Albert, the firm of Baumann Brothers had little in the way of formal training, but had been involved in more urban and public projects than any other firm around. They collaborated on the Borches Block, just north of the Square, with its immense stone arches, probably the most talked-about recent building in the immediate vicinity.

The fire department left the Square at the time of the construction of the Market House, due to the fact that its fire trucks were seen as a "constant menace to passers by," ending 30 years of occasional noisy excitement on the Square, but opening up new opportunities for building design that interested Mayor Heiskell. Heiskell recommended one design feature: that the ground floor of City Hall be incorporated, for the first time, into the market part of the Market House. It was no longer used for firetrucks, anyway. Heiskell said he wanted to be able to stand on Union Avenue and see through the long building, all the way to Wall.

The city sold $30,000 in municipal bonds to pay for the building, which Baumann is said to have patterned after Sixth Street Market in Cincinnati.

Construction came in stages, as the old Market House was demolished in stages. Some historians cite reason to believe the old place wasn't torn down in its entirety—that perhaps the antebellum single-story middle section was retained in the 1897 design, and survived as long as that building did.

Market Square was in some awkward disheveled state for most of that year, which turned out to be one of the strangest years in Knoxville history.

≈

It was hard to consider positive improvements in a city frequently called to react to bizarre emergencies. Some were tolled by an urgent clanging from the City Hall's bell tower.

William Gibbs McAdoo was the son of an old Knoxville figure of the same name, a prominent attorney and professor who, a secessionist, had taken the family deeper South at the outbreak of the Civil War. The son spent his earliest years in Milledgeville, Georgia, the former state capital. In 1877, after a 15-year absence, the McAdoos returned to Knoxville, with a teenager in tow.

Young McAdoo, a UT grad, established Knoxville's first electric streetcar line in 1890, but had been embarrassed when his business plan failed, and he had to sell the system to a deep-pocketed investor. Sure that he knew what he'd done wrong, he launched a second plan, to build a second, competing streetcar line—apparently without doing all the required paperwork. He hired 300 workmen and, on a night in early 1897, started with a little surreptitious construction work on Depot Street.

When dawn broke and the authorities were alerted that McAdoo was building his freelance streetcar line on an unauthorized street, police attempted to arrest his

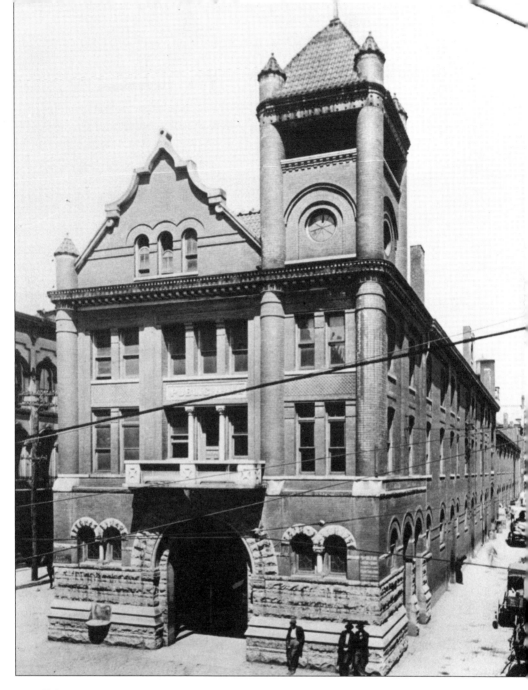

A well-known ca. 1909 vertical photo of the 1897 Market House, a building Cormac McCarthy, in the novel Suttree, *described as "the markethouse where brick the color of dried blood rose turreted and cupolaed and crazed into the heat of the day form on form in demented accretion without precedent or counterpart in the annals of architecture." High above the entrance is the inscription, "*PUBLIC HALL.*" McClung Historical Collection.*

men, setting off a riot, known as the Battle of Depot Street. It left one worker dead and several injured. McAdoo appealed to a county judge, who ordered his men freed. For a time, the city police and county sheriff's deputies were in a standoff on Depot Street, under orders to arrest each other. McAdoo himself was under arrest, and dragged to City Hall.

Later on, the same man would build, quite legally and in the daytime, the first subway under the Hudson River. About 20 years after his hour in jail on Market Square, President Woodrow Wilson overlooked McAdoo's criminal record to allow him to marry his daughter. He had also selected McAdoo to be his Secretary of the Treasury; in that role, he was instrumental in the founding of the Federal Reserve System, of which he was first chairman. Still later, he would co-found United Artists, and be elected U.S. Senator from California; he ran two credible campaigns for the Democratic nomination for the U.S. presidency. McAdoo was quickly freed on bond that day in March, 1897, but he's likely the most famous man who ever checked in at the Market Square calaboose.

Hardly a month later, the bell rang another alarm; this time its meaning was probably more obvious to the people of Market Square, because they could smell smoke. A fire, started in an oil drum behind a small hotel on Gay Street, parallel to Market Square, attacked the hotel, then consumed an entire block. Fire engines went screaming, and Knoxville's few underequipped firemen did what they could, but it wasn't enough. The city had to wire to its hated rival to the South, Chattanooga, for assistance. By the time it was over, the Million Dollar Fire was the most ruinous fire in Knoxville history.

Knoxville needed a pick-me-up, and it was already taking shape on Market Square.

≈

The new Market House opened just in time for Christmas-shopping season, on December 2, 1897. A marble tablet high on the façade heralded this "PUBLIC HALL."

A lengthy program of speakers alternating with musical performances heralded the new building. An estimated 3,000 Knoxvillians crowded into the new building to hear well-known speakers like Mayor Heiskell and former Mayor William Rule, but the most inspiring speech belonged to Dean Henry H. Ingersoll, of the UT Law School. He described the gathering in an expansive way that seemed to describe the daily population of Market Square itself.

"Today no Republican or Democrat, no gold-bug or silverite, no Methodist or Baptist, no Calvinist or Lutheran, no Catholic or Protestant, is here—but only Knoxvillians. Today none claim to be native or naturalized, Southern or Yankee, rich or poor, Irish or Swiss, white or black, or high or low, but everyone is proud to be a citizen of Knoxville and to share her renown."

He added, "This Market House is not only of public but of universal use—a house for all, and will be used every week by every family in the city."

The Market House was a wonder—like other market houses perhaps modeled on Fanueil Hall, it had farmers' stalls on the street level, 57 of them, and a substantial auditorium on the second floor.

"Knoxville's magnificent new market house is open for business," led the *Knoxville Journal*, adding that it "will go down on the pages of municipal history as marking one of the epochs in the progress of Knoxville during the closing years of the nineteenth century. It is metropolitan, strictly up to date, and will meet the demands of the city until it shall have increased three times its present size...."

By the middle of the 20th century, the Market House would strike many who beheld it as a sort of sub-architectural freak, a mongrel with perhaps three too many architectural styles. But the people of 1897 agreed it was a wonderful, modern, and even graceful building. Headlining "Knoxville's Elegant New Market House," the *Knoxville Morning Tribune* stated, as if it were a matter of fact, "the building is treated in the Romanesque style and is kept pure and free from all superfluous ornamentation."

Baumann and company had made perhaps too efficient use of Market Square. With the old City Hall, the brick leviathan stretched from Union to Wall, obscuring the older architecture along the sides of the Square, forcing traffic jams along the alleys on either side, and filling up the remaining open space—an amenity that Knoxville, a city that even sympathetic visitors were astonished to find had no real public parks, may not have fully appreciated. There was hardly any place left for Indian doctors and Mexican bands. But in 1897, any criticism was swamped by gratitude and praise. The prediction that it would serve capably until the city was three times its size would prove to be, roughly, accurate.

By the end of the century, it was becoming clear that what Knoxville had at the northern end of Prince Street was not just a marketplace. Most cities had a marketplace of some sort. Market Square was something different, a unique oddity almost universally remarked upon by strangers. It was different from all other marketplaces in America; some liked that fact, and some, for reasons of their own, didn't. It was hard to put a finger on exactly what made it different; Market Square, as a whole, was an odd arrangement of buildings, to be sure, with the newest one the oddest. Maybe it was merely the unusual, almost hyper-urban density of a place originally plotted for a much-smaller town—and that those two acres might actually be visited by all 75,000 people who lived in Knox County in any given week, as its promoters expected, was almost plausible. Maybe it was its astonishing ethnic diversity unexpected in a region not known for ethnic diversity. But it wasn't just that contrast. Market Square could exhibit a cultural diversity unusual even in big cities, not only in skin color and its Babel of accents both foreign and domestic which were certainly present on the Square—but also because it hosted a large contingent of Americans rarely represented in other downtowns: dirt farmers from the hills, people who by their dress and curious accents maybe stood farther apart from the American mainstream than some immigrant ethnic groups did. And in many stalls and shops of Market Square, they were in charge. In the century to come, tourists and poets would remark upon them, sometimes with a condescending smirk, sometimes with a rare awe. But among their customers were ladies with parasols who sent their daughters to Vassar and summered in New York and depended on a chauffeur waiting at the south entrance. If society ladies knew about nothing else, they knew about fresh food, and no one could be certain they had prepared the perfect banquet or reception unless they'd visited Market Square.

Exactly what was different about Market Square, or whether it was something the city should be proud of or ashamed of was something that would divide, perplex, and infuriate Knoxvillians for a century to come.

CHAPTER 4

"The Most Democratic Place on Earth"

Progressivism, Max Arnstein, and "the White Way"

T he Turn of the Century, the much-heralded fin d'siecle, was a time of rapid, sweeping changes to business standards and labor laws, a time of idealogical foment and idealistic thought and several rival forms of progressivism. Americans believed that anything was possible, and at times, especially on Market Square, faith came easy.

The people of 1900 didn't often use the word *diversity* to convey a desired end. Four years after the U.S. Supreme Court upheld the constitutionality of segregation, Knoxville was becoming more and more divided by race. But occasionally, on Market Square, the mixture of people could be exhilarating. "Market Square is the most democratic place on earth," declared a writer for the *Knoxville Journal & Tribune* in 1900. "There the rich and the poor, the white and the black, jostle each other in perfect equality, and the scenes during the busy hours of the afternoon are always worth watching."

Knoxville seemed to have no limits in 1900, and municipal optimists could already see the day when the wonderful new Market House would be replaced with something even grander. According to predictions offered in the newspapers at the opening of the century, some expected that by 2000 the Market House would be replaced by a new one, stretching from Clinch to Vine Street, four blocks in all. It would be, one writer said, a lot like St. Peter's Basilica. The wag may not have been altogether serious, but they were idealistic times.

As it was, the new, modern, Market House, with its public auditorium, was often an interesting place to be. The produce was the daily attraction, and by 1900 Knoxvillians were routinely boasting, as if it were a matter that could be looked up in the almanacs, that Market Square was "the best market southwest of Norfolk" or "the South's greatest inland city market," comparable only with the famous French Market in New Orleans.

A period promotional booklet remarked that "Visitors who go through the Market House wonder at the great quantity of everything…. In this big building is found an exposition of the products of field, farm, orchard, and garden that can be raised in one of the most fertile regions in the South…. The wonder increases as they view the half-mile of wagons packed closely on the sidewalks of the Square…. The scene is not one that can be viewed in other cities."

The era's boasts about the Square were about its almost encyclopedic supply of things to eat. However, because Market Square was a gathering place for disparate people, it was also, inevitably, a marketplace of ideas.

Knowing where it was easiest to find a crowd, suffragists sometimes set up their soap boxes in the Market Square area. Lizzie Crozier French, the persuasive young teacher and single mother who became Knoxville's leading feminist, is the middle woman depicted since 2006 in a statue on the Square's southern end. Since the 1880s she'd often spoken nearby, to passing crowds. By 1900 Knoxville was generally open-minded on the issue of women's suffrage; French almost certainly had a hand in tipping the state decisively into the pro-suffrage category in 1919, and Tennessee's uncertain swing toward suffrage enabled the nation itself to pass the 19th amendment, for the first time allowing women to vote, about 40 years after she started preaching equality on the streets of downtown Knoxville.

The second-floor Market Hall, in particular, served as a platform for some of the progressive movements of the day. Pictures of its interior are rare, and it's unclear exactly what it looked like in the earliest days. According to the original specifications for it, it could reputedly accommodate as many as 1,000, though whether comfortably seated, uncomfortably seated, or standing is unclear; some later memories make it sound smaller than that. The modest-sized room could enhance the dramatic energy of a speech by William Jennings Bryan, the king of all charismatic progressives, who spoke there at least once—or former Tennessee Governor Bob Taylor, who was in some respects our own version of Bryan, who could leave audiences weeping with joy.

Lizzie Crozier French (1851–1926), the maverick early feminist who found some receptive crowds for her message on Market Square. Daughter of a lawyer and former congressman, she worked as a teacher for years, and as a widowed single mother, raised a child, but remained a major community leader throughout her life, and served as a lobbyist for women's issues even in her 70s. She is the central figure in a statue honoring Tennessee suffragettes installed on Market Square in 2006. McClung Historical Collection.

Among the many programs held in the Market Hall auditorium were some of the early exhortations for conservation or pacifism, some campaigns for universal public education, and some of the early warnings about air pollution which, in those days, was called *smoke*. Previously, cities had seen smoke as a sign of progress, even exaggerating dense black factory smoke in illustrated city profiles, but by 1910, an idealistic University of Tennessee professor named J.A. Switzer was giving grave speeches at the Market Hall, illustrated with moving pictures, about the "smoke nuisance."

The New York-born Switzer, the Cornell-educated professor of "experimental engineering," would as an old man be thickly involved in an idealistic project called TVA, but in the Progressive Era, the smoke nuisance was his favorite subject, unless it was another, that of the Junior Republic movement, a pre-Boys' Town ideal that troublemakers from the slums should be taken out into camps in the clean country air, and allowed, within reason, to govern themselves. In general, Switzer thought fresh air was a good idea all around.

In August, 1904, one Harry McKee spoke at the Market Hall, a lecture which aroused perhaps more interest than most visitors with a cause. McKee was a socialist, and his subject was the death of capitalism. McKee would soon gain some minor fame as a socialist leader in California. A sometime delegate to national Socialist conventions in the era of Eugene V. Debs' quixotic runs for the presidency (Debs campaigned in Knoxville, too), McKee twice ran for Congress, coming in a very distant second, and was once jailed for inciting to riot. At the Market House, that evening in 1904, he called capitalism "anarchy gone mad…a system which makes men, both capitalist and laborer, hoggish and selfish and brutal." He promoted the collective ownership of business and labor.

In Market Square, the man seems to have found an audience, if only for a moment. His apparently well-received talk got coverage in old Captain Rule's Republican paper, the *Journal and Tribune*.

In the year 1904, when child labor was still a reality and few government controls on quality were in place, even conservative Americans suspected radical change was inevitable; and before the Bolshevik revolution and the subsequent Cold War, socialism had wide credence, even in middle America, as a promising idea.

Naturally, the Square became a hub for union organizing. In 1913, the national Central Labor Union held a streetcar strike meeting openly at the Market House. One of the speakers was popular local labor leader John T. O'Connor, the Irish immigrants' son who later became mayor of Knoxville.

Of course, some new ideas presented on Market Square came in forms that didn't require much concentration to understand; around 1907, many may have gotten their first close-up look at the new internal-combustion automobile when a mustachioed young driver brought one to the Square, apparently on a dare, to race a small ox, ridden by two farmboys, Bill and John Winkle. The ox, of course, won.

In November, 1909, Booker T. Washington spoke in the Market Hall. The 53-year-old author of *Up from Slavery* may have been the best-known American of color at that time, popular with blacks and progressive whites, among them Theodore Roosevelt, who a few years earlier had honored him as the first-ever black guest at the White House.

It was an odd morning speech, to conform to Washington's train schedule and previous commitments at Knoxville College, but despite the "inauspicious hour," he drew a "packed house, including 300 white people, some of them ladies." Reports of the capacity of the Market Hall are variable, and the proportion of black attendees is not recorded. Washington himself arrived at Market Square with a retinue of more than a dozen, including medical academics from Tuskegee and Meharry, reporters for the *New York Evening Post* and other papers, and Robert E. Park, the well-known sociologist and author, then teaching at Harvard. After an opening by the Ford Quartet, Knoxville Mayor John Brooks said, "It's not often that Knoxville has the opportunity of greeting a great leader among men."

In his speech, Washington boosted education and hard physical labor, but said, "We are going to live together here in the South as black people and white people. We can live separately socially, and are going to do so. No reasonable Negro desires

The ox-versus-car race around Market Square in 1907 was a memorable stunt from the dawn of the automobile age. Bill and Jack Winkle, are astride their impressive pet, perhaps the last animal to win a race with a car in Knoxville. McClung Historical Collection.

to have social intermingling with the white people of the South. What the Negro is interested in is to be sure that his life, liberty, and property are protected by the officers of the law...."

Soon, younger blacks, like W.E.B. Du Bois, would criticize Washington's accommodating perspectives harshly—but in 1909, Washington was reaching conservative white audiences who weren't used to listening to black men speak. However, over the next 40 years, Knoxville would become only more segregated, and Knoxville may or may not have suspected it, but in 1909 the era of black representatives answering roll calls at Market Square's City Hall was already over.

~

Perhaps the most astonishingly successful political movement in Knoxville history coalesced on Market Square. The Women's Christian Temperance Union had kept its most visible permanent presence as a restaurant they had hosted on Market Square since the 1880s, spurred on by a visit from the famous feminist and prohibitionist Frances Willard; a well-known photograph shows prohibitionist Vera Smith waving a large American flag and leading a mainly male crowd in song, perhaps a hymn of sustenance.

When the effort gathered steam in the new century, some of its most dramatic moments were on Market Square, a safer and more savory spot than some of Knoxville's other saloon districts, which the WCTU used as a sort of focal point for parades, lectures, and demonstrations.

In 1901, when well-known Wild West outlaw Harvey "Kid Curry" Logan shot two police officers in a Central Street saloon, barely three blocks east of Market Square, the women gained a powerful symbol, a real-life cautionary tale which was useful to them, considering they still had no vote. Much of the debate of whether the sale of alcohol should be entirely abolished in Knoxville was held in the public auditorium of the Market House. Mayor Sam Heiskell was a well-known opponent of prohibitionism. By 1907, there were an estimated 114 legal saloons in downtown Knoxville alone, and they were, for the most part, good municipal citizens, and, more importantly, dependable sources of tax revenue.

One night in the Market Hall, when partisans of both factions packed the hall, Heiskell stood up to say a few words in favor of some other solution than an outright saloon ban.

The women in white ribbons chanted, "Har-vey Lo-gan, Har-vey Lo-gan." It was the name of the murderous outlaw and known drinker, also known as Kid Curry. Captured by a posse a few days after he wounded the Knoxville cops, the train robber and former hit man for Butch Cassidy's Wild Bunch was held and tried on various federal charges in the Custom House's courtroom (now the McClung

Collection's reading room, scene of much of the research for this book) until he escaped the Knox County Jail in June, 1903. He was never seen alive again. Logan was believed by some to have died by his own hand during a shootout in Colorado the following year, by others to have escaped to South America to rejoin Butch and the Sundance Kid.

Men found it difficult to counter that comparison. The prosperous Knoxville men of 1907, in their starched collars and bowler hats, didn't want to be like Harvey Logan, at least not in any way they'd be willing to admit to women. And the women had a better point than may be obvious to moderns. Knoxville had an impressively high murder rate in 1907, higher than it has ever been, and saloons were indeed involved, directly or indirectly, in a lot of deadly violence. In many cases of husbands and fathers unable to control their saloon habit, it also drained household incomes, or caused men to stray, morally or physically, leaving women alone to tend to their children. During the thick of the debate, in November, 1904, the sheriff busted a third-floor gambling den near the Square on Union, at the old White Elephant Saloon. Outside the saloon he made a pile of gambling equipment and furniture, including a roulette wheel and a pool table, and burned them in the street.

Not all of the movement's leaders were women; in the early 1900s, the convincing voice of Southern prohibitionism, journalist and former U.S. Sen. Edward Ward Carmack, boosted the cause. The handsome, charismatic, mustachioed Carmack had recently lost a campaign for re-election, but as editor of the *Nashville Tennessean*, he was pushing his crusade to abolish alcohol wherever he could.

When he spoke at the Market Hall, on March 9, 1907, it was reportedly the biggest crowd the place had ever seen. Even standing room was at a premium, and men and women crowded the stairs up to the auditorium just for the privilege of catching a thrilling phrase.

Old Captain Rule introduced him. Former Mayor Rule had not been the most outspoken prohibitionist in Knoxville, and his paper ran ads for alcoholic beverages, but by 1909 he seems to have been sympathetic to the idea of banning it all. And he was a fellow journalist who had known Carmack for 20 years, and held him in high esteem. Carmack was met with a room full of applause. He spoke forcefully.

"It seems to me impossible that this great and magnificent gathering would not presage a complete and final victory for our cause and the utter extinction of the saloon in this great community," Carmack declared. "It will be the most glorious day that ever dawned upon the people of the city of Knoxville." He was frequently interrupted by applause.

University of Tennessee Professor Philander P. Claxton, the nationally known advocate for public education, followed with a perhaps less stirring talk, with statistics, noting that 56 murders in Knoxville in the previous three years had originated in the saloons or under the influence of whiskey. To many thoughtful citizens, including some drinkers, banning saloons began to seem an urgent solution.

When the day of the referendum came, just two days after Carmack's talk, women couldn't vote, but their husbands could. Through marches and persuasive lectures at the Market Hall and elsewhere, they mustered enough male allies to vote Dry.

By the end of that year, all 114 of Knoxville's saloons, including five on Market Square and several others nearby, closed forever. Not until 65 years later would Knoxville's liquor laws be nearly as liberal as they had been before 1907.

Carmack, a lifelong Middle Tennessean, hinted he was contemplating a move to Knoxville. A year later, though, after venting some anger in print at a political rival and wet advocate, he was shot and killed in downtown Nashville. His sudden death is believed to have helped the passage of statewide prohibition in 1909. Some saw him as a martyr, and the state legislature erected a prominent statue of him on the capitol grounds in Nashville.

Temperance activist Vera Smith singing hymns of inspiration to a mixed-race but primarily male Market Square crowd, early in the 20th century. Though the temperance movement was dominated by women, who were not allowed the vote, prohibitionists successfully persuaded Knoxville's male electorate to ban saloons in 1907. McClung Historical Collection.

Prohibition changed the face of Market Square, closing both saloons and liquor dealers, like Horne's, the wholesaling stalwart that had long anchored the northwest corner. General Horne didn't quite live to see it. He had died the previous year, to be buried at Old Gray, beneath one of the most striking stones in that graveyard full of sculpture, a marble statue of a dashingly bearded Confederate soldier holding a rifle and wearing an officer's broad-brimmed hat and a buckle inscribed C.S.

It's certain that some liquor sales, even in bar settings, survived local prohibition, on Market Square and elsewhere. Author James Agee's childhood memories of a visit with his father to a Market Square bar, as recounted in his novel, *A Death in the Family*, are at least credible. At least one saloonkeeper, William M. McIntyre, stayed on in his same old establishment at 21 Market Square, but now advertising his place as a billiard hall. If Agee's description of a post-prohibition Market Square bar is real, it may be that one.

But Red Mike's had closed. Members of the Cullinan family continued to live upstairs at 15 Market Square, but after 1907, Mike Cullinan disappears from the local records.

Another era ended the same fall that prohibition went into effect; Peter Kern, the jovial spirit of Market Square for the previous 40 years, died, a few days before his 72nd birthday, which was Halloween. A whole generation of men who had been energetic young entrepreneurs on an unfinished, frontier-like Market Square in the days after the Civil War was passing from the scene.

No one would fill Kern's role as the de facto host and prime celebrant of Market Square, exactly, but another imaginative entrepreneur with a German accent was already bringing a different kind of energy to the Square.

~

Max Arnstein was a Jewish immigrant from Germany whose arrival in Knoxville was as accidental as Kern's had been. Though he had associations with New York, Arnstein had run a small store in Anderson, SC, in 1888 when a trusted business associate, Herman Baruch—uncle of the major financier Bernard Baruch, who was then a young man, not yet famous—offered Arnstein a partnership in a business venture in Birmingham. Arnstein and Baruch set out for Alabama on the trains, which then took them through Knoxville. They had a layover here, and Baruch looked around and said, "Max, this looks like a good town, there's lots of stores to rent. Maybe we can find a good store here." Baruch and Arnstein, originally a retail clothing store on Gay Street, was a success—it was said that Arnstein's smile had much to do with his success—and became Arnstein's when Baruch retired in the 1890s.

In 1905, Arnstein set out to build a grand new store, Knoxville's first "skyscraper," by the standards of the day, and looked in the direction of Market Square.

After some controversy within the congregation, the Second Presbyterian Church, outgrowing its 1860 chapel, chose to move. Its 80 years on the corner had included the entire history of Market Square, but the church finally sold its prime commercial acreage at Prince and Union. The sale financed most of the construction of a much-larger stone gothic church around at Church and Walnut.

What became of the graveyard on the corner has some mystery connected with it. Some graves are known to have been distributed, at the families' behest, to Old Gray, plus the two new graveyards farther out, New Gray and Greenwood. The most famous of the graves, that of General Sanders, was missing for decades until a plain regulation stone with his name on it turned up in the 1960s, at the U.S. cemetery in Chattanooga, a location that has puzzled researchers. Whether all the graves were removed before the excavation for the Arnstein project is a matter of faith.

Max Arnstein acquired the property, and, just across Union from Market Square, on the spot which had recently been a graveyard, he built a seven-story brick building to house both Arnstein's posh department store and numerous offices. To design his grand opus, he hired the prestigious New York firm of Cleverdon & Putzel, who had been among Manhattan's leading architects of the 1890s. Several of the firm's surviving buildings are restored and pointed out on architectural tours of New York today. By 1900 Cleverdon & Putzel had designed several of the new buildings called "skyscrapers," including the 12-story Astor Building on Broadway, buildings built taller than buildings ever had been before, thanks to their new steel-frame construction.

That technology had never been tried in Knoxville before, but Arnstein's wealth and connections made it happen at the corner of Prince and Union. Upon its completion, the Arnstein Building was not only the tallest building in Knoxville, even taller than the Vendome apartment building around the corner on Clinch, it was widely acknowledged as Knoxville's finest piece of architecture. Mayor Heiskell himself, risking the alienation of local architects, declared it so: "Architecturally, the gem of Market Square is the Arnstein Building, which is worthy of any city, and which showed great courage and faith in the future of Knoxville on the part of its owner to construct...."

The Arnstein would enjoy its status of Knoxville's tallest building for only a couple of years, as other steel-frame structures rose on Gay Street—but Max Arnstein ran his department store there for almost a quarter century, until his retirement at age 70. To young Knoxville women of wealth, Arnstein's offered newer, higher fashions than had been available at Miller's or George's. Arnstein's saved some debutantes the bother of a shopping trip to New York. The department store's retail sales were concentrated in the building's lower floors; the upper floors were the offices of various professionals, including physicians, architects, insurance men, music teachers and, for a time, a chemistry laboratory. For a while, the sixth floor hosted the headquarters of city schools, the superintendant's office and the Board of Education.

Along the way Max Arnstein became intimately associated with Knoxville's Jewish community, helping to found the Arnstein Jewish Community Center, originally located downtown but still thriving in the 21st century in West Knoxville. It was here that he met a contemporary who was a former Market Square character, though long since moved away: Adolph Ochs, whose daughter would call the Knoxville merchant "Uncle Max."

～

Meanwhile, as always, other new businesses were sprouting on the Square. Few expected much when Ira Watson, a bushy-eyebrowed former schoolteacher from Ohio, began selling "distressed stock" out of one small storefront at 11 Market Square. He'd first come to town around 1907, and did most of his early trade on the fly, but later opened a permanent store, first on Wall. Records disagree, but Watson's Market Square store seems to have opened around 1913. He sold mainly stock from businesses that had suffered fires or floods or had declared bankruptcy, and was thus able to sell high-quality goods, albeit a sometimes odd assortment of them, at a very low price.

Watson's was never a fancy place, but Watson himself lived a glamorous life from a Cole Porter song. He and his wife, Eva, had no children, didn't really settle in Knoxville, and never stayed anywhere very long, taking regular vacations to Atlantic City and Louisville, to see the races. When in Knoxville, the Watsons kept adjoining suites at the Farragut Hotel, at Gay and Clinch, where they were known to share their passions for bridge and piano. They eventually made a home in Birmingham, while their nephew and great-nephew, both named Forrest Watson, settled in Knoxville and shepherded the expansion of what became a multi-state chain, based at the headquarters store on old Market Square, which over a period of about 75 years expanded to take in a whole series of adjacent buildings on the west side.

One building that catches the eye of architectural students is on the Square's northeast corner, with entrances on Market Square and Wall Avenue. At four full stories, it's the tallest building on the Square, and features some cast-iron construction and hints of a stylish architect's work. That architect's name is unknown, as is the date of its construction: records indicate it was built between 1890 and 1903. Though sometimes called the Woods & Taylor building, after the clothing store located there for a quarter century, that firm wasn't the first in this building. It had hosted various dry-goods merchants before 1907, when it opened as the original location of another big department store S.H. George, well-known to Knoxvillians of the first half of the 20th century, especially for its later Gay Street store. Woods & Taylor, which moved in ca. 1913, advertised as "Dependable Outfitters: Correct Clothes for Men and Women." That store seems to have gone out of business during the Great Depression, promptly replaced by another men's clothing store well-known to a postwar generation as Bowers. The building eventually boasted a customer elevator, an unusual amenity for Market Square.

Benjamin Bower (1891–1981), son of a recent British immigrant clothier, was a World War I veteran who saw the potential of army surplus. A pioneer local pilot, himself, Bower is credited with spawning Knoxville's aviation boom of the 1920s with an influx of inexpensive surplus airplanes and airplane parts. He also founded the Camel Tent Company. But here on the Square he was best known for his way with army surplus clothing, and at turning around castaway goods into useful merchandise he appears to have been something of a genius.

The Horatio Alger stories popular at the turn of the century were often assumed, then and now, to be an American myth. But Market Square seemed always to have some crypto-fictional, novelistic dynamic to it. Somehow, several ambitious folks went, literally, from rags to riches, almost without leaving this block.

J. Frank Walker's story is one that Mr. Alger himself might have had trouble swallowing. A kid from a poor cotton-farming family in North Carolina, he was nine when his struggling family moved to Knoxville in 1890. He went immediately to work, first as a water carrier on construction projects. At 14, he was living on his own, working for his bed at Mrs. Gentry's boarding house on Market Square. He later got work as a "roustabout" at Biddle & Moulden's dry-goods store at 24 Market Square, and improved his living conditions, working up to a $2 a week boarding house just around the corner on Union. At 19, lying about his age to sign some papers, he opened his own furniture store on Market Square, carrying everything from small kitchen utensils to, according to a newspaper story, "suites of mahogany furniture of period designs, many of which are upholstered in rich velour." He worked with a manufacturer to develop a stove "specially built for the Appalachian district," and known as Walker's Economist Range. Walker was also the Knoxville agent for Brunswick phonographs, a state-of-the-art brand. Many Knoxville-area people probably bought their first record players at Walker's store. By 1920, it had expanded to cover the addresses at 29, 31, and 33 Market Square; Walker built one of the buildings, a four-story addition, himself. Walker was a proud self-made man who, even when his company got big, never had any use for a board of directors. He was fond of quoting Henry Ford: "A board is just a plank with splinters in it."

≈

By 1905 or so, Market Square had been intimately associated with every local immigrant culture except maybe one. The small but commercially dynamic Greek community, when it first formed in Knoxville around 1900, congregated mainly near the train station, especially on the 100 block of South Central. Around 1909, a couple of Greek immigrants named Paskalis—or something like that—acquired the former Horne liquor wholesale space at #37 Market Square and opened a restaurant which would become a major institution in the Knoxville Greek community, and to downtown itself.

Actually, the first proprietor listed in the city directory is Haralacos Paschalio, though he may be the same fellow who's listed in the same book as Harris Paskalis. Knoxville seemed to know him better as "Harry," and his brother as "Gus." They

The tallest building on the Square, 36 Market Square, at the northeast corner. Sometimes known as the Woods & Taylor building, after the department store which occupied it longer than any other, this photo shows an earlier period, around 1910. It was the original location of S.H. George's, one of Knoxville's most popular department stores of the 20th century. George's was here until the store moved to a larger building on Gay Street around 1912. McClung Historical Collection.

shared the space, for a short time, with an Italian confectioner named Samuel Armatta (whose name was sometimes spelled with different vowels). The Armattas, ice-cream makers and confectioners, would be much more strongly associated with the Old City area, where their name is still visible in the brick on the side of Sullivan's Saloon.

The Paskalises, by whatever spelling, ran their restaurant until about 1915, whereupon they disappear from Knoxville records. It's unclear exactly when their restaurant became popularly known as the Gold Sun, whether during its original Paskalis era or just after, when the Tampas and Cavalaris families were in charge of the place.

The name "Gold Sun" is familiar to generations of Knoxvillians, but may seem odd, given its location. Always in the shade of the Market House, it was never a sunny spot; even its side windows on Wall Avenue offered only northern exposure. The name may have been a joke—or a dare. See, as early as the Paskalis brothers were, they weren't the first Greek restaurateurs on Market Square.

By 1906, there was a restaurant at No. 8 Market Square run by one Costa, or Custa, Constantine. The spelling of his first name was variable—and probably not very important, considering that everyone called him Joe, and as he got older, Daddy Joe. Before there was a Gold Sun, Constantine's place was known as the Silver Moon. Though forgotten now, it was a familiar spot on the east side of the Square for more than 20 years, when Constantine moved a few yards around the corner, on Union, and opened a place called Daddy Joe's.

The Gold Sun was a lively and well-run place, unusual in several respects; it was open 24 hours a day, and hardly ever closed at all. They were known to let customers order things that weren't even on the menu. If a man at a table insisted on some red snapper, for example, the waiter wouldn't shrug; he'd just step out the door to the fish market section of the Market House, and buy some snapper fresh for the customer as he waited at his table. Handy access to the markets made the Gold Sun's menu, for practical purposes, infinite.

They also made a point to offer Mediterranean food, especially certain lamb dishes, to immigrant communities who wouldn't otherwise have access to it: fellow Greeks, as well as Italians, and, in years to come, some Syrians and other Arabs. Greek specialties were never on the menu, at least not until later in the century, but were available for the asking.

∽

Electric lights had been introduced to Knoxville in 1885, and public streetlights were common throughout downtown in the mid-1890s, supplanting the flickery gaslights of a former era. For some aspirants to urbanity, though, it wasn't nearly enough. New York had a stretch of Broadway lit so bright it was called the Great

White Way. Many Knoxvillians, especially Max Arnstein, were familiar with the sheer spectacle of city streets brilliantly lit at night—and excited about the effects it might have on retail in Knoxville.

In August, 1911, Knoxville prepared for its biggest party in history, the second Appalachian Exposition at Chilhowee Park, an opportunity to brag to the nation about the industry and natural resources of the area, due to open on September 11. Much of the planning for the festival took place in offices in the Arnstein Building; Lalla Block Arnstein, Max's wife, was involved, serving on its Women's Board; later, she would be the first woman elected to serve as a representative on Knox County government.

In preparation for the estimated hundreds of thousands of tourists expected for the exposition, Knoxville boosters hastened to spiff up downtown, the locus of the hotels where most of the exposition-goers would stay, to make it look as impressively urban as possible.

Previously, the Square had generally operated under an every-man-for-himself ethic, but in 1911, a private group of merchants organized as the Market Square Business Men's Club, led by Max Arnstein. Its first order of business was to make Market Square Knoxville's "White Way"—with the addition of 82 large additional streetlights. It was undeniably amazing. The *Journal & Tribune* ran a cartoon of a weeping moon, as below, heartless Knoxville declared, "We don't need you anymore."

Later on, Gay Street, with its brightly lit movie theaters and other nocturnal amusements, would be better known as "Knoxville's White Way." But for a while beginning that evening in 1911, the distinction "White Way" belonged to Market Square alone. It may not have been something Market Square was especially famous for after that one night.

The era of idealism may have seen its peak in 1913, the year of the National Conservation Exposition at Chilhowee Park, an enormous event that for two months entertained one million visitors. It was planned from its headquarters, on the top floor of the Arnstein Building, with the help of nationally noted conservationist Gifford Pinchot. Though the exposition itself was three miles away, Market Square was decorated for the duration with extravagant flags and bunting, topped with a "large Knoxville flag" flying over the Market House.

It may seem a sad irony that the Progressive era coincided with the practical end of the first civil rights era—and the end, for several decades, of elected black participation in city government. Knoxville blacks continued to vote, and get elected, for several years after Jim Crow laws elsewhere in the South disenfranchised them. But in 1912, the city shifted from a 12-member Board of Aldermen to a five-member City Commission. It was said to be a more efficient way to run a government, but one casualty, intended or not, was elective black participation.

The last black member of City Council to take a seat in Market Square's City Hall was a memorable one. Henry M. Green, a respected local surgeon, served from 1908 to 1912. Well known far beyond Tennessee as an expert on diseases related to poverty, Green was chairman of a National Medical Association commission on the then-rampant vitamin deficiency pellagra.

～

Markets were open every day, but no day like Saturday. By 1915, the *Journal and Tribune* said, "The Saturday-morning market, with the presence of hundreds of rural neighbors, and the big crowds of buyers, is one of the picturesque things for which the city of Knoxville is famed. Every visitor who comes to the city for even the briefest of visits must be shown the Saturday-morning market…."

The approach to Market Square along Union Avenue from Gay Street, in May, 1913. This block had once hosted saloons, but also law offices, including that of pioneering black attorney William F. Yardley. Visible on the left is the Arnstein Building; Kern's is on the right. The building in the left foreground is on the present site of Krutch Park. McClung Historical Collection.

In July, 1915, the city augmented the women's rooms on the ground floor with pretty swank-sounding "rest rooms" on the second floor. Descriptions of it make it sound like a phenomenon beyond mere plumbing. "The rest room on the second floor of Market Hall…is a somewhat belated tribute of appreciation to the rural women who have for many years contributed greatly to the success of the market. Though being late in establishment, it is a handsome atonement…. There are comfortable rocking chairs, couches, tables decorated with flowers, the late periodicals, and a lavatory. A colored maid is in attendance to give assistance and to see that everything is kept clean and orderly. There are window boxes, which give an artistic and home-like touch to the rest room."

One early group of farm women was observed, late that summer, at about noon: "There were several young mothers with small babies, nursing or entertaining them until the father 'hitched up' to leave for home. Some were reading or looking at the pictures, and a few nodded in their chairs. There was a small social group, and a good deal of discussion about local church and school affairs. The rest rooms will be the means of broadening the acquaintance of rural women. They will enjoy the interchange of ideas and benefit by an exchange of experiences."

It might take an idealist to believe that a visit to Market Square could improve the lives of country women, but it was an age of idealism.

~

The Great War came, and went—and the influenza epidemic came and went, killing about 160 in Knoxville, about the same number of local men who died in the trenches in a few months in 1918. When thousands of soldiers returned on the train one famous day in 1919, Market Square celebrated with the rest of downtown, which hosted the biggest outdoor banquet in the city's history.

Later that year, though, just before Labor Day, a group of angry white men gathered on Market Square, attempting to recruit a lynch mob. A white woman had been murdered in her bedroom, on the northeast side of town, and a black man had been arrested for the crime. Market Square merchants may have heaved a sigh of relief when the crowd, growing in size, left the Square, heading south, toward the jailhouse on Hill Avenue. They wouldn't accomplish their purpose that night, but they'd set off a night of violence that provoked the governor to send in the National Guard and left several dead, most of them blacks killed by whites, and caused thousands in property damage. The riot shocked Knoxville, which had boasted that racial violence was impossible here.

Market Square escaped the worst of the looting, which was over on Gay Street, and all of the killing, most of which was over on Vine and Central. The Square was, after all, still the headquarters of the police. But Market Square would never be the same after 1919, the year of the national Red Scare, when the city, like many American cities, began to fear not only blacks, but foreigners. In 1920, city boosters began to brag about the fact that Knoxville was whiter than most cities in the South, and, perhaps exaggerating the matter, bragging that Knoxville was overwhelmingly native-born. No longer would immigrants or blacks sit on City Council, and in the decade to come, foreign accents on Market Square became more the exception than the rule.

William Jennings Bryan, perennial presidential candidate and pacifist former Secretary of State who had quit the Wilson administration over the decision to join the war, spoke that fall at the Market Hall, and drew a big crowd, but perhaps didn't generate the charismatic fervor he was able to evoke a decade or two earlier.

The war, and the Red Summer riot of 1919 seemed a decisive end to an era when unlimited improvement seemed possible.

A Versatile Setting

I n American literature, Market Square may be East Tennessee's most-described spot. Few blocks anywhere have a richer literary heritage. For more than a century, its human color has caught the attention of writers of different genres and eras. Market Square appears, in thick detail, in at least five novels that received national or international attention in their time, as well as a memoir or two. One could walk into any good bookstore in America and reasonably expect to find at least one book that offers a rich description of Market Square. The best-known passages are in three well-known novels by Knoxville's two best-known novelists.

Its literary associations run deep. Market Square co-founder William Swan, author of legal books and co-editor of the secessionist journal The Southern Citizen, was a plausibly literary fellow. The best-known East Tennessee writer of the 19th century, humorist George Washington Harris, was surely familiar with this real-estate project of his political allies Swan and Mabry. Market Square was just congealing when he left town around 1861; in his fiction, his few mentions of Knoxville evoke a pre-Market House era.

Of likely literary connections in those early years, the most intriguing comes from around 1867, when an English girl named Fannie Hodgson, a teenager who lived in the Clinton Pike area—near what would later be Knoxville College—picked wild berries and grapes to sell for pencils, paper, and stamps, basic supplies for an aspiring writer. It's not clear whether Fannie herself did the selling; the scant records suggest she may have counted on some neighbors, a couple of young black girls who were sisters, to make the trip to Market Square. But with the proceeds, Fannie Hodgson was able to *mail off her first story submission, a revision of a short story she'd written when she was even younger, back in Manchester, England, called "Miss Carruthers' Engagement."*

Godey's Ladies' Magazine, *one of her quarries, liked the story, but noting the Knoxville postmark, wrote back that the story "is so distinctly English that our reader is not sure of its having been written by an American.... Will you kindly inform us if the story is original?"*

Hodgson assured them that it was. She would soon enough be known as Frances Hodgson Burnett, one of the most successful female writers of her time, author of Little Lord Fauntleroy, The Secret Garden, *and* A Little Princess.

Whether she was the one who actually sold the grapes on the Square or not, she was certainly familiar with the place. Her widowed mother had moved to Knoxville at the end of the Civil War mainly for the security of her brother's successful business; by 1865, Frances's uncle, William Boond, had a successful business as a "Grocer, Provision Dealer, and Commission Merchant" at the corner of Gay and Union, hardly a block from the market. And the Square's newspaper, the Chronicle, *published a few of her short travel pieces, describing a return trip to England.*

Frances Hodgson Burnett lived in Knoxville until around 1877, and set one novel in a war-devastated, Knoxville-like town called Deslisleville, but did not reference a Market Square.

The first known description of Market Square in a novel comes from a long-out-of-print curiosity called The Seas of God, *published anonymously in 1915. A literary romance of intercontinental adultery, with overtones of corruption and philosophical turbulence, it concerns a woman from a college town called Kingsville who eventually lives in London with her lover. The book received international acclaim in its own day, and even earned comparisons to Tolstoy's* Anna Karenina.

The author was later revealed to be former Knoxvillian Anne Armstrong, who would be best known in her own lifetime as a business scholar, among other distinctions the first woman to teach a business class at Harvard.

"The Market Square was full of loafers when she came to it—negroes and poor whites. Miserable-looking white beggar girls accosted her with their whining, 'Miss, gimme a nickel.' She made her way hurryingly into the big Market House and made purchases at various stalls. As she emerged into the narrow, cluttered thoroughfare that ran on four sides of the Market House, she paused.... Inattentively picking her way among the huckster's wagons, one of them almost backed into her...."

Later, when she is suffering some moral regrets, expressing themselves as homesickness, she confesses to her lover, "'Why Ransom, there have been times when I've felt I'd rather—I'd rather'—her voice shook with stifled sobs—'be back in Kingsville and be one of those miserable little waif dogs that used to pick up scraps around the Market House than to be the grandest person in the world anywhere else!'"

In a nonfiction book, the memoir More Lives Than One, *drama critic, biographer, and naturalist Joseph Wood Krutch (1893-1970) remembers Market Square at roughly the same era:*

"The farmers of the surrounding country drove their wagons in at night, slept in them in the public square, and were ready the next morning individually to offer for sale a few bushels of green beans, a few pounds of homemade butter, a few dressed chickens, and a dishpan of lye hominy covered with a piece of cheesecloth to keep it moist. I can still see my father moving from wagon to wagon, snapping the beans to discover which were the freshest, bending the breastbones of the chickens to find the youngest."

A crowded day on the east side of Market Square. Visible are Biddles' Department Store, a dry-goods merchant at No. 18–20; a cigar shop; Hall's clothing store; and Kenny's Coffee Co. And, to the far right, part of a sign for Harbison's, one of a few downtown merchants mentioned by name in James Agee's Pulitzer-winning novel, A Death In the Family. *A sign on the Market House advises a speed limit, even before automobiles were common: "$5 – $50 Fine to Ride or Drive Faster Than a Walk on Market Square During Market Hours." McClung Historical Collection.*

It was Krutch's brother, Charlie, who willed the seven-figure gift the city used to establish Krutch Park, which since its construction in the early 1980s has become something like a southern extension of Market Square. Krutch's father, who was picky about his chicken, would later be killed in a freak elevator accident at the old Empire Building on Market Street, about two blocks south of the Square.

The best-known single description of Market Square in literature comes from Chapter One of James Agee's Pulitzer-winning novel, A Death In the Family, *as assembled from notes just after the author's own death and published in 1957.*

The novel, which appears to be strictly autobiographical, is about Agee himself, a little boy named Rufus (Agee's middle name) in the book. He and his father, Jay, have set out on foot from their Highland Avenue home to see a Charlie Chaplin movie on Gay Street.

The setting is May, 1916, just before the death, in an automobile accident, of Agee's father—and within that date is a puzzle.

"They turned aside into a darker street, where the fewer faces looked more secret, and came into the odd, shaky light of Market Square," Agee writes of the father and son, just as they leave the movie theater known as the Majestic, a small, storefront place on Gay near Wall. "It was almost empty at this hour, but here and there, along the pavement streaked with horse urine, a wagon stayed still, and low firelight shone through the white cloth shell stretched tightly on its hickory hoops. A dark-faced man leaned against the white brick wall, gnawing a turnip. He looked at them low, with sad, pale eyes. When Rufus's father raised his hand in silent greeting, he raised his hand, but less, and Rufus, turning, saw how he looked sorrowfully, somehow dangerously, after them. They passed a wagon in which a lantern burned low orange; there lay a whole family, large and small, silent, asleep. In the tail of one wagon a woman sat, her face narrow beneath her flare of sunbonnet, her dark eyes in its shade, like smudges of soot. Rufus's father averted his eyes and touched his straw hat lightly; and Rufus, looking back, saw how her dead eyes kept looking gently ahead of her."

The father says, "Well…reckon I'll hoist me a couple." And the narrator follows as "They turned through the swinging doors into a blast of odor and sound. There was no music: only the density of bodies and the smell of a market bar, of beer, whiskey, and country bodies, salt and leather; no clamor, only the thick quietude of crumpled talk."

The puzzle concerns the existence of a bar, on Market Square, and therefore within sight of the police station, in 1916; the city had voted to abolish bars in 1907. It may be a vividly imagined error by Agee, who knew his father drank but perhaps didn't research Knoxville's political history for the book. Agee was just a kid at the time of the setting, and when he wrote his novel, he lived in New York. However, considering that very little in the autobiographical novel is invented, it's just as likely that he described one of several openly tolerated speakeasies in the downtown area.

If there were such an amenity on Market Square, ca. 1916, we can only guess where it might have been. At least one well-known former saloonkeeper, John McIntyre, was still keeping a business listed as a "billiard hall" at 25 Market Square during that period.

At some later time—the next day, according to students of the text—young Agee returns to a very different Market Square, the daytime place of clothing shops, with his Aunt Hannah, who was more indulgent than his own mother, to buy a sporty hat. They'd been shopping in stores on Gay Street that didn't interest the kid when "[S]he compressed her lips and, by unaccountable brilliance of intuition, went straight past Miller's, a profoundly matronly store in which Rufus's mother always bought the best clothes which were always, at best, his own second choice, and steered him round to Market Street and into Harbison's, which sold clothing exclusively for men and boys, and was regarded, by his mother, Rufus had overheard, as 'tough' and 'sporty' and 'vulgar.'

"And is was indeed a world most alien to women; not very pleasant men turned to stare at this spinster with the radiant, appalled little boy in tow...."

That description contains another puzzle. In Agee's youth there was, indeed a prominent store called Harbison's, just behind Miller's, anchoring the southeast corner of Market Square in 1916—but Harbison's motto was "Nothing But Shoes." It was not likely a place you'd go if you were thinking about hats.

The puzzle has been the subject of at least one research paper, which concluded that Agee was mistaken about the name, probably remembering Edington's at 12 Market Square, which sounds, in advertisements, more like the shop Agee describes.

At the store, wherever it was, Aunt Hannah bought the boy the hat he really wanted, "a thunderous fleecy check in jade green, canary yellow, black and white, which stuck out inches to either side above his ears and had a great scoop of visor beneath which his face was all but lost. It was a cap, she reflected, that even a colored sport might think a little loud...."

In 1937, Annemarie Schwarzenbach came to town. Now a tragic literary heroine (she died in a freak bicycle accident at age 34) with a cult following, the Swiss writer was a lesbian, and a daring German-language novelist and journalist. Her American travelogue, Jenseits von New York (Beyond New York), *has never been translated, in full, into English, but was republished in German in 1992. During a visit to Knoxville, she referred to "the old market hall where the mules and vegetable carts of the farmers stand and where on Saturdays the American Legion holds its patriotic speeches and dances": the American Legion Hall was then on the second floor of the Market House. She also mentions "a garishly lit movie house where love stories and Wild West movies from the good old days are playing," probably a reference to the Brichetto brothers' Crystal, and "cheap displays of ladies' fashions and drugstores...."*

Knoxville's first home-grown literary hero after World War II was David Madden, born in 1933, who was well known as a writer in Knoxville even as a teenager. He earned national praise for his short stories in the '60s. One 1967 story, "A Piece of the Sky," apparently set in the '50s, includes a sultry nocturnal scene that refers to Market Square's "vegetable trucks parked in the dark" and the "white brightness of the Gold Sun Cafe." In 1974, Madden published something like an autobiographical novel, Bijou. Knoxville is disguised in the book, which slightly distorts the city and renames most landmarks, but the Market House appears as it really was, circa 1946; it and its environs are among the haunts of Madden's teenaged protagonist Lucius Hutchfield:

"Lucius enjoyed passing through the ancient, three-story, block-long, brick Market House, its arched ceiling looming over them, a line of rough little tables running down the spine of the building where country women sold butter, eggs, shelled walnuts, jams, and honey. Permanent butcher and flower and fruit stalls and restaurants and lunch counters on each side. They walked along the sidewalks flanking the Market

Market Square attracted everybody. In this photo, which a poster in the rear suggests was taken during World War I, two ladies emerge from their chauffeur-driven Renault with baskets, prepared to do some shopping in the Market House. The distinctively designed car appears to be a 1914 Renault limousine, a French-made car which was a rarity in Knoxville, and an expensive one. McClung Historical Collection.

House where produce and flower trucks, mostly canvas-covered Ford pickups of the '30s, were parked, backed up to the curbs, their overladen tailgates hanging heavy, the country folks standing by, ready to sack up some pole beans or okra. The police loved to park at each end of the Market House, where the ornate fountains attached to the sooty brick walls were dry.

"The Bijou Boys walked past the Jewel, a hole in the wall so tiny it seemed almost a playhouse, the symphonic background music, the shooting and the galloping reaching out to them over a loudspeaker above the sidewalk, and a few skid-row stores down, past another hole in the wall that sold tobacco, practical jokes, and Trojan rubbers, the Ritz, the Jewel's twin, owned by two Italian brothers, where they heard only the sound of spurs clinking on a boardwalk and Charles Starratt as The Durango Kid was featured on a poster." (Starratt played the Durango Kid in a series of Westerns made from 1945 to 1952.)

Though much of Madden's descriptions of the fictional Cherokee, Tennessee, are fictional, the Brichetto brothers were the proprietors of movie houses on Market Square in the 1940s. The Jewel likely represents the Crystal; the Ritz, the Rialto.

Richard Marius mentioned Market Square, in passing, in his final novel, An Affair of Honor, as a place where a character finds a tuxedo to rent in 1953.

Much-praised novelist Cormac McCarthy described the Square in greater detail than any novelist before or since, and in more than one novel. Both The Orchard Keeper (1965) and Suttree (1979) include scenes on Market Square, described in dense and colorful detail.

In his first novel, The Orchard Keeper, McCarthy describes Market Square as it was in 1940; McCarthy was a child of seven at the time, but his father worked at nearby TVA, and the author likely drew from personal memories of the Square during the prewar era. He describes the trek of a young character, a country boy who's in downtown Knoxville looking for a trap for muskrats.

"He went up the far side of the square under the shadow of the market house past brown country faces peering from among their carts and trucks, perched on crates, old women with faces like dried fruit set deep in their hooded bonnets, shaggy, striated and hooktoothed as coconut carvings, shappy backlanders trafficking in the wares of the earth, higgling their goods from a long row of ancient vehicles backed obliquely against the curb and freighted with fruits and vegetables, eggs and berries, honey in jars and boxes of nuts, bundles of roots and herbs from sassafras to boneset, a bordello of potted plants and flowers. By shoe windows where shoddy footgear rose in dusty tiers and clothing stores in whose vestibules iron racks stood packed with used coats, past bins of socks and stockings, a meat market where hams and ribcages dangled like gibbeted miscreants and in the glass cases square porcelain trays piled with meat white-spotted and trichinella-ridden, chunks of liver the color of clay tottering up from moats of watery blood, a tray of brains, unidentifiable gobbits of flesh scattered here and there.

"Among overalled men and blind men and amputees on roller carts or crutches, flour and feed bags piled on the walk and pencil peddlars holding out their tireless arms, past stalls and cribs and holes-in-the-wall vending tobacco in cut or plug, leaf or bag, and snuff, sweet or scotch, in little tins, pipes and lighters and an esotery of small items down to pornographic picture books. Past cafes reeking with burned coffee, an effluvium of frying meat, and indistinguishable medley of smells."

That reference to "hole-in-the-wall" tobacco stores may be a very inside joke. A cigar store at 19 Market Square was actually called The Hole In the Wall. Madden made the same sort of backwards pun in his own description of Market Square.

McCarthy continues: "Under the Crystal's marquee of lightbulbs a group of country men stood gazing hard past the box office where a tired-looking woman sat beneath a

The south end of Market Square, ca. 1930, with the 1897 Market House, the Square's most conspicuous feature for more than 60 years. Kinney's Shoes and Miller's Bargain Annex are visible at right. Note "Deadly Autos" sign on the Market House itself; it reported the traffic-fatality toll for the year. McClung Historical Collection.

sign: Adults 25—Children 10 —watching the film through a missing panel of curtain. Sounds of hooves and gunfire issued onto the street. He couldn't see past or over them and went on by, up the square, until he stood before a window garnished with shapes of wood and metal among which he recognized only a few common handtools…. he went in. His footfalls were muffled on the dark oiled floors, bearing him into an atmosphere heavy with smells of leather and iron, machine-oil, seed, beneath strange objects hung from hooks on the ceiling, past barrels of nails, to the counter. They were hanging down by their chains and looking fierce and ancient among the trace chains and harness, bucksaws and axehelves…."

McCarthy's fourth novel, Suttree, *is much more concerned with urban Knoxville, and Market Square appears repeatedly. Early in the novel, the fisherman Cornelius Suttree approaches the Square with a sack of fish to sell.*

"Market Street on Monday morning, Knoxville Tennessee. In this year 1951. Suttree with his parcel of fish going past the rows of derelict trucks piled with produce and flowers, an atmosphere rank with country commerce, a reek of farmgoods in the air tending off in a light surmise of putrefaction and decay. Pariahs adorned the walk and blind singers and organists and psalmists with mouth harps wandered up and down. Past hardware stores and meatmarkets and little tobacco shops. A strong smell of feed in the hot noon like working mash. Mute and roosting pedlars watching from their wagonbeds and flower ladies in their bonnets like cowled gnomes, driftwood hands composed in their apron laps and their underlips swollen with snuff."

So three of the most detailed descriptions of Market Square all come from the '40s and early '50s, a period no one would suggest was a high point of Market Square in terms of politics or culture or commerce or aesthetics, but when it was, nonetheless, distinctly fascinating for its characters, and in part perhaps because of its decline or, as McCarthy called it, its "light surmise of putrefaction and decay."

It was precisely during that era that the second floor of the storied old Kern Building became the new home of an almost-forgotten institution called the Knoxville Metaphysical Library. A public amenity associated with the local Bahai faith, it was previously located in the Cherokee Building, two blocks south, but moved to Market Square around 1947, where it stayed for four or five years before vanishing altogether. Its unusual collection included works of modern philosophy as well as ghost stories, and might have been an ideal spot to contemplate the mysteries of Market Square.

This was also the Square that attracted poet Carl Sandburg, who rejoiced in the unvarnished oddity of it. The famous Chicagoan first visited Market Square around 1940, about the time he was moving to what would be his final home, in Flat Rock, North Carolina. In a letter to a friend, he described it as the only place he'd ever been, in a central business district, where one could buy hazelnuts, black walnuts, and ginseng. He had friends in Knoxville, including Harbrace grammarian John

Hodges, and apparently made a point to visit Market Square whenever he was in town. Sandburg gave a talk at UT in late 1957, at the height of the controversy over whether to demolish the Market House. "It's a worthy and dignified landmark, and belongs among these mountains," the poet said.

In 1961, however, soon after the demolition of the Market House, well-known New Yorker writer Phillip Hamburger found on Market Square only further reason to be skeptical about Knoxville's efforts at urban renewal:

"Where the old market place once stood, a bright new mall is being erected, with suitable arrangements for the piping in of music. Flower cars are still angle-parked near the site of the old market place both day and night. By day, they are filled with fresh flowers. At night, they are just empty automobiles, angle-parked. Many of them have been parked in the same spot for years, exercising squatter's rights. They are not moved at night because they cannot be moved. Their motors were long ago taken out."

Hamburger apparently caught that dead-truck era of Market Square at the very end of it; the derelict-truck era did not survive long into the '60s.

The spruced-up Market Square Mall of the '60s, '70s, and '80s may have been something the Chamber of Commerce was sometimes proud of, but it seems not to have been the sort of place that inspires novelists. It's interesting that three of the best-known descriptions of the Square, by Madden and McCarthy, were written in the '60s and '70s, the Mall era—but they each harked back to much-earlier eras. Still, through all the changes, Market Square may have kept some of its literary magnetism.

In 1999, author Norman Mailer took a slow stroll through the Square and remarked, "Knoxville is very lucky to have a place like this." He led his talk at UT that evening with a description of Market Square that, unfortunately for us, was not saved for posterity, except for his opening line: "I had a very agreeable experience this afternoon." The gist of Mailer's talk was that Market Square was an authentic urban space holding onto its own against encroaching soulless architectural modernism, presumably represented by the TVA buildings.

In recent years, Market Square has been mentioned a few times as a lunch locale in Richard Yancey's mostly humorous "Highly Effective Detective" series of novels about a bumbling gumshoe named Teddy Ruzak whose office is in the Ely Building, on Church near Market Street. Ruzak refers to the Market Square street-corner preacher and has conferences at a place called Market Square Grill, which sounds like Market Square Kitchen, as well as the real-life Tomato Head. In Jefferson Bass's 2009 "Body Farm" mystery Bones of Betrayal, *adjacent Krutch Park makes a cameo, and the following novel* The Bone Thief, *includes a Market Square scene. Jon Jefferson, the freelance writer who is, with William Bass, half of the novel-writing team that makes up Jefferson Bass, was a familiar figure at the patio of Preservation Pub as the series was becoming popular.*

Market Square has served several novels as a scene, and has played a biographical role in a few author's lives, but until recently no well-known writers known to have lived and worked there.

In her bestselling 2010 memoir, Committed, *popular confessional writer Elizabeth Gilbert, the author of* Eat, Pray, Love, *includes an autobiographical detail that surprised many of her Knoxville fans. Speaking of her inspiring but problematic relationship with the mysterious Brazilian-born Australian lover she called "Felipe," the major character of* Eat, Pray, Love, *she writes, "I took a temporary job teaching writing at the University of Tennessee, and for a few curious months we lived together in a decaying old hotel room in Knoxville." Naturally, that room was on Market Square. Gilbert taught graduate-level fiction writing at UT during the spring semester of 2005. In the book she adds no further detail about the actual place she lived, or what made those months "curious"—but the iconic author confirms that she lived on the third floor of the St. Oliver, the eccentric hotel in Peter Kern's old building on Market Square, for about five months. Her lover, whose real name is José Nunes, joined her for the final few weeks of that period.*

She found the place with the help of her colleague, novelist Michael Knight, who had described the eccentric hotel and the fact that Patricia Neal was sometimes spotted there. Gilbert replied, "It sounds like the kind of place a writer might go to drink herself to death," and took it. Knight had expected her to stay there only a few days, but Gilbert was delighted with the eccentric perch and made it her Knoxville home. She later wrote that she lived on pickles, carrot sticks, microwaved eggs, and tea, while trying to learn Portuguese. When Nunes joined her, he gazed down from the windows at Union Avenue traffic, awed that American drivers seemed to obey traffic rules. It was during the time that she finished writing Eat, Pray, Love, *and there that she received the letter confirming it would be published. "I sent the editor the first draft of my book from Knoxville, I think," said Gilbert in an e-mail conveyed via Knight, for the purpose of this book, "and it was definitely in that room that I received his marked-up version of the manuscript, along with a note saying that he loved the book, which made me so relieved I cried."*

She suspected the St. Oliver's first-floor library to be haunted. "Whenever I came home at night, I would run past that room, frightened. I could never figure out any system as to why it had the books it had. They were utterly random books." But she concludes, "I have really fond memories of those months. It was an important haven, during an important transition."

Eat, Pray, Love *turned out to be an international bestseller, one of the most popular nonfiction books of the 21st century's first decade; in 2010 Gilbert's story was released as a major motion picture.*

CHAPTER 5

"A Town Within a Town"

The End of City Hall, the Beginning of Picture Shows, and
"Strange and Old-fashioned Ways"

Prince Street became known as Market Street as a result of World War I. It made sense, certainly, that this street that ran all the way from the riverfront wharf to Vine Avenue should be named for its primary objective and obstruction: the Market, which was then at its height. But the chief motivation for the change may have been hatred for the German Kaiser Wilhelm, who was born a prince. Many Americans saw the Great War as a war against the antiquated and corrupt monarchies of the Old Country. Knoxville didn't have a prince and didn't need a Prince Street.

So the century-old strip of pavement known as Prince was suddenly Market Street. It's unlikely that anyone remembered that, more than a century earlier, the next street over, Gay Street, had been called Market Street—or that, a half-century earlier, some called part of Wall Avenue by the same name. This time, it stuck.

It was during the war that an unprepossessing insurance lawyer from Connecticut, staying in a downtown hotel for a few days on business, wrote a short and mostly rapturous description of verdant Knoxville in the springtime. Wallace Stevens, successful attorney, moonlighted as one of the two or three most influential modern American poets. It's believed that this business trip inspired one of his best known (and most puzzling) poems, "The Anecdote of the Jar." "I placed a jar in Tennessee /

And round it was, upon a hill…." He seemed bewitched with Knoxville, which he said reminded him of the Erie, Pennsylvania, of his youth. But his description of Market Square seems ambiguous.

"There are a few rich people, but…the farmers in the market, which I shall walk through in the morning, are the most extraordinary collection of poor people, living off the land, to be found in the whole country."

This new definition of Market Square as a most extraordinary collection of poor people would be a recurring theme for most of the rest of the century. Previous newspaper accounts sometime spoke with condescending wonder at the arrival of mountain farmers at certain selling seasons, but in the 20th century, the poor seemed more and more a fixture of the Square, on both sides of the market counters. Their eccentric dress and manners often comprised the chief impression visitors took away. It was, perhaps, not what Max Arnstein and his Market Square

A scene of the east side of the Square, ca. 1930, showing the Millers Annex; the Slipper Shoppe; Lane Drugs, which replaced G.W. Albers; the Model, a ladies" dress shop; and the Deitch Department Store, which was advertising an 88-cent sale. The family-owned store at Nos. 18-20, run by Gustave, Benjamin, and Nathan Deitch, was a durable Market Square institution. McClung Historical Collection.

Businessmen's Club had intended, just a few years earlier, when they heralded the Square's electric-lit White Way.

Market Square could still cough up a cosmopolitan innovation now and then. The name "Piggly Wiggly" makes kids giggle, on trips through small towns in the deep South, but in 1920, Piggly Wiggly was something like an avant-garde grocery store, introducing a major innovation that latter-day shoppers take for granted: self-service shopping. Previously, groceries operated something like a reference library. Customers asked a grocer for individual items; he'd bring them to the counter and then ring them up. Founded in Memphis in 1916, Piggly Wiggly offered customers the chance to push a cart up and down aisles and pick things off shelves. One of the first two Piggly Wigglys in Knoxville, and presumably one of the city's first two self-service groceries, was just off Market Square, on the 500 block of Market, next to Arnstein's.

However, the Roaring '20s never got very roaring on Market Square. Soon supermarkets were popping up everywhere, hundreds of stores in Knox County alone, stocked with passably fresh produce, tropical fruit, specialty meats, the things people rich and poor used to come to Market Square for.

Worse, as more and more people every month seemed to be driving cars into town, the Square itself was beginning to seem problematic. Farmers had begun driving motorized trucks, no longer horsecarts, but they'd still park them in the alleys on either side of the Market House, often so many of them that the lanes were impassible by vehicles, and difficult even for pedestrians. The congestion was bad enough, but many of the trucks were "dead wagons," incapable of moving. It says something about Knoxville's character that city leaders complained bitterly about Market Square's peculiar clutter of machinery and humanity for decades without doing anything forceful to curtail it.

The congestion was such that various plans offered top-down ideas whose end seemed to be to rid the alleys alongside of the Square of squatters—but, carefully, without passing any personal judgment on the squatters themselves.

One which got some momentum in the mid-20s was to provide limited outdoor cubicles, in glass-covered covered "arcades"; it would seem an improvement for the farmers, but they'd no longer be able to leave their trucks in the alleys. After the newspapers offered illustrated explanations of how it would work, nothing ever came of it.

In 1924, a new face showed up at City Hall. Louis Brownlow, the city's first City Manager, was a progressive from St. Louis. (A distant cousin of the Parson, this Brownlow had never lived in Knoxville before he was hired to run the city.) He had lots of ideas, but one of the first was for the city's officers to find another place to do business, and leave their cramped offices on Market Square. City Hall had been built to serve a town of hardly more than 5,000, with scant city services;

Knoxville was now an undeniable city, nearing a six-digit population. Brownlow's long-term plan was to build an even larger building than the School for the Deaf, in a sweeping, modernistic re-imagining of Knoxville. In the beautiful, streamlined, art-moderne Knoxville of Brownlow's dream, Market Square would not necessarily play a major role.

On February 10, 1925, at Brownlow's behest, city government moved away from Market Square, into the recently vacated School for the Deaf building, the old "Asylum," a few blocks to the northwest. Not far, but it wasn't the same as when mayors and city councilmen were on the Square every day.

City Hall's almost 60 years there had been dramatic. While City Hall was on Market Square, Knoxville had grown from a weary and shell-shocked town of about 5,000 to a booming, if imperfect, city of 100,000. Within the sounds and odors of the daily market, the Board of Aldermen had welcomed electricity, fresh water, sewage treatment, public education, the first public parks, the first asphalt-paved roads for automobiles, the first hospital, the first public transit systems. They saw the biggest annexations in the city's history, of Fort Sanders, of North Knoxville, of Sequoyah Hills, even of the remote areas beyond the river that would be called South Knoxville. No part of the city's 220-year history has been as municipally momentous as the one-quarter of it that transpired on Market Square. Knoxville became a city during the time that its headquarters was right there, in an odd little building on the north end of Market Square, alongside Asylum Avenue.

Perhaps little of the city's progress can be ascribed to the location of its leaders, at the time they made their proposals and cast they votes yea or nay; progress was mainly a function of the times. Then again, decisionmakers never had to speculate about the city and its people; they walked through the thickest part of it when they came to each meeting. If any alderman ever wished to take a semi-scientific referendum on any issue, he could accomplish it during a cigar break—there was always a plausibly representative sample of voters handy, just outside. Entering or exiting the offices meant running a gauntlet of constituents: allies, perhaps, or opponents, from every walk of life. On Market Square, Knoxville was never an abstract concept.

∾

The evacuation of city offices was a symbolic blow to Market Square, which was no longer the center of municipal power. It also may have meant the Market House didn't get as much regular maintenance as it had previously. Partly due to the prevalence of the electric media of radio and telephones, the Market House may have seemed less vital in the 1920s, but attracted some important public gatherings nonetheless. None were more important than the public meetings promoting a major project which started as a grass-roots effort, a Great Smoky Mountains National Park—the triumph of the conservationist movement that had been familiar on Market Square since before World War I. Knoxville conservationists like pharmacist David Chapman, industrialist Willis Davis, and his politician wife, Annie Davis, exhorted their fellow citizens to get involved is this major park movement, unusual among national parks in that it began with private donations and volunteer efforts of people in the region.

Probably one of the last big political rallies ever witnessed in the Market House book-ended the prohibition era. After the repeal of national prohibition, the matter was coming up for a vote on prohibition in the state, and many of the

The west side of Market Square in 1930, showing part of the Kern building, then home to C. W. Henderson's produce; Emery's 5 and 10, which survives in the 21st century on Chapman Highway, is next door. The Ziegler building then housed the Covington Supply Co. Note that Market Square stalwart Watson's is known as "Watson's Salvage Store." The conspicuous "22's" appear in a poster for a highly publicized circus scheduled for August 22. McClung Historical Collection.

aging temperance activists harbored real hope that in spite of national legalization, they could keep Tennessee dry. Jefferson McCarn, known to some as "Old Rose," was a diminutive, white-haired attorney from Nashville known as the former U.S. Attorney-General for the pre-statehood Hawaiian Islands, remembered for having succeeded, for a time, in banning boxing there. Misty-eyed Tennesseans remembered him better as the prosecutor who had secured a conviction of Robin Cooper for the 1908 slaying of prohibitionist hero Edward Ward Carmack— who had spoken on Market Square just before another alcohol vote, back in 1907. McCarn spoke in the same auditorium 26 years later, on July 6, 1933. An old-fashioned man in an old-fashioned venue, McCarn didn't draw nearly as big

Perhaps the best-known interior shot of the Market House. Long after Kern's Bakery, moved to a larger plant on Chapman Highway, after being sold to other families, the Kern name kept a presence on Market Square at its stall inside the Market House. Both of Knoxville's best-known bakeries, Kern's and Swan's, are visible in this shot. A New Deal-era National Recovery Administration poster in the background suggests this photo was taken in the mid-1930s. McClung Historical Collection.

a crowd to the auditorium, about 125 by one newsman's estimate. "I would rather live and take my chances with the people of Tennessee," he said, "than go to hell" with the ban-repealing nation. Repeal passed in the city of Knoxville, failed in Knox County beyond city limits, and passed in Tennessee. Beer would soon be legal again in Knoxville; stronger drink would have to wait a few more decades.

It was the end of another era, both for the idealistic prohibition movement and for the once-thrilling Market Hall lecture. Though the auditorium would be used through the '30s, especially for country-music shows, there was less demand for it. Other, much larger and more comfortable auditoriums, like the extravagant Riviera, which opened in 1920, and the Tennessee in 1928, hosted the big events; though both were mainly movie theaters, both occasionally featured talks and concerts and talent shows of a sort that might previously have been held at the Market Hall. More competition came from the times; evening public events were scarcer, in general, as more people stayed home to listen to broadcast talk and music on the radio. The number of chapters of fraternal organizations which had once flocked to meeting halls on the Square in the evenings seemed to dwindle during that era, as well. In the 1920s, Market Square got quieter at night.

Under the almost futuristically visionary plans of City Manager Louis Brownlow, Knoxville seemed poised to take bold steps into a bright future. Brownlow's men worked in a wide periphery around Market Square, with new emphasis on the river and Henley Street, prospects on the riverfront, and improvements to the parks and suburbs. They worked on grand plans to restyle the city of Knoxville. Although the big plans didn't bother Market Square much, they didn't include it, either. The City Planning Commission's thick report, released in 1929, outlines assessments and rec-ommendations for Knoxville in an otherwise forward-thinking and comprehensive way—but hardly mentions Market Square. It's not shown in the report's photographs. It's not even labeled on its many maps. Whether planners considered Market Square an asset or a liability is unclear; they just preferred not to mention it.

The modern world was flowing around Market Square, leaving this antebellum relic tucked away, discreetly out of sight.

Some of the old stalwarts slipped quietly away. J.S. Hall's, which had sold cloth-ing on Market Square since the Civil War, and had recently used "on the Square" as its motto, moved to Gay Street in 1924. J. Frank Walker opened a whole new, much larger store on Gay Street in 1927, and though he kept an interest in Market Square business, concentrated his attention on Gay.

In 1928, the year Max Arnstein reached the age of 70, he closed his huge and glamorous store; he and Lalla moved back to New York.

Kern's, which had been the anchor of Market Square since its early days, and to some extent its inspiration, sold out, in 1925, to a company that was mainly in-terested in the bread side of the business. The new corporate Kern's leased out the once-famous street-level footage. By 1928, Kern's old confectionary had become

The Smoke House: a "Cigars, Tobacco, and Soda Fountain" sort of place, appended with a poolhall, perhaps in the same section where the ice-cream saloon used to be. The Kern building's third floor became a speakeasy. In 1931, Kern's left the building altogether, moving into a modern factory building on the new Chapman Highway, and the storefront at No. 1 Market Square became familiar, to those too young to remember the congenial old German baker Peter Kern, as a Cole's chain drugstore.

Kern's did keep a vigorous presence on the Square for years to come, by way of an impressive stall in the Market House. For years, Kern's maintained a rivalry with the other major bakery in town, Swan's, which also had a large and well-kept counter in the same big room.

About the same time Kern's moved, the federal government built a large new postal facility on Main Avenue, and evacuated the old Custom House; for the first time in 60 years, East Tennessee's busiest post office was no longer within view of Market Square.

Those who did still bother to look noticed that the Market House was showing some wear. City Hall's bell is likely the one mentioned in Leola Manning's blues song, "The Arcade Building Moan" ("Listen how the bell did ring . . . . ") tolling news of that fatal disaster around the corner on Union Avenue in 1930. By the early '30s, the old bell tower would be condemned as unsafe; the huge City Hall bell, which had rung alarms for disasters early in the century, had hung silently in recent years. It was outmoded by modern electric alarms and radio communications, for one thing. And if someone actually did try to pull the chain and ring it again, the 2,600-pound bell might well plummet through several rotting floors of old city hall. To eliminate that hazard, the city just removed it, and gave it to the Burlington Fire Station in East Knoxville, where it remained for several years. Later still, it traveled to rural Kingswood School in Grainger County, where it served for years as a puzzling lawn ornament.

～

Market Square wasn't dead or dying after 1925, but its claims to being modern and dynamic and central to Knoxville business were just a memory. To many young Knoxvillians of the early supermarket era, it was hardly even that.

Some stores in the old Victorian buildings along the sides catered mainly to the farmers who came to sell. By the 1920s, at least two permanent stores on Market Square sold mainly seeds, with others nearby on Wall. Historians have observed that Knoxville took on more of a rural character in the 1920s, as an agricultural depression, combined with the failure of some mines in the region, sent thousands of country people looking for work and a new life in the city. The phenomenon was nowhere more evident than in Market Square, the spot several farmers had been most familiar with for years. The country people who had once been exotic visitors to the Square came to be more and more its everyday clientele. The Square did retain some aspects of its famously cosmopolitan diversity—many of its merchants were Jewish, and at times that group, rare elsewhere in the region, seemed to dominate Market Square retail, especially in dry goods—even as the everyday customer base became more "country." Merchant Abe Schwartz opened a stylish-looking Ladies Ready-to-Wear shop on the west side; mid-century shoppers recall that he catered mainly to black women. Several businesses, both local and chain retail shops, catered to the poor and advertised their low prices in the names of their stores: it was the era of the 5 and 10-cent store, and several Market Square stores heralded that banner proudly.

Around 1923, Louis Lippner, a kosher butcher originally from Vienna, Austria, opened a meat market in the Market House. Occupying several stalls, it offered a kosher side and a non-kosher side. Eventually augmented with a fish market, the Lippner family, including other members like Isadore and Harry, would be among the best-known and best-remembered venders in the Market House for as long as it existed. At their stalls, the Lippners were known to offer free lessons in kosher preparation for those who were interested.

Writers came to Market Square just to describe it—a sure sign that the Pride of the City was becoming quaint. Perhaps even self-consciously quaint. Eccentrics make good newspaper copy, and Market Square, hardly a five-minute walk from both the city's newsrooms, was a dependable mine for reporters. Sometime in 1929, a young writer named Bert Vincent made his first visit to the Square. A Kentuckian, he'd spent the years since the Great War as a lumberjack and vagabond reporter, working for papers around the country. He loved rural ways, and found them on Market Square. Over the next 40 years, the *News-Sentinel* reporter would become Knoxville's most popular newspaper columnist, and an unofficial citizen of Market Square.

At the very end of the 1920s, on December 8, 1929, the *New York Times*, which still boasted Adolph Ochs' name at the top of its masthead, ran an unexpected essay called "In Old Knoxville Market: Mountain People of Strange Old-Fashioned Ways Come There to Gossip and Trade."

The author was Rosa Naomi Scott, a sometime short-story writer, sometime Knoxvillian. Her essay is maybe the richest description of the Square of that era, with more detail than any that came before it.

"One short block from Hope's clock in Knoxville, Tenn.—the hub of the city—you get an amazing glimpse of two long lines of vegetable-filled trucks, wagons, and rusty automobiles that make Market Square," she wrote. "In a city overhung with quaint atmosphere and in its picturesqueness a monument to the ease of settled ways, nothing is more characteristic…."

"Sharply detailed pictures stand out. A covered wagon—the pioneer wagon to a T—arrests you, and a wagon with a huge umbrella over it. A woman with hair that is still her glory, done in a clumsy knot, does a brisk business…. A tiny old woman sleeps sitting by a truck, her head carefully propped on her wagon. A rattle-trap automobile with bottles of honey has a guardian so bent and odd that if fitted with a broomstick she might fly back to her hills."

The images are so similar to James Agee's, in his famous description of ca. 1916 Market Square in *A Death in the Family*, you might well wonder whether the author used Scott's piece as a prompter. Or maybe he just remembered some of the same people.

A lot of the Scott essay is perhaps authentic dictation of country people's speech: "'Whom do you sell to,' you ask a woman selling dahlias. She looks like an antique rag doll, but her answer is pat. 'Common class of people, lady. Them as can't buy at—.' She mentioned the best florist in the city."

The Market House always seemed like a country place. In the stalls, merchants sold freshly butchered meat, and chickens—the chickens were displayed on ice, with a damp cloth over them to keep them cool. Customers were welcome to handle them, to test them for freshness.

The first memory most regulars offer of the Market House in the middle of the 20th century, was the smell—or as some prefer to describe it, the stench. It seems to have affected different people differently. Some remember fish as the chief smell, some mention manure, but there were many others: the building offered an especially aromatic coffee house. Some customers remember the smell would cling to their hair and clothes long after they left; customers would walk into clothing stores, and a clerk would remark, not altogether happily, that they'd obviously been in the Market House. They smelled of recently cleaned fish and raw meat.

~

Market Square had an influence that by the 1920s and '30s may have been felt more in the countryside than in the city. Cherel Henderson, director of the East Tennessee Historical Society, remembers her mountain grandmother's life changed when her husband came back from Market Square with some new city technology: a washboard. Previously the family had washed their clothes by beating them with sticks.

Writer Florence Cope Bush wrote of Sevier Countians of the early 20th century who regarded Market Square with both fascination and fear. Perhaps with good reason, country people didn't trust city people. The rumor in the hills was that if farmers fell asleep by their wagons on Market Square, they'd be kidnapped, spirited away in a sack, and dissected by medical students from the college. On a marketing weekend, many farmers sat up awake all night.

Many of the farmers who brought produce to the Square came back home with food, too, especially two exotic delicacies: white bread, previously unknown in Tennessee, and bologna. "After a steady diet of pork and chicken," Bush wrote,

This scene of unidentified Market Square farmers dates from 1928, judging by the license plate. No longer touted as a cosmopolitan urban center, by the '20s the Square was attracting photographers and writers who relished its country flavors. This one scene suggests some cultural diversity even among the farm families. On the left, a man grasps green beans from farm baskets in an old-fashioned, hoop-style covered wagon. The boy on that side is barefoot. The family on the right has a modern automobile, and flowers in a vase on the hood. They're selling a variety of root vegetables, greens, and peppers. The well-dressed boy, hands in pockets like a downtown businessman, wears a political button on his shirt. On close examination the face on the button looks like 1928 Democratic nominee Al Smith, whose candidacy was popular in the rural South. McClung Historical Collection.

"this spicy, firm sausage was a treat to look forward to all year." Any farmer, upon his return from Market Square down in Knoxville, was expected to bring enough bologna sausage for everybody back home.

~

One evening in 1935, a young man whose face was not as familiar as it would be 10 or 20 years later trudged onto the Square, fresh off the train from Bulls Gap, Tennessee. Cold and exhausted, he made his way into one of the few places lit up late at night, the Gold Sun. The counterman took pity on him, gave him a sandwich, and said if he didn't tell anybody, he could sleep under a table. Archie Campbell would be grateful to that kindness to a stranger for the rest of his life.

A talented singer and comic, Campbell would become a popular radio entertainer in Knoxville, especially on WNOX. Also a public servant, he would be elected and re-elected to Knoxville School Board—before he went on to greater fame as a comedian, on the Grand Ole Opry and the popular national TV show "Hee-Haw."

Times were tough, but they never seemed quite as tough at the Gold Sun, which through these lean times had become the worthy standard-bearer of Market Square tradition, the place people went to see old friends. The Knoxville Congressional district's representative from 1919 until 1939 was the colorful, tobacco-chewing Republican J. Will Taylor. He loved the Gold Sun, had a meal or two there every time he was in town, and used the place as a sort of informal campaign headquarters. Maybe it's not surprising that many years later, a member of the family that ran the Gold Sun would be a prominent Republican politician, herself.

At the Gold Sun, customers kept an eye out for famous visitors, whether Republican politicians or big-time sports figures. Bandleader Guy Lombardo came by the week he did a show at UT, around 1940. Sometimes local country musicians would drop in after a show at the WNOX Mid-Day Merry-Go-Round, future legends like Chet Atkins and Roy Acuff. The Gold Sun was one of local sports promoters John and Gus Cazana's favorite places, and when they were squiring around visiting celebrities, like George Zaharis, Babe Didrickson, or even semi-retired boxer Jack Dempsey, they'd bring them by the Gold Sun.

The place was owned, then, by the Cavalaris family. John Demetrius Cavalaris had come to Knoxville back in 1916 to work with his cousins. He'd fought the Turks in the Balkan Confederacy Wars; on a reunion trip back to Greece in 1939, his daughter fell for a man named Peroulas, whom she married and brought back to Knoxville. His name would later be visible on Market Square.

Several other Greek-owned restaurants appeared in the vicinity. The Biltmore opened in the side of the long building that fronted at 2 Market Square, around

1933. It was, according to the promotional literature, "a well-appointed cafe, with the privacy of booths, where a glass of cheery Budweiser (which it specializes) makes one feel in tune with the infinite!" The proprietor, who was from the Peloponnesian town of Tripolis, Greece, was named Christ Anagnost. His brother, shaven-headed George Anagnost, had earned the sobriquet "Chili King." Two of the Biltmore's specialties, besides Budweiser, and advertised in big words outside on Union Avenue, were CHILI and TAMALES. Whether this spot was the origin of the old Knoxville favorite, the "Full House," is anybody's guess.

~

Market Square has always been adaptable in ways that Charles Darwin would have admired; every reverse seems to come with some new mutation, some new way to survive and prevail. By the late '20s, there weren't many things that had happened anywhere in Knoxville but had never happened in Market Square—but one did when Tim W. Smith moved into one of Walker's old buildings and opened something called the Rialto. Right by the farmers' trucks, on the spittin' side of Market Square, it was a movie theater. Showing cowboy silents and other popular movies of the day, it was a popular attraction that commenced a whole era of movie theaters on Market Square. It's an era scarcely remembered except by those old enough to have made a habit of them.

In 1930, movie theaters were much more diverse in size and quality. The Tennessee and Riviera were the queen movie theaters of Gay Street: huge, posh, grand, stylish palaces that would seat as many as 2,000 for the same feature and awe them all. Less conspicuous were several other movie theaters that set up in old storefronts, usually playing second- and third-run films, hits from last year or even two or three years before. They made a brisk living on the fringes. Following the Square's 5 & 10 trends, a cheap cinema at No. 29 opened under the name the Dime Theater. It was short lived.

Despite the complication of transforming retail space to movie theaters, Smith's Rialto didn't stay put; it slid around a little on the Square's west side. The few old enough to remember the Rialto may well be puzzled by conflicting memories of it. It was at No. 31 only until 1934, when Smith moved to the perhaps more-visible space, near the front of the Market House, at No. 5. At that location it seems to have doubled as a sort of third-rate vaudeville house; a 1937 photo advertises a performer named Cotton Watts, a bawdy clown who was more often associated with the Roxy on Union. (Watts later had a strange second career as a blackface comedian in B movies.)

Later, around 1940, the Rialto moved to the old building with a grandiose front at 19 Market Square.

After his first move, in 1935, Smith got some competition, when the Brichetto brothers, Italian immigrants Lawrence and John, moved into his original Rialto and reopened it as the Crystal. They'd had a previous theater half a block away on Gay Street when they were forced out by Miller's expansion, and chose to open on the Square. The Crystal was known as a B-movie "western house" which showed mostly cowboy movies and other genres that appealed to the thousands of boys who always seemed to be footloose, with a quarter or two in their pockets, in downtown Knoxville, especially on a Saturday. Lawrence Brichetto was a tinkerer, and seemed to have fun coming up with promotional attractions to bring the kids in. Speakers in the Square, broadcasting the soundtrack from the movie inside, would draw attention. When he showed *The Mummy,* with Boris Karloff, he wrapped a mannequin in gauze and set it in a coffin. A speaker inside, emitting sounds from the movie, could be activated by a switch.

For about a decade, there were two movie theaters on the west side of Market Square. The Rialto closed around 1945, as Smith concentrated his movie concerns on the suburbs. Television arrived in Knoxville late, in 1953, and took its toll on Knoxvillians' casual viewing habits; TV was especially hard on the second-run theaters, as people were less likely to pay even a quarter to see an old movie. The Brichettos kept the Crystal going at 31 Market Square until 1957, long after most of downtown's small movie theaters had closed. Market Square's movie-show era lasted about 30 years.

In the '30s, '40s, and '50s the west side of Market Square was known as the spittin' side, for its tendency to draw tobacco spit. Bunny Brichetto, whose family's movie theater was on that side, recalled, "The west side was more country. The other side was more sophisticated." It seems to have been mainly a 20th-century designation; of course, both sides were lined with farmers' trucks.

The '30s saw an elegant-sounding arrival in the old Kern building, on the third floor which had once been the Oddfellows Hall. Ledgerwood Studios, a.k.a. Ledgerwood School of Dance, moved into 403½ Union around 1934. J. Frank Ledgerwood, whose brothers had run an apparently successful piano and organ store at the other end of the Square, just around the corner on Wall, since 1911, was the dance instructor during those days when Knoxvillians watched Fred and Ginger dance on the big screen. Ledgerwood advertised, "Tap, Toe, Ballroom / Piano and Vocal Exercises," and eventually a "Gymnasium." The floor below may have been a noisy place at times. The Ledgerwood Studio moved to Gay Street in the early '40s.

It may be Ledgerwood's that's the "dance hall" some old timers would later remember, vaguely, from this period. Or it might be the American Legion hall, referenced by Swiss travel writer Annemarie Schwarzenbach in 1937. The veterans' group that often sponsored dances was based on the second floor of the Market

House in the 1930s and '40s. Though the old Public Hall seemed to be used less and less for the general public, other veterans' groups kept their headquarters up there, including the local chapter of the veterans of the Spanish American War.

Even in the Square's neglected years, new things moved in. The White Stores, a major local grocery chain of the mid-20th century, opened one of its early stores at 25 Market Square around 1927, and remained somewhere on the Square for several decades. Several stores of the new era were national chains, like Ben Franklin, and other small five and dimes, "Cash stores." Brothers Benjamin and Gustave Deitch, at 18-20, sold women's clothes; the Hub Department Store, at No. 29, specialized in work clothes. Beginning in the late '30s, Bowers' thrived as an outdoorsy store in the tall building at No. 36; it was a place where kids and their mothers came to get scout uniforms. And Miller's, the Gay Street champion of middle-class posh, opened its Annex on the Square's southeast corner, offering no-frills bargain shopping and, for a time, shoe repair.

One of the first stores in what would be a Knoxville-based regional chain, Edgar L. and Russell V. Emery opened Emery's 5 and 10, around 1930, at 7 Market Square, with a nearly-everything motif. Emery's would be a Square stalwart for 30 years.

Around 1934, a bespectacled young man from Illinois named Robert Wadlow appeared on the Square. He was then just a teenager, working for national shoe company Peters Shoes, not one of the first 1,000 guys who had come to Market Square to sell shoes. But he was certainly the tallest. In fact, Robert Wadlow became the tallest man in the history of the world, one inch shy of nine feet tall. He would have had to crouch to enter the Market House.

~

The end of national prohibition permitted beer (and beer only) in Knoxville, for the first time since 1907. The first bar to reappear on the Square, in 1933, was at 3 Market Square, part of the old Kern's front, a place called Perry's Beer Garden, run by one Harry Saltos. It lasted for only a couple of years. It wouldn't be the last, but for the rest of 20th century, bars wouldn't be as popular on Market Square as they had been before 1907.

The reformist spirit of temperance survived, in a way, in one warning that's legible in many old photographs of the Union Avenue area. In a city without another obvious gathering place, the south end of the Market House may have been the single most conspicuous spot in town, and by 1930, that brick wall bore a grim reminder, updated regularly, and headed DEADLY AUTOS. Beneath, arranged almost like numbers on an old-fashioned baseball scoreboard, was a running tally of the number of people who had died in automobile accidents in Knox County, by month and year.

Coinciding with the end of prohibition was the beginning of a new institution which would change Market Square, and much of the Mid-South, for decades to come. The Tennessee Valley Authority, the New Deal agency created in the famous first 100 Days of Franklin Roosevelt's administration, moved into the neighborhood. Knoxville was to be the federal agency's headquarters, but in 1933, TVA was building dams, not downtown buildings. By the mid-'30s, TVA occupied several buildings downtown; its main headquarters was in the New Sprankle Building, on Union a

In 1937, at the height of the popularity of film stars Fred Astaire and Ginger Rogers, the old Kern building, no longer a bakery, hosted the Ledgerwood Dance Studio, a lively sounding place that must have had gymnasium-like amenities. The sign advertises "TAP, TOE, BALL ROOM, PIANO-VOCAL EXERCISES, CONSTRUCTIVE, REDUCING, UP-BUILDING ATHLETICS, HAND-TENNIS." *On the ground floor, longtime tenant Cole Drugs, and, next door's Corkland's Shoes, then advertising a close-out. McClung Historical Collection.*

block west of the Square, but TVA also occupied the Daylight Building across the street, the old Customs House—the main post office had just moved over to Main Street—and perhaps most impressively, the Arnstein Building, where the agency sometimes exhibited its grand plans in Max Arnstein's old display windows. TVA's thousands of employees would be a daily presence on Market Square for the rest of the century.

Author James Agee would later describe the complex Market Square of his childhood in a Pulitzer-winning novel. In 1935, though, he was a young journalist then working for Henry Luce's groundbreaking business magazine *Fortune*, returning

This 1930s scene of the Square's west side shows Jacob Licht's fruits-and-vegetables shop and the Rialto Theatre, one of the movie houses run by the Brichetto brothers on the Square. The movie advertised, Two Outlaws, *starring Jack Perrin, was a silent that came out in 1928, 10 years before the date of the photo. Though it was unusual for cinemas in the late '30s to show old movies, Market Square's theaters did tend to show second, third, and fourth runs films, especially westerns. Despite what looks like warm-weather clothing, a sign for one store advertises an "August Closing Sale." McClung Historical Collection.*

home to write the second of two long analytical feature articles about the national phenomenon known as TVA. He describes the approach to TVA's headquarters: "walk up sooty Gay Street and turn down smudgy Union and past Market Square straight on to the New Sprankle Building…." where TVA chairmen Arthur Morgan, Harcourt Morgan, and David Lilienthal kept their offices. At age 25, Agee's dismissively sparse description of downtown Knoxville, which had deteriorated since his childhood, seems to betray no sentimentality on the author's part, but it was probably honest. After a visit to TVA headquarters about the same time, journalist Ernie Pyle remarked that Knoxville might well be the dirtiest city in the world. Downtown, suffering from the Depression but also neglected by Knoxville's gentry, many of whom were then preoccupied with suburban houses, gardens, and clubs, and, more nobly, a Herculean project called the Great Smoky Mountains National Park, was already on the decline.

A 1939 master's thesis written by UT graduate student Victor Albert Hyde, who would later be a professor of urban and regional planning at the University of Illinois, referred to the Square in socioeconomic terms and anthropological condescension: around the old farmer's market, "a commercial area has grown up quite distinct from that of near-by areas, in which goods of a less specialized and lower price are sold, in response to a limited market presented by the weekly influx of farmers to the city."

Those farmers weren't necessarily limited to Knoxville's metropolitan region. As memories of musical legend Charlie Louvin prove, some farmers drove all the way from Sand Mountain, Alabama—about 150 miles—to sell on Market Square. He and his father and brother Ira regularly drove their truck up to sell sorghum at the regionally famous market.

Also in 1939, the New Deal Works Progress Administration published its guide to Tennessee. The author of its section about downtown Knoxville is unknown, but it offers a glimpse into the operations of the Market House, and the daily activity around it:

"The stalls in the Market House are leased to merchants and in the center aisle 104 tables are allotted free to farm women for the display of their produce. In this section and in the free curb market outside, where farmers sell their wares from wagons, trucks, and cars, no produce that has been 'jobbed' is permitted for sale…."

The anonymous writer went on to describe the market's unique character.

"Market Square and its environs form a town within a town. Here, only one block from Gay Street, the talk is of the weather, of the price of corn, of stockbreeding and other matters important to the farmer. At noontime, the women who run boarding houses on the second floors of the buildings around the square descend to the street and dong their old-time hand bells. Meals in these houses are 15 cents for 'all you can eat.'"

It's a rare, and late, description of the Square's venerable boarding houses, which seem to fade from view after World War II.

By then, Market Square had become a rural microcosm in the growing city. By the 1930s, the Square was no longer the cosmopolitan urban center known to Kern and Arnstein, at least not exactly. The middle class that had once counted on Market Square both for routine grocery purchases and for fancier imported goods were beginning to think of it as a simpler place, good for produce and raw materials for a recipe, but not necessarily inspiration. Suburbanization was underway, and by 1939 people who had cars—the middle class—found it easier to do their shopping in the literally hundreds of grocery stores, with free parking lots, that had sprung up near residential neighborhoods all over the county.

Though a few thousand still lived downtown—some of them were elderly affluent folks who preferred not to move—by 1940 a downtown residence was no longer fashionable; downtown was more and more the domain of the carless poor. Though some exacting cooks admitted there were things they could find only at the Market House, the era of the downtown public market had peaked.

It was in 1940 that Market Square got the first of several visits from a former Chicagoan who might have passed for a farmer, but looked familiar, especially to the library ladies over at Lawson McGhee. Carl Sandburg, who had just moved to his beloved goat farm south of Asheville, had friends in Knoxville, and developed an immediate fondness for Market Square. The man who wrote "I Am the People, the Mob" grew to love the place and the people who worked there. He said he especially appreciated the fact that there was one place in the world where you could buy ginseng in a central business district.

Despite the fact it was not necessarily part of the average Knoxvillian's week, or because of it, Market Square remained a dependable source for local color. In August, 1942, the *Knoxville Journal* noted that "Market Square is probably the best-known Knoxville institution."

World War II affected Market Square as it affected every neighborhood in Knoxville, but the Square played its own specialized roles in the war effort. Probably one of the last times the old public auditorium area of the Market House was busy was during the war, when it hosted the headquarters of the American Legion, Disabled American Veterans, and the American Red Cross—as well as the post of the graying local veterans of the Spanish-American War.

Most of the young men of the Square, city boys and country boys alike, went off to the the latest war, as their fathers had, a generation before. One was a UT engineering grad, originally from Fountain City, named Warren Nichols. Though his degree was in engineering, he went to work for Watson's around 1940, and became an assistant manager. He apparently liked retail, and didn't use his engineering degree until he joined the army in 1943; he became a lieutenant in the 159th Combat Engineers. It turned out that the retailer was cool under fire. He did some important reconnaissance behind enemy lines during the Battle of the Bulge, and later, under fire in the dark, he directed an infantry crossing of the Rhine near Remagen. He earned both a bronze star and an oak-leaf cluster, cited for "his cool manner and fearlessness."

After almost a year in combat in France, Luxembourg and Germany, Nichols returned to his old job in retail on Market Square, and spent 42 years at Watson's, eventually becoming a vice-president and board member of the company.

≈

During World War II, Cas Walker opened a store at 35 Market Square. The famous grocer-impresario-demagogue who had come from rural Sevier County in the 1920s seems to have been a reluctant downtowner. Reversing a tedious retail pattern, Walker opened his first stores in the suburbs and only later tried downtown. By the time he opened his Market Square store in the early 1940s, he had long been well known for his chain of a half-dozen stores in North and East Knoxville.

According to legendary TVA planner and urban observer Aelred "Flash" Gray, Walker's Market Square store eventually served as a "social center....for the type of people referred to in Knoxville as 'country people,' or 'Cas Walker voters.'" Market Square, as it had developed in the 20th century, "was a symbol of the old Knoxville, an outlook and way of life which Cas Walker articulated and represented."

It may have helped his political career. Walker's first election to City Council came about the time his Market Square store opened; a short time later, he was elected mayor of the city, only to be recalled for malfeasance after 11 months in office. His unprecedented 35 years in City Council were mainly a record of voting against things; he would make one of his most dramatic stands in a vote against a major proposal for Market Square.

Somewhere along the way, perhaps much earlier than this era, one particular corner earned a reputation for street evangelism. "Preacher's Corner," as it has been understood to several generations, is at the intersection of Market and Union. Which corner is favored by the preachers sometimes migrates; for many years, it was at the southwestern corner, in front of the Arnstein, that a street preacher, sometimes a different one every day for a week or more, would hold forth, especially at lunchtime.

It may be here that British author Malcolm Muggeridge encountered a downtown street preacher, described in a 1947 travel journal. In both *The Orchard Keeper*, set ca. 1940, and *Suttree*, set ca. 1951, novelist Cormac McCarthy describes street

Titled "Knoxville, Tennessee, 1946," this photograph, taken in the Square's southwestern corner, is the work of Henri Cartier-Bresson (1908-2004). One of the most praised photographic artists of the 20th century, the French photographer was on his famous tour of the U.S. when he stopped in Knoxville at least long enough to take this shot.

The identity of his ambiguously elegant subject is unknown. This photograph was published in a 1999 issue of American Photo. *Cole Drugs, visible in this photo, was in the Kern Building; Southern Credit Jewelers was next door. ©Henri Cartier-Bresson/ Magnum Photos.*

preachers in the Market Square vicinity; in *Suttree,* the protagonist walks "among vendors and beggars and wild street preachers haranguing a lost world with a vigor unknown to the sane."

In 1946, a French photographer named Henri Cartier-Bresson arrived on the Square with a Leika. It's possible that he heard about the place from his friend Jean-Paul Sartre, who had probably at least seen the Square the year before, when he was staying at the Andrew Johnson Hotel and attending meetings at TVA headquarters on Union. Whatever enticed him, Cartier-Bresson came to Market Square in 1946 and got a photograph he called "Knoxville, Tennessee, 1946."

It's an image of a beautiful woman with a stylish '40s coif. She's wearing an eyepatch, and sitting in the driver's seat of a beaten-up pickup with chicken crates on the hood. In the background is the old Kern Building, a.k.a. Coles Drugs. It could have been titled, "The Spirit of Market Square."

CHAPTER 6

Remember the Market House

Visions of Modernism in the '50s:
Of Demolition, Parking Garages, and a Mall

By the middle of the 20th century, Market Square was the crazy aunt in Knoxville's basement. Newcomers remarked on it, sometimes in fascination, sometimes in humor, sometimes in horror, at the rusty trucks and chicken crates and squatters who seemed defiantly out of step with the modern world, and with a city struggling to join the modern world and share America's sleek new lines of postwar prosperity.

Some newspaper columnists, a few aspiring novelists, and apparently the occasional French photographer, were fond of her; some even loved her particular brand of disorder. Market Square was authentic, perhaps even unique among American blocks. Its denizens were admirable and independent-minded hill-country bohemians. To many of the buttoned-down businessmen of Knoxville, though, they were living representatives of a backward stereotype, and impediments to municipal growth.

To writers, generally, and some of the new celebrants of Appalachian culture, they were mainly fascinating. To bankers and entrepreneurs and politicians anxious about Knoxville's long-term prospects, they were unsettling. The sharp, outspoken disagreement about the fate of Market Square represents, once again, its unusual place in the public's democratic heart. The postwar years were a time when citizens were enduring radical changes, for the most part without newsworthy objection.

Interstate construction and urban renewal were destroying generations-old neighborhoods; without major protest, people picked up and moved on. The silent majority met the early motions of desegregation with a shrug. Knoxvillians faced the possibility of nuclear war, and the likelihood that Oak Ridge would be an early strike target, by reading about bomb shelters and evacuation routes in the evening newspaper, just before supper.

But when it came to the fate of Market Square, everyone had a strong opinion, one generally immune to persuasion. Most would keep their opinions for the rest of their lives.

In 1947, an unusual book called *Inside U.S.A.,* came out, to nationwide interest. The author, respected travel writer John Gunther, had surveyed almost all the cities in America. He pronounced Knoxville the "ugliest" in the entire nation. He wasn't very specific, but it was clear that he was referring not to Cherokee Boulevard or the Holston Hills Golf Course, or Fountain City's duck pond, but to downtown, where he spent his visit. Though his comments were sharply condemned by right-thinking Knoxvillians, they formed a context for much of the civic discussion in Knoxville for decades to come.

Downtown had been losing its affluent residents for more than 25 years, and now that more and more Knoxvillians had private automobiles in this prosperous postwar era, commercial development in the suburbs was also drawing customers away from the center. In 1947, Sears opened a major store on North Central; though it was less than a mile northwest of downtown, Sears represented a major departure for Knoxville and its traditional shopping patterns: it featured the first giant free parking lot many Knoxvillians had ever seen. Many more would follow, especially to the north of town, and, increasingly, to the west. For the first time, it was now possible to live in Knoxville and rarely ever come downtown, and many seemed happy with that option. By the 1950s, most of the goods traditionally available in Market Square were also available in the supermarkets and strip-mall stores of the new suburban residential areas.

Just as some glib civic boosters tried to find ways to assure that the John Gunthers of the future would look past downtown to beautiful suburban Knoxville, via Dogwood trails and the like, more ambitious city fathers tried to find a way to fix downtown.

With its narrow streets, unusual dearth of parks, and seemingly permanent layer of soot, downtown had problems all over, but in the center was Market Square, where the alleys on either side of the weird old Market House were always jammed with farmers' old trucks, some of them no longer functional. It may have seemed the handiest culprit.

The word *eyesore* didn't quite cover the matter. Market Square was, by some accounts, an exceptional concentration of blight, a sort of urban pustule. What do you say to a curb merchant who likes his spot so much he sells his truck's engine, so it can't be moved? The daily ragged line of rusting Fords and Chevys up and down twin Victorian alleys of clutter and gloom could make the uniformity and utility of a junkyard look good, by comparison.

The Market House itself had been deteriorating since the '20s; the many amenities of the second floor were all but forgotten. The American Legion had abandoned it. The famous Public Hall hadn't been used as such since the War, except that, for a time, the intrepid congregation the Calgary Church of the Nazarene met somewhere on the floor. One business held out on the second floor, known as Jessie's Lunch Room, and later Williams' Lunch Room. In directories it was discreetly marked *(c)* for "colored."

Prostitution, pornography, and gambling crept in around the edges. The Roxy, a sleazy burlesque house, had surfaced in the '30s around the corner on Union, catering both to frat boys and farmers. Everybody had a story of rats running across their shoes, in the Market House, and even in the movie theaters, and would tell them with relish.

It didn't help that they'd shut down the trolley line that went by Market Square in 1946. Everybody was getting cars, and for the first time, Knoxville needed lots and lots of parking. The Market Square area hardly had any.

The city's approach says something either poignantly polite or cowardly about Knoxville's heart. In another city, the farmers' rusty trucks might have been towed away, their owners fined or even jailed, concrete barriers placed to prevent their return. In Knoxville, though, for several years, decades, in fact, beginning in the 1920s, authorities tipped their hats and stepped politely around them—but then, safely back in the office, considered plans that seemed designed to make their lifestyle impossible. They attacked not the people, but the circumstances that allowed them to be there. The plan to abolish the Market House as Knoxville knew it paralleled urban renewal—which was never characterized, in so many words, as a way to remove poor people from sight.

~

By 1949, City Councilman, former City Manager, and recently disappointed mayoral candidate George Dempster had begun formulating an idea to tear down the Market House. He would come to believe that the best thing for old Market Square was a large, modern parking garage.

No ogre and no simpleton, Dempster had been a strong voice for progressive change in Knoxville for decades. Son of Scottish immigrants, he was a former railroad laborer who had worked on the Panama Canal, and as a young man had formed the Dempster Construction Company, whose best-known product was his own invention, the Dempster Dumpster.

During the city's progressive city-manager form of government in the 1920s and '30s, Dempster had served in that top job, overseeing major projects like the Henley Street Bridge (later formally renamed the George Dempster Bridge) and McGhee Tyson Airport, and had been instrumental in the establishment of the Great Smoky Mountains National Park. Finally elected mayor at age 64 in 1951, Dempster would spend much of his term trying to find ways to reinvent Market Square. At the top of his agenda was what he considered a necessity, the demolition of the Market House.

In early 1950, the Knoxville Parking Authority advised razing the Market House and replacing it with a 350-space parking garage. Nothing happened right away; Dempster said he was negotiating with the Swan and Mabry heirs for a quit-claim deed. There was, at one time, a city offer of $140,000 for the document, which was said to be agreeable to all the heirs but one, whom attorneys were having difficulty contacting.

With the question on the table, other ideas flowed in. The North Knoxville Businessmen's Club proposed tearing it down just to make a wider business street. Other proposals called for the long-discussed Civic Auditorium to be built there.

Meanwhile, a number of rural residents, farmers who sold at the Square, organized a committee to oppose the plan; Tom McCammon, the chairman, claimed he had been selling vegetables on Market Square since 1895. The committee's attorney, Frank Flynn, declared, "When cities destroy landmarks of importance, they destroy part of the city." The Association for the Preservation of Tennessee Antiquities, Daughters of the American Revolution, and the United Daughters of the Confederacy publicly opposed the plan to demolish the Market House.

A half-block away, Gay Street merchants, for reasons that might be obvious, were said to quietly favor the parking-garage idea. Miller's had been dropping hints about moving out of the downtown area, but promised to stay put if the Market Square parking garage went in. Predictably, some merchants questioned the motives of those who declared the Market House was an institution worth saving. Jeweler Harry Busch declared the only antique thing about the Market House was "the smell of that fish from one end to the other."

Those who favored demolition suddenly found many urgent reasons to get the job done quickly, claiming many of the hucksters who exploited it maybe weren't even farmers, but opportunists selling wholesale produce for a quick profit; in many cases, it was apparently true, but Knoxville shoppers had knowingly tolerated it for decades. Others complained of the place's sanitary issues, the sellers' standards for health and safety which wouldn't have passed a restaurant inspector's visit. By the end of 1950, Market House merchants had hastened to clean up their act. Hot-water taps, for sanitary washing, were on their way. Fish was no longer cleaned in the open with customers hovering. Raw chicken was no longer kept out on ice, but in insulated boxes. Merchants had to get health cards, based on a physical exam and a chest X-ray, presumably to detect tuberculosis. A regimen of rat poison was a major setback for the Square's once-arrogant rodent population, at least for the time being. "Rats used to run over the customers' feet, but I haven't seen many rats lately," boasted one merchant.

Mayor Dempster kept juggling ideas. He offered to build another market house outside of the downtown area. Another idea which gained some credibility was to tear the Market House down and build the parking garage, but reserve the ground floor for farmers' produce sales.

The *Knoxville Journal* advised the city to move cautiously: acquire the rights to the property, they suggested, but don't change it any time soon. Reaction from individual newspaper columnists was more personal.

Journal columnist Sherlock Hope wrote in 1950, "Some call it an eyesore, a monstrosity that hopelessly snarls downtown traffic, an ugly relic that should be torn down—the quicker the better, an antiquated thing that no longer serves a useful purpose but has been taken over by bogus farmers who use it to peddle produce they did not grow and, subsidized by city taxpayers, unfairly compete with established businesses. Others affectionately regard it as a symbol of Knoxville…."

"Bless its old brick hide," wrote young *News-Sentinel* columnist Carson Brewer in 1954.

The *News-Sentinel's* Lucy Templeton, the much-beloved grande dame of newspaper columnists, and the only one with the guts to suggest, in 1947, that John Gunther had a point, argued that the Market House was iconic. "It has changed less and is more typical of Knoxville than any other spot…." At 77, she may have been almost old enough to remember when, in 1900, another columnist had brought up St. Peter's Basilica in a tongue-in-cheek comparison to the Market House. "It is not grand like Trafalgar Square, St. Peter's, or Rockefeller Center," Templeton wrote. "It is ugly and dirty, but it is the town center…. It is not only our civic center, but the rallying point for Knox County."

She acknowledged, though, that it might be best to tear down the existing structure. "It should be improved, and not abolished," she wrote. Admitting that she did most of her shopping in the supermarket, she pointed out that even in 1955, "there are certain things I cannot find in these markets…. For these things I go to Market Square."

It was then hardly more than half a century old, and Knoxvillians of the 1950s were not accustomed to regarding buildings of the 1890s as "historic." "Historic" was colonial or antebellum, and except maybe for Blount Mansion, Knoxville just didn't have historic stuff. When a few raised the flag of historic preservation in connection with the Market House, a flabbergasted Dempster protested that the Market House was hardly older than he was.

It says something about Knoxville's attitude toward its history that most people in the 1950s, even newspaper columnists with access to archives, seemed not to have any idea how long the Market House had been there. Such details apparently weren't easy to come by in newsrooms. After some research in the McClung Room at the library, some wags pointed out that the Market House actually wasn't quite as old as Mayor Dempster; the Market House, pronounced historic, had been built when Dempster was 10. He might even have been in the crowd at Mayor Heiskell's dedication ceremony; he just didn't remember it. But the sly remark supported his point.

Into the fray stepped Harvey Broome, the 52-year-old lawyer, author, conservationist co-founder of the national Wilderness Society. He sent an interesting letter to the *News Sentinel*, and the afternoon paper published it alongside another one, from Kansas City, titled, "Market House called Rat Hole by Visitor; Mayor Is Praised."

Referring to an effort to start a UT archaeological museum which became the Frank McClung Museum, Broome noted that the city was overlooking an existing asset. "One of Knoxville's distinctive attractions known to artists, photographers, muralists, housewives, and townspeople, and appreciated by such well-known persons as Howard Zahniser and Carl Sandburg, is already in existence, not in some out of the way place but in the heart of Knoxville." Zahniser was, with Broome, a leader of the Wilderness Society, and editor of *The Living Wilderness*. He had been impressed with Market Square on a visit. His greatest fame would come later, as the chief author of the U.S. Wilderness Act, signed by President Johnson in 1964, but to Broome, Zahniser was already heroic in 1955.

It's clear in context that Broome's paean was at least as much about Market Square as the Market House.

"Knoxville's market place is as distinctive as Charleston's Battery, the New Orleans French Quarter, Cincinnati's Fountain Square, and San Francisco's cable cars," Broome wrote. "It has market displays as colorful as any in Mexico or Guatemala. Its displays of greenery at Christmas time bring the forest to the center of Knoxville and the offerings of bright flowers in February awaken the spring in all of us. Where else in the heart of Knoxville can one find such homely things as sassafras roots, sorghum molasses, holly and hemlock, or such exotic things as Provolone cheese, sunflower seeds and Alaskan crabs? Here country people meet townspeople, and it is good for both of them.

"It may not be too important to keep the present building…. However, old Knoxvillians have a sentimental attachment for that building because of its memories of mass meetings, political gatherings, investigations, lectures on temperance, tuberculosis, Alaska and far places, mass meetings on the Great Smokies Park, school entertainments, poultry shows and fiddlers' conventions. The old building is rich with tradition and I think few of us would like to live in a place that does not have traditions and sentiment….

"Perhaps the old building should go, but not the market place…." He went on to propose rebuilding a market house, perhaps with parking on the second or third floors. "Save Knoxville's heart; save its countryside distinction; save the City of Knoxville $150,000; preserve the meeting place of town and country…."

Eventually Carl Sandburg himself, in town in 1957 for a speech at UT, weighed in on the issue, describing his affection for this place, unusual in his experience, where you could still find hazelnuts, black walnuts, and ginseng in a central business district.

Most pleas to save the market didn't insist on saving the 60-year-old building exactly as it was. But Charles Patton, the elderly *Journal* columnist, pointed out in 1955 that the building's unusual stone arches were "of special interest to strangers, but the average Knoxvillian scarcely pauses to appreciate the work of skilled [craftsmen] of an earlier generation."

More and more desperate toward the end of the decade, Market House advocates looked into the idea of preserving the building for architectural reasons.

Knoxville's architect laureate in 1958 was 70-year-old Charles Barber, co-founder of the firm of Barber & McMurry, which had designed many of Knoxville's uncontroversially handsomest public buildings and private homes. Asked to give it a close look and appraise it for preservation, he offered a response of almost Confucian simplicity:

"For sentiment's sake, keep it if the people wish," he said, "but not for its architectural value." Though other architects might have agreed that the Market House was a mongrel of a building, and not architecturally important, Barber was perhaps not a perfectly neutral authority; architect Albert Baumann, co-designer of the Market House, had once been Barber's chief rival.

≈

Other thoughtful citizens worked on a compromise. One of the most appealing, to modern eyes, might have been one put forth by the Area Improvement Committee in 1958. Composed of an interesting array of citizens, including the young modernist architect Bruce McCarty and popular historian Betsey Creekmore, the group came up with an interesting proposal. Though it proposed razing Market Square's most architecturally distinctive, if not distinguished, features, the north and south ends, it would preserve a length of its central portion, like a simple two-story Victorian building. "Remove the ends of the Market House, retaining the center section only, and beautifying the area around the building as Knoxville's first pedestrian mall—a beauty spot in the heart of downtown."

The 1958 proposal submitted to the Mayor's Greater Knoxville Development Committee may be the first use of a word that had never been mentioned in connection to Market Square, or, for that matter, in connection to Knoxville. The word was *mall*. Though that word was just coming into the American lexicon in reference to a new retail phenomenon up north, the covered "shopping mall," the committee's use of the word was more in the sense of its original meaning, a long open pedestrian space in an urban setting—like the Mall in Washington, D.C. The word had originated in London, 300 years earlier, to refer to an open space big enough to play the croquet-like game known as pall mall.

The Downtown Knoxville Association considered still another proposal, to tear down not only the Market House, but all the buildings in the vicinity of the Square: the Kern, the Gold Sun, everything. An out-of-town consulting firm that had studied the issue, Larry Smith & Associates of Seattle, discouraged that idea.

Meanwhile, throughout the decade-long controversy, the Square continued to do what it did best—bring disparate people together and sell them a wider variety of things than they could find in any comparable patch in East Tennessee. Market Square stalwarts like Bowers' sold outdoor gear and Boy Scout uniforms. The Vogue sold dresses to minority women. Watson's sold its unpredictable array of distressed merchandise.

One of the best examples of how Market Square worked was one odd but also definitive incident that occurred well under the radar of the Dempster administration, in the summer of 1954, just before the second round of sparring between the Square's warring factions, when the astonishing popularity of a new independent-label record among the diversity of city and country types on Market Square launched RCA's interest in Elvis Presley (see pp. 64–65). In RCA's experience, Market Square was both a microcosm af America and a musical portal that was receptive to the new.

~

Jack Dance had defeated Mayor Dempster's re-election bid in 1955. On Market Square, Dance pushed an amended plan to leave parking out of the equation, at least on Market Square proper—areas could be cleared for parking elsewhere—but proceed with demolition of the Market House, to render an open space, a mall. Dance was deeply interested in the idea of urban planning; he revived an old Louis-Brownlow-era idea, a Metropolitan Planning Commission, and laid groundwork for a Civic Coliseum and Auditorium.

Dance died, suddenly, in office, in 1959. His successor was John Duncan, who pushed forward with the same policies concerning the proposed "Market Square Mall." As proposed by architect David Liberman, it would be an open pedestrian space, with a small market shelter at one end.

Almost all City Councilmen were in agreement; the defector was the Council's perennial Nay, Cas Walker. He had once favored the plan, but preferred the parking-garage idea. He had kept a grocery store on the Square, and admitted he didn't like the idea of city-subsidized rivals, farmers, right outside his door. Duncan's order to demolish the Market House with "all practical haste" passed City Council on November 26, 1959, 6-1.

Hugh Sanford, the 80-year-old polymath industrialist, piled on, seeming to echo Dempster's personal resentment of those who would consider any 60-year-old building historic, calling the Market House "not an antiquity, and of no historical value."

Demolition seemed a fait accompli, but there was still considerable resentment about it from those who still wanted to save the building. One stall operator, M.T. Scalf, protested, with a Cold War allusion: "The whole thing was done just like in Russia—behind closed doors." A petition started making the rounds, to save the Market House.

Exactly two weeks after the City Council vote, as the Square was decorated for a Christmas holiday that some already suspected might be the last for the Market House, a fire broke out in the old upstairs of the building in the northwest corner.

Later suspicion of deliberate sabotage would be rampant, given the timing. But soon after the fire, a 14-year-old Young High freshman named Tommy Hope confessed. Apparently bored, he'd gone up to the balcony above his parents' flower stall to smoke a cigarette, and put a match to some wax-coated flower-wrapping paper, just to see what would happen. It spread suddenly, much quicker than he expected.

In the future, the shorthand version of the story would be that the Market House burned down, but that wasn't the case. Firemen were on the scene quickly, and doused the fire before it had consumed the long building, most of which was untouched. Some looked at the building and, even in those conservative days, considered it reparable; the damage was estimated at $20,000. The fire had severely damaged about 16 stalls on the west side, but for the next two months, many farmers elsewhere in the building came back to work. The petition to save the Market House had collected a reported 7,500 signatures. "It'll be Remember the Market House at the polls next time," warned one advocate. "If the present city administration wants to go against the large majority of the people and tear down the Market House, all right. But the time will come when they will be sorry."

On December 20, Bert Vincent ran a bitter column, quoting longtime sellers, who were weeping in their stalls. "I've been in this Market House since 1890," one said, a little overdramatically, as the edifice had been built in 1897. "That has been 70 years. It is a crime to tear the old place down. It is the same as home to me."

Vincent added, of this place which had been his beat for over 30 years. "It is our heritage. And it has been the pulse, the heart of the city.... Ah, *tempus fugit*, and how fleeting is sentiment, history, and fame!"

Ben McMurry, Charles Barber's partner, was leader of the East Tennessee chapter of the American Institute of Architects. "We do not know what we can do yet, but our chapter would like to work as a group and try to make the square as beautiful and modern as possible if the Market House is torn down."

The Market House being demolished in 1960 after a decade of controversy. In the foreground is the Greek-owned Gold Sun, open 24 hours for most of its history. The most durable restaurant on Market Square in the 20th century, it long claimed to be Knoxville's oldest restaurant, with a founding date of 1907. It survived the mall era, later to be known as Peroulas. The Arnstein Building is visible in the background. McClung Historical Collection.

As the 1950s became the 1960s, Mayor Duncan resolutely pushed past the concerns of the preservationists, historical groups, old-time sentimentalists, and newspaper columnists, and gave the stall tenants until February to get out.

Paul Hope's flower shop moved into 24½ Market Square and stayed there for more than a decade. Tommy was relieved to have confessed, but classmates never let him forget it; he was accused, apparently unjustly, of setting another fire at Young High. For the rest of his short life, he was reportedly never very happy.

Market Square in 1960, just after the controversial demolition of the 1897 Market House. Visible on the east side are a few shoe stores and Bowers, "Home of Low Prices." It's hard not to notice the Kern's Bread truck in front of the Gold Sun, probably making a delivery to the 24-hour diner. Kern's, which operated a large shop in their own building on the Square for more than 60 years, then maintained a strong presence as one of the most popular stalls in the Market House for 30 more years, was still making an appearance here after the demolition of the big building—almost a century after Peter Kern's arrival on the Square. McClung Historical Collection.

Under a billboard-sized banner with a happy cartoon figure and the words "Another NEW KNOXVILLE DEVELOPMENT," bulldozers scraped away the old Market House, into heaps of ancient brick that would be used in the construction of a new Holiday Inn on Chapman Highway—right near the big 1930s building that housed the modern Kern's Bakery.

The Center of Festivity

B efore Market Square offered much in the way of shopping options, even before it was fully built out, it seemed a fitting spot for civic celebrations. Of all holidays, the one Knoxvillians celebrated most regularly during the city's first century was the Fourth of July. When the local fire companies launched its first annual Fourth of July Parade, in 1859, the new marketplace seemed a handy starting point. "The Procession will form in Market Square, at 11 O'Clock precisely," they advertised in the Whig. It was an impressive parade, incorporating Mayor James C. Luttrell and his aldermen, as well as the mayor and aldermen of incorporated East Knoxville, a procession of mounted "Fire Police," marching bands playing "martial music," and the holiday-decorated engines of Fountain Fire Co. #1 and Niagara Fire Co. #2. Even though those pre-war days were unnerving for patriots, the parade was a great success. "All was order and good cheer," reported the Whig. "Indeed we have never seen a procession here to imposing, and so generally admired."

It's hard to prove that Knoxville owes its entire sense of Christmas holiday festivity to Market Square—but then again, it's hard to disprove it. Before Market Square, Knoxville didn't do much for the holidays.

Among Knoxville's original citizens of the 1790s, the minority who were religious tended to be stern Presbyterians who, like many American protestants, regarded Christmas as a corrupt old-world holiday, fatally infested with paganism. They sometimes celebrated patriotic holidays, including Thanksgiving, but in only a desultory sort of way. Celebrations of Christmas, condemned by stern protestants, were rare or unknown in Knoxville before the 1840s.

The arrival of German immigrants in the 1840s and '50s seemed to have played a role in changing that—the German society Turn Verein held annual Christmas Balls. Before Knoxville had radio or phonographs or even regular vaudeville theaters, the only institutions that regularly exposed Knoxvillians to other cultures were the newspapers and Market Square.

It's natural that, from the early days, Market Square set the stage for both Thanksgiving and Christmas, being that the holidays both involved feasts: merchants stocked up on turkeys, geese, ducks, and hams for both holidays. Also, a fact that dependably surprises 21st-century people is that fresh oysters were considered a holiday staple; shipped in regularly on the train, they were available on Market Square, both in the Market House and in some of the shops around it. (Turkey was generally available, but often associated with Northern feasts; it but did not become established as the definitive holiday entree in Knoxville until around 1900.)

And it's not surprising that Peter Kern, the kindly mustachioed German who had celebrated Christmas in his youth, would be spotted in the thick of it, as a holiday provocateur.

If Peter Kern's ad in the Knoxville Chronicle *of December 13, 1871, repeated a week later, wasn't the first advertisement that referenced Christmas, it was likely the most exuberant in Knoxville's history up to that point. At a time when few December retailers offered Christmas specialties, and fewer advertisements even mentioned the holiday, Kern's went:*

"THE HOLIDAYS! CHRISTMAS IS COMING AND ALL ARE PREPARING FOR IT. PETER KERN, DEALER IN CONFECTIONARIES, FANCY GROCERIES, FIRE-WORKS, TOYS & C. *West Side of Market Place,* OFFERS A MAGNIFICENT ASSORTMENT OF GOODS FOR THE HOLIDAY TRADE *Which cannot be surpassed in East Tennessee in quantity, quality or price." It goes on, a full vertical column. "Fancy Articles Useful as well as pleasing to young and old…. Christmas Presents. There is not an article to render the children joyful, or those of larger growth happy, that cannot be found in my establishment. My assortment of Christmas Presents consists of almost every imaginable variety, and have been selected with special reference to the trade of the season…."*

Kern's yuletide announcements would be an annual feature in the newspapers. He later styled his store, credibly, as Knoxville's "Christmas Headquarters." No individual had a greater impact on our celebration than German immigrant Peter Kern, who was likely the jolliest Knoxvillian of his era. He was a portly fellow with an Old World accent and an apparently perpetual gleam in his eye; if he'd had a white beard, and not just a graying walrus mustache, kids would have mistaken him for Santa Claus himself.

Kern did much to promote the extravagant celebration of Christmas, which naturally boosted his own business in candy and cakes. His newspaper ads, which often featured a different illustration every day of the Christmas shopping season, are generally the most eye-catching of any.

Other specialists tried to improvise new traditions, perhaps none more daring than Market House butcher Paul Huray, who by the mid-1890s was building fanciful holiday sculptures composed entirely of sausage, sometimes in multiple exotic varieties. Sometimes he sculpted festive pigs, made of sausage. In 1896, Huray raffled off a "novel Christmas tree" from the skin of a hog, stuffed with 17 different kinds of sausage, among them garlic sausage, German blood sausage, head cheese, meat pudding, and sundry wursts.

Since it was past the growing season for most vegetables, much of the Square was given over to the sales of yuletide greenery, and Knoxvillians knew Market Square was the best single place in East Tennessee to shop for wreaths, garlands, holly, mistletoe, and Christmas trees. They were usually cedar trees in those days, and Market Square trafficked them in the hundreds. A reporter in December, 1898, remarked that Market Square "looked like a forest: a cold, damp, forest."

The permanent shops along the sides had Christmas sales, of course, and as if to prove it wasn't all for the money, George Houser, proprietor of the venerable Farmers and Traders Saloon on the west side, offered annual feasts for the poor; in 1896, for example, he barbecued a hog, a calf, a deer, a bear, and 25 possums—with sweet potatoes, as you'd expect—and fed it all to the masses on Christmas Day.

In years to come, the Salvation Army would provide the feast, sometimes at the Armory Hall on Market Square; on Christmas Day, 1905, they fed 700 there.

The reason that Kern also advertised fireworks at the holidays might not seem immediately apparent. But when Christmas finally caught on in the previously protestant and abstemious parts of the South, including East Tennessee, fireworks were part of the Christmas party—as Kern may have learned when he lived in Georgia. Christmas Eve, in particular, was a noisy night.

We don't know whether Kern ever shot off firecrackers on Christmas Eve back in Zwingeberg, but his store carried an extravagant array of fireworks; he knew that in Tennessee, fireworks were as much a part of Christmas as the candies and pies he sold.

His 1871 "CHRISTMAS IS COMING" ad describes "FIRE WORKS of all kinds, among which are the familiar FIRE CRACKERS, ROMAN CANDLES, BENGAL LIGHTS, PHAROAH'S SERPENTS, CHINESE LANTERNS, SKY ROCKETS, SILVER SHOWER CANDLES, TORPEDOES, BALOONS & C."

Things got out of hand on one unseasonably warm Christmas in 1893. Unhindered by the unpleasant weather that in previous years may have controlled the celebrations, joyously riotous mobs swarmed downtown setting off various festive explosives, shattering windows and damaging some storefronts with blasts, setting a couple of buildings ablaze, and even injuring some of the policemen called in to quell the mobs. The city prudently banned fireworks afterward—the actual detonation of them, not the sale. Former Mayor Kern kept selling fireworks at his bakery.

Exotic fruits were already a Christmas tradition by the late 19th century, and Kern stocked Christmas oranges, advertising 10,000 of them in December, 1896. Kern's was always the place to go, as a reporter described it that year, "a bower of beauty... running over with precious humanity."

Pickpockets were rife on the Square, and the callaboose was never more full than it was in the days leading up to the holiday, often standing-room only with prisoners whose chief crime was, as the police were fond of euphemizing, "too much Christmas."

One of the richest descriptions of Market Square during the holiday season comes in an unsigned vignette in the Journal & Tribune *from 1900. "There are other places in the city, but during the holiday season there are none equal to Market Square. The stores on each side are filled with seasonal merchandise, and more than filled with customers, the nearly 60 stalls in the Market House being piled high with seasonal delicacies of nearly every imaginable kind....*

"On Saturday night, the market is thronged until after 10.... The country wagons and their proprietors always present something new and attractive to the student of mountain life. Many of these old dilapidated wagons, drawn sometimes by an ill-matched span of mules, sometimes by shaggy mountain ponies, and not infrequently by a yoke of steers, come from 60 to 80 miles away, from the heart of the Great Smokies, with their loads of Christmas cheer, fine close-braided evergreens for Christmas trees, high stacks of dark green holly with thick clusters of brilliant scarlet berries, great bundles of dull-green mistletoe with its waxlike white berries.

"Scores of these wagons, laden with their loads of spicy fragrance, come creaking in over the long [Gay Street] bridge...every morning just as the first faint streaks of dawn begin to appear in the eastern sky, rumble slowly around the first corner into Prince Street, and then...up to some position in the market.

"Some of the mountaineers are curiosities in themselves.... They never think of paying for a night's lodging for themselves, but will curl up somewhere in or under their wagons on the square, wrapped in an old quilt or blanket, where they appear to spend the night very comfortably, and certainly cheaply.

"With the coming of the holidays, these peculiar types increase on the market, for the men who bring the holly and mistletoe are by no means the same men who make a business of coming into the city three or four times...a week to peddle some of their surplus farm produce. These mountaineers seldom visit the city except at holiday season...."

It closes with a quote mentioned elsewhere in this narrative, but it bears repeating: "Market Square is the most democratic place on earth. There the rich and the poor, the white and the black, jostle each other in perfect equality, and the scenes during the busy hours of the afternoon are always worth watching."

In 1929, the Square was on the decline in some respects, but Christmas was still a big deal. In her New York Times *essay about the Square, Rosa Naomi Scott* wrote, "In Autumn chinkapins, chestnuts, homemade hominy and pumpkins then fill the market. Later the mountaineers come down for Christmas, with lumbering wagons of holly, glistening mistletoe, wild red berries and galax leaves. Lank and gaunt they stare at the towering Christmas tree on the square. But the charm of the old country's firesides, of snapping wood, the magic of aromatic Christmas cedars and hemlocks cling to these wagons and their gray, raw wardens from the hills."

Of course, Knoxville's small Jewish community celebrated their own holidays, some of which emphasize traditional Jewish specialties. Before Knoxville had a kosher grocery, the Lippner family, who kept a stall in the northern end of the Market House, advertised all sorts of meats, but reserved half of their shop for kosher foods. The Lippners were known to be expert in preparation of kosher specialties, and sometimes offered demonstrations there in the stall for preparing pickles or corned beef.

A postcard probably produced very soon after the 1897 construction of the Market House offers an unusually comprehensive view of the Square. Note the patriotic bunting on the Kern building, which was characteristic, especially on patriotic holidays. Courtesy of Mark Heinz.

Market Square was a venue for secular patriotic holidays as well, like the aforementioned Fourth of July. Celebrated much more in post-Civil War Knoxville than it was in most of the Deep South—in several states, former Confederates effectively banned the U.S. patriotic holiday for more than three decades after the war—the Fourth always elicited yards and yards of bright red, white, and blue bunting on Market Square, and sales of fireworks at Kern's, which was crowned for a while with an electric American flag. (No one was more overtly patriotic than Peter Kern; as a German who'd been a Confederate soldier, he may have felt had had something to prove.)

Knoxvillians celebrated other secular patriotic holidays on the Square as well. Knoxville began celebrating Lincoln's Birthday in the 1890s, perhaps a little quicker than most of the South did; some of those early celebrations were on Market Square. At the centennial of Lincoln's birth, on February 12, 1909, the Union-veteran organization Grand Army of the Republic presided over an evening entertainment in Market Square's auditorium which included musical recitals, patriotic sing-alongs (the YMCA glee club helped), and speeches. One of the addresses given that day was "Lincoln as a Man," by attorney John Webb Green. (As an old man 50 years later, Green would lead the legal opposition to an out-of-town white-supremacist group attempting to block efforts to desegregate local schools.) In 1909, Green, son of a Confederate officer killed in the war, declared, "the South has thrown off its prejudices" and "now regards Lincoln in his true light."

It's significant, and surprising, that among the crowd was to be a delegation of Confederate veterans. However, bitter winter weather dampened the expected standing-room-only crowd, and newspaper accounts don't mention the graying grays' reaction to the new holiday.

Kern's seemed to try to make a sales event of even minor holidays. By the turn of the century, Kern's was advertising "Valentine novelties," including candies for Knoxville sweethearts. And a 1910 ad goes, "When Planning Your Washington Birthday PARTY Be Sure To Consult KERN'S. Their stock of novelties is complete." What sort of novelties Knoxvillians might have in mind on the minor patriotic holiday isn't obvious, but across the Square, Kenny's was advertising "George Washington buttons."

In the early 20th century, Kern's also assisted in a February 22 tradition since lost: the "Martha Washington Tea." Presumably it was a women's home event which required special treats.

The foreign-born Kern seemed to dare native-born Americans to outdo his displays when he decorated his famous building for the patriotic holidays like Fourth of July, which saw his building, which for a time wore a large electric flag on the roof, dressed in red, white, and blue bunting. A few holiday parades commenced from the Square, near his store.

As far as Peter Kern was concerned, his place was essential shopping for nearly every holiday. In 1899, he advertised his Confectionary.... For Thanksgiving." The ad explains, "Our ice cream and cakes are indispensable for a good Thanksgiving dinner." Then Kern adds, "We will have in large supply all grades of fresh oysters in bulk for Thanksgiving."

St. Patrick's Day was once celebrated by Knoxville's dynamic Irish community in a bombastic way, with big parades and late-night balls at the Lamar House which went well into the wee hours. However, the tradition seems to have been most popular with the original immigrants. By the early 20th century, when most of the first generation were dwindling and getting on in years, March 17 became a more modest celebration, often held at the Market Hall. Some would remember group sings there of "I'll Take You Home Again, Kathleen."

On one peculiar occasion, it may have been what Market Square didn't offer that may have had the biggest influence on the national celebration of a national holiday. Each May beginning in 1866, Decoration Day was the holiday put aside to decorate the graves of Union dead with flowers, most of them purchased from Market Square's flower vendors by the women's auxiliary of the Grand Army of the Republic, made up chiefly of wives and widows of Union soldiers. According to one interesting telling of the story, it was a disappointment in 1874; because of a drought, flowers were scarce in the market. One young Knoxville widow named Laura Richardson, a member of the committee in charge of decorations, had a desperate idea. After she found a large quantity of toy flags in an unnamed downtown store, she convinced her colleagues that the best way to memorialize the dead that year would be to decorate the graves at the National Cemetery with small flags.

All of that story appears only in a 1942 article published in the National Tribune, in Washington, DC, and the article claimed Mrs. Richardson's effort was the origin of the flag-planting custom on the holiday now known as Memorial Day. The story can only be partially confirmed through local sources; there was indeed a Union war widow named Laura Richardson living in downtown Knoxville in the 1870s; but in 1874, the year listed in the story, the flower supply was reportedly "bountiful." Her innovation may have come later.

Several holidays faded somewhat in the late 20th century, but through thick and thin some farmers always showed up to sell wreaths and other evergreenery, and the city almost always offered some sort of an observance of Christmas on Market Square, like a Christmas-tree lighting. Crowds were respectable if not festively huge. For a few years in the 1980s, the city sponsored an artificial ice-skating rink. Weather and technical problems forced an end to the custom, but it returned after the Square's 2004 reopening, as more gift stores opened and Market Square seemed to be redeveloping a holiday-shopping gravity of its own.

In the 21st century, the holidays have returned to the Square in ways in which Peter Kern might have approved. During the Christmas season of 2005, a few downtown businessmen, led by Larson Jay, a maverick filmmaker (his feature movie project,

That Evening Sun, *would garner national praise in 2009), opened the outdoor skating rink. The idea was first launched to unprofitable response in the late 1980s, but new lower-cost freezing technology and a new, more favorable attitude toward the Square seemed to suggest it would work better this time, and it did. Within a year, Holidays on Ice seemed something like a Christmas tradition. One holiday rarely celebrated in public, however, was New Year's Eve. Market Square seemed Knoxville's handiest equivalent to Times Square, attempts to get something going there saw only a little success, at first.*

The year 2007–8 saw the first big city-sponsored New Year's Eve celebration on the Square, featuring live bands, and a lighted ball dropped from a crane. Thousands attended, and the several bars which had remained open all night emptied into the Square. The celebration was more ambitious the following year. The first "First Night" festival featured music in the open Square, again, but this time a dozen interior venues featured bands, dramatic troupes, dancers, and film, much of it on Gay Street or

A Homecoming, of Sorts: At the first "First Night" festival, popular performer Webb Wilder is onstage as thousands of revelers watch 2007 become 2008. Adolph Ochs, who began his long career in journalism on Market Square, launched the famous Time Square New Year's Eve party soon after buying the New York Times *in 1896, but midnight New Year's Eve parties were rare on Market Square until the twenty-first century. Courtesy of Tinah Utsman.*

Clinch—but the center was always *Market Square*, where early-evening fireworks celebrated the holiday for sleepy kids, and where bars emptied at midnight for more fireworks and the ball drop, this time done from the top of the Arnstein Building.

While a few found the celebrations, especially the ball drop on Market Square, a little derivative, it had an authentic source. Max Arnstein's friend, New York Times publisher Adolph Ochs, had started the tradition in 1904 as a way to market the Times and, his creation, Times Square. And Ochs, of course, began his career in journalism just after the Civil War, on a different Square, Knoxville's Market Square.

CHAPTER 7

The Mall

Dogwood Arts, TVA, Ronald Reagan,
and the Talk of America

L ike several other modernizations to downtown, Market Square Mall, finished in the first year of an optimistic new president's administration, seemed a wonderful vision of the modern New Frontier. "Umbrellas" of clean white concrete offered shelter here and there, collecting to form a roof for those farmers who, leaving their rusty trucks elsewhere, still came to sell produce on the Square.

In the center, an oval fountain was lined with tile. According to the *Journal*, "underwater lights make it especially beautiful at night. Trees and shrubs give a calm and peaceful environment to the mall where shoppers may move from one store to another without worry of traffic or other distraction."

A block of old buildings down on Walnut were torn down to provide a broad, almost Sears-sized space of surface parking. There would be free parking for Square customers, with a minimum purchase.

The *Journal* called it "Magnificent: Who'd believe it? This beautiful oasis from the hustle and bustle of downtown city life is located in the heart of Knoxville…. Now the artistic sidewalk canopies, pavilion roof, fountain, walkways, trees and shrubbery make it a showplace and real tourist attraction…. A neat, small brick building at the north end of the Square provide clean toilet facilities, but eliminates a loitering place...." The reporter also describes "a beautiful blue tile fountain, grassy areas to carry out the suburban theme, benches and then trees and shrubbery...."

"Operation successful: the heart of the city has been repaired. The patient is making a remarkable recovery and can be expected to be better than ever."

Naturally, Cas Walker was bitter about the whole thing. He'd been an early supporter of tearing down the Market House, but preferred the parking-garage idea. "I'm pleading with you to change your minds before you make a fatal mistake," he had said to his fellow councilmen before registering the sole vote against the project.

Walker, who had never been too keen on downtown to begin with, made good on his promise to quit the Mall, claiming inadequate parking, and predicting the demise of downtown. "Knoxville's on wheels," he said. Nobody's going to hang

Market Square Mall under construction. The sign in the center boasts, "Another New Knoxville Development / Congratulatons from the Knoxville Chamber of Commerce." (The Chamber would actually move its offices to the Square after the 2003 facelift.) On the left, the old Kern building is almost forgotten as such, now home to Rexall Drugs, and upstairs, an optical shop and the Knoxville Beauty School. Farther down is Snyder's Department Store. On the right side of the Square is long-time women's wear merchant, The Vogue. This image shows the original course of Market Street, north of the Square; before TVA's massive landscaping ended Market Street at the Square more than a decade later, Market Street continued North, climbing a slight hill. McClung Historical Collection.

around downtown when they can drive somewhere else. The building he left at 35 Market Square remained empty for much of the decade.

The Grand Opening was a two-day "festival" on the last weekend of October, 1961, with barbershop singing, the Central High marching band, and speeches from Mayor John Duncan and others. Popular insurance man and amateur artist Russell Briscoe, who made a specialty of neo-primitivist historical scenes of downtown Knoxville, was MC. Carried live on Channel 6, it all led into a square dance, with breaks for Bill Dooley, the juggling clown, until 10 that night. Dooley's real name was Paul Hope, the florist; his son was the kid who'd started the fire that had destroyed a portion of the old Market House.

"Market Square Mall takes on the appearance of a park at night, a good place to relax…. Moon watchers are likely to find the mall a favorite place…. Waters playing in the fountain…offer a feeling of tranquility. Underwater lights add to the fountain's beauty at night."

The Square's merchants ran an ad in the papers, "Thank You Knoxville for co-operation, loyalty, and goodwill in making DOWNTOWN KNOXVILLE THE TALK OF AMERICA."

It was an exaggeration, maybe, but not an unsupportable lie. In its early years, Market Square did get some flattering press around the South, from Daytona Beach to Roanoke, where the *World-News* averred, "If Knoxville can do it, so can Roanoke." In a later profile of Market Square Mall, the *Spartanburg Herald* asked, in 1964, "Why Not Make Downtown the Best Shopping Center of All?"

A few months after the opening, the *Atlanta Journal-Constitution* ran a full-page color photo of Market Square Mall with the caption, "New Life for the Heart of Knoxville," referring to "beautiful Market Square Mall, where trees grow, flowers bloom, fountains splash, and people enjoy themselves in the center of town."

Market Square Mall even got some positive international press, in papers in Winnipeg and Melbourne.

Of course, "Market Square Mall," the fresh new phrase tripping off Knoxvillian lips in 1961, was technically a redundancy. Throughout the English-speaking world, after all, most "squares" are understood to be pedestrian malls, from Trafalgar Square in London to Washington Square in New York. By the definition of *mall* as an open space in an urban setting, most urban "squares" were in fact more mall-like, in the original sense, than was Market Square Mall, with its clusters of permanent concrete umbrellas—so the term was also, arguably, a misnomer. But to those who remembered Knoxville's distinctly different Market Square as chiefly a place with a giant building on it, the word *mall* may have served as an important signifier that it was now a different, more open sort of place. It was a break with the past, and a signal to Middle Class suburbanites that Market Square was now modern, clean, and safe to return to.

The '60s was also, coincidentally, a decade when another retail concept, the enclosed suburban shopping "mall," the outsized shopping center with giant parking lots and big chain stores, swept the nation. Market Square Mall would stand in as a face-saving consolation in a city that hadn't been able to put one together yet.

Regardless, the word *Mall* seemed something to be proud of. It was the New Frontier, and the year 1961 was also the year that Knoxville, at long last, was a swinging, sophisticated city, allowing package liquor and wine sales for the first time since 1907. One of the first new package stores in Knoxville was the Caracostis family's "Mall Package Store." Other businesses picked up on the theme. Watson's 50-year-old store was suddenly "Watson's On the Mall." Peter Kern's lovely and historic old building, which still hosted mainly Cole's Drugstore, was renamed the "Mall Building"; at the time, the renaming didn't strike anyone as an indignity.

A surprisingly verdant perspective on Market Square Mall, from a 1960s postcard. The "concrete toadstools" lining the Square seemed modern in 1961, but would prove less and less popular as the years went by. The building in the rear was the old T.E. Burns specialty-grocery building on Wall Avenue, which was torn down in the 1970s before the construction of TVA's headquarters. Courtesy of Mark Heinz.

The Mall reportedly boosted Market Square-area business as much as 24 percent in the first year, and more the second, despite the fact that the mix of businesses had hardly changed. Market Square was still, mainly, Watson's and Bowers' and Miller's cut-rate annex.

The Dogwood Arts Festival, spurred on in part by John Gunther's 1947 outrage, began as a series of automobile-driven dogwood trails in the prettier neighborhoods of town. When it first added a public festival component, in 1962, the Market Square Mall seemed an obvious nucleus for it. Beginning in 1962, the festival sold plants and flowers on the Mall, as craftsmen demonstrated painting, woodcarving, and pottery. For the first few years, Dogwood Arts was a resounding success, with flattering profiles in the *New York Times* and *Better Homes and Gardens*. The magazine *Tennessee Conservationist* ran a photo from the year before of a woman painting a scene of plant vendors on the Square, creditably in the style of Matisse. The caption was "University of Tennessee art student finds inspiration for her talents in the flower and vegetable venders on Market Mall, which during festival season becomes a 'Greenwich Village of the South.'"

Aging *News-Sentinel* columnist Burt Vincent remained skeptical of the space which had taken the place of his beloved, authentic Market House, but his younger colleague Carson Brewer became a great advocate of the Mall.

Meanwhile, the heirs of Joseph Mabry, who averred that they were disappointed with the design of the Mall, filed a suit claiming that the open-sided covering did not constitute a "Market House," as delineated in the original deed. One of the complainants, incredibly, was Churchwell Mabry, who claimed to be Joseph Mabry's son.

A visitor might not have heard quite as many different accents on Market Square Mall as might have been evident 50 years earlier, nor were the few country people who still did come to sell produce quite as exotically antique as maybe they had before. Market Square Mall may have seemed a safer, more predictable place than old Market Square had been, and in some respects it probably was.

To the minority of Knoxvillians of the 1960s who were lovers of Victorian commercial-vernacular architecture, one of the worst things about the Square was that the concrete toadstools obscured the facades, and in many cases proprietors finished the modernist conversion by adding obscuring paneling of plastic, aluminum, or concrete, often trying to force horizontal lines on the old buildings' original vertical ones, as if to make the place look fresh and new.

Still, the Mall was never exactly a sanitized, homogenized version of the Square. Watson's, now the flagship of a 40-store chain, grew during the Mall era to take in five old west-side storefronts, and remained an unpredictable shopping adventure. The store carried an always-surprising variety of stylish furniture, clothing of random but sometimes very fine quality, sometimes-exotic kitchenware, and other odds and ends. Some likened the Watson's experience to exploring an especially well-laden shipwreck.

Further, much of Market Square's mid-20th-century seediness survived around the fringes of the Mall. One of the first new businesses to open after the demolition of the Market House was called the Star Stag Bar. It would become a fixture in the northwestern quarter of the Mall as an unreconstructed beer joint,

An aerial shot of rapidly changing Market Square around 1962, when it was by then becoming a better known as "the Mall." Concrete polygons, later excoriated as "toadstools," served as both modernist decoration and post-Market House shelter for farmers who still sold their wares here. During that urban-renewel era, the city was almost desperately trying to "modernize " downtown Knoxville, which was already suffering from competition with suburban attractions. This image shows the almost-forgotten blocks of Market Square along Wall, Commerce, and Vine Avenues. McClung Historial Collection.

and whether the city liked it or not, one of the Mall's most durable businesses. An upstairs establishment nearby on the west side was advertised as a "sports center," usually code for a billiard hall and gambling joint. Prostitutes were known to make connections on the Mall. In the early '70s, a place on the east side called the Hang-Up was a clothing store with a counterculture reputation; it somehow mutated into a restaurant and arcade and, in the early '80s, a hip, albeit short-lived, nightclub.

Near the Star bar, later on, was the Bargain Box, a charity-run thrift store intended to help the poor. It was assumed the poor still frequented Market Square, even in the shiny new Mall era, and in fact they did. One reason was that the Square offered the only handy public restroom downtown, and it was close enough to the bus-transfer point on Gay that it afforded many a relieving layover.

And the Mall era brought some bona-fide new institutions. In 1963, just in time for Beatlemania, Tucker's Record Store opened on Market Square, first in a small slot on the east side, later moving to a larger space on the west. It developed a reputation for stocking at least one copy of nearly everything. Tucker's lasted for an impressive quarter century. To the ever-more rebellious younger generation who might have thought the new Mall seemed designed for housewives, Tucker's allowed the Mall at least a hint of cool.

And any place that still supported the Gold Sun could lay a claim to authenticity. Even if they chose to close at night occasionally; in 1969, the Peroulas family had a lock installed on the front door of 37 Market Square, for the first time in 60 years.

Market Square retained its ability to surprise. On a lucky day, there was still that once-characteristic out-of-nowhere development now and then that could give the credulous the notion that Market Square was the center of the universe.

In 1963, a TV trailer, showed up, shooting pilots for a new Allen Funt TV show. Funt was then at the peak of his fame as the creator of Candid Camera, and had come up with an idea for a new reality show called "Tell It To the Camera." Funt himself was probably not present; the man in charge was Sam Orleans, the jovial, rotund documentarian who was Knoxville's only independent filmmaker at the time. The idea was to find angry people on the street and get them to sound off on camera. It was perhaps an idea before its time—but the results of the Market Square Mall shoot are obscure. The show never aired, and Orleans was killed in an airliner crash a few months later.

One of the most unlikely of Market Square's many random visitors arrived on an April morning in 1970. A city delegation led by Mayor Leonard Rogers escorted actress Ingrid Bergman to a grassy spot in the southwest corner, presented her with a silver shovel, and invited her to help plant a dogwood tree. Calling it a "lovely idea," the legendary Swedish actress complied as local

TV cameras rolled and a crowd of 400 watched. Bergman was in town for the world premiere of her movie, *A Walk In the Spring Rain,* most of which had been filmed in the area a year earlier. The premiere was the first such event not held at the Tennessee Theatre; befitting those suburban days, it happened at the Capri-70 in Bearden, and the actress seems to have spent most of her time socializing in suburban settings. But someone thought it symbolically important that a distinguished visitor come downtown and make some sort of memorable visit to Market Square.

Columnist Carson Brewer, who was present, was skeptical of the planting technique, and predicted the tree would not survive. Indeed, the Bergman Dogwood, which stood near the old Kern building, seems to have vanished not long after its high-profile planting.

~

Descriptions of the Mall in the 1960s were almost unanimously positive, and several businesses, like Watson's, did very well. A 1967 thesis for a masters in planning degree describes the Mall in glowing terms, as an outstanding success. In the early '70s, however, came the first intimations that maybe the 1961 reconstruction was, perhaps something like its predecessor the Market House, a fashion victim.

The early 1970s saw a rash of demolitions which removed entire blocks from the northern parts of downtown for the construction of Summit Hill Drive, with talk of a massive TVA headquarters project in the offing. The newly formed preservationist group Knoxville Heritage enlisted a Nashville consulting firm, Architect-Engineer Associates, to come to Knoxville and assess the state of architecture in the downtown area. The only building on Market Square, besides the Arnstein, that impressed the consultants was the Kern Building and, to a lesser extent, its balconied neighbor at 5 Market Square. In April, 1974, they released a report of what they'd seen, a booklet called "Historic Buildings of Knoxville, Tennessee."

"Though only one is of sufficient merit to stand on its own, the buildings in Market Square taken together do provide an interesting and fairly unified visual experience," they wrote. "However, much of this effect is destroyed by the intervention of several irrelevant modern storefronts, and by concrete parasols which tend to stifle the individuality of each building."

That comment disparaging the Mall's celebrated modernist hallmarks might have startled the few who read it. A decade earlier, the world was telling Knoxville how wonderful the concrete parasols were. "Modernizing" old buildings by covering them with plain sheeting of glass, concrete, or plastic, was still considered an improvement as late as 1974, when one of West Town Mall's developers bought the ornate beaux-arts ca. 1905 Miller's Building, around the corner from

Market Square Mall, then proceeded to destroy much of the exterior, covering the whole with reflective glass in an attempt to make it more "modern" and therefore marketable.

By then, the new, modern West Town Mall was changing Knoxville's shopping habits again. The first enclosed shopping mall in the region opened in 1972, inevitably drawing business from this old mall and the rest of downtown and, for Knoxvillians, redefining the meaning of the word *Mall*. Suddenly the old Market Square Mall, the much-envied triumph of '61, was looking small and shabby.

Despite its early fame, and initial success in improving business—and some published claims that the Mall had no vacancies—City Directories indicate that the Mall usually had several vacancies throughout its career. Market Square Mall may have been successful for several of its businesses, most of which had been there before, but it never quite reached the crest of success Knoxville expected of it.

However, it could still impress some. In the 1977 study, *For Pedestrians Only: Planning, Design, and Management of Traffic-Free Zones*, published by the Whitney Library of Design, Market Square Mall was listed as one of several successes. "An open-air market, where farmers sell their own products, plants, and flowers, stands at the north end of the mall. Pedestrian amenities include pastel colored sidewalks and a continuous canopy to protect shoppers from inclement weather...." One of the authors of that book, by the way, was a young Gianni Longo, the urban planner and pedestrian advocate later credited with helping to spur downtown Chattanooga's revival. More than 20 years later, he would spend more time in Knoxville, shepherding the Nine Counties One Vision project.

The book includes a massive amount of data from hundreds of different sources. However, they may have gotten some rosy pictures of the Square: "Vacancy rates in…Knoxville, Tennessee, for example, dropped from 25 percent to zero during the first year of their pedestrian district's existence."

And the photo they used to illustrate the lively mall was apparently not a very fresh one; in the background is the old pre-TVA T.E. Burns building on Wall Avenue, which had been torn down half a decade before the book's publication. The book's description may have been the last nice thing published in the national media about Market Square Mall.

There would be other, more extravagant proposals to take Market Square Mall's apparent success and spread it across downtown. One proposal, taken seriously for a time in the '70s, stretched the pedestrian concept all the way up and down Market Street. Another called for an East-West Mall, which would intersect with Market at Church. They were earnest ideas.

But it's not the people with ideas that make the big changes. Those usually come from the people with the money, and it helps when they have the backing of the federal government. Easily the biggest change after the Mall came in 1974-76, when

TVA cleared a few square blocks of buildings just to the north to build its massively plain white headquarters buildings.

It may seem ironic that throughout the ambitious eras of building dams that received international acclaim and even inventing model towns, like Norris and Fontana, TVA's leadership had been content to keep its offices in several unconnected older buildings, built for other purposes, like the old post office and the old Arnstein department store, as it was long rumored that TVA would move its headquarters from Knoxville to Muscle Shoals, Alabama. TVA was past 40 years old when the agency finally got around to building its first permanent, consolidated headquarters.

Knoxville cajoled TVA into keeping its headquarters in downtown Knoxville, perhaps offering a bit too much: to tear down several distinguished old buildings along Wall Avenue, close old Commerce Street and the northern part of Market Street altogether, and donate to TVA those city blocks and their commanding eminence over Market Square.

Among the buildings in TVA's way was the Hotel St. James. Still advertising as "Fireproof," 70 years after its construction, the hotel had added a further inducement: "Located near Knoxville's famous Mall." That was probably the St. James's last advertising slogan. Knoxville's first all-concrete building was said to be a difficult demolition project.

Knoxville was anxious about losing so much residential and retail vigor to the suburbs, and looked to TVA, perhaps a little desperately, as a savior.

TVA's new headquarters would be a plain, modernist complex dominated by two almost-cubical white towers which, in the wake of the Energy Crisis, were said to maximize energy efficiency. The city did have the gumption to insist that the section between the buildings be open to pedestrian access from Market Square to the north— but when it was all done, the link was designed in such a way, with a surprising altitude of a hill that hadn't existed on northern Market Street before, and switchback steps, that the section between the buildings looked like a private plaza. It would rarely be used by the public for routine access to the Square, which was, for the first time, inaccessible by street from the north. TVA's project blocked the Square from any northern view—from anywhere other than TVA itself, that is. It's not surprising that the 120-year-old Market Square was informally redefined as a TVA amenity, sometimes pointed out to visitors as "where TVA people have lunch," or "TVA's backyard."

From the completion of its looming headquarters buildings in 1976, TVA dominated Market Square. The agency employed about 3,000 in the twin towers, and most of them seemed to find their way daily to Market Square Mall. Most businesses, even the famously 24-hour Gold Sun, concentrated on the lunch crowd, and the hundreds of ID-wearing TVA employees who flowed into the Square every weekday at noon. Old Watsons, which had once been busy all day, still did good business, but mostly at the weekday lunch hour, cutting its evening hours back to two nights a week, then one—as managers reluctantly accepted that, despite the construction of the big parking lot on Walnut, and the Mall's lighted fountain, most of their retail customers in this new era were just commuters who worked downtown. At certain times in the late 1970s and '80s, Market Square could look desolate: utterly abandoned in evenings and for much of the weekend. But on a nice weekday, lunchtime could look like a daily festival, albeit a sober, official-looking sort of festival.

The agency brought new layers of history to the Square. TVA moved into its new headquarters in the midst of its biggest controversies, perhaps, since its inception. One was the relatively new Browns Ferry nuclear plant, which had soon after its completion suffered major damage in a fire that its opponents believed could have been catastrophic. The other was Tellico Dam, TVA's first big dam project since World War II. It was almost complete, but was facing fierce opposition from all points of the political spectrum: from farmers and property owners, from custodians of Cherokee heritage, and especially from environmentalists concerned that the project could extinguish a recently discovered species of unusual fish called the snail darter. That controversy in particular garnered national interest, with even Supreme Court Justice William O. Douglas taking sides and pleading with TVA to quit the project.

Once again, Market Square became, as it had been many times before, the scene of sometimes angry political demonstrations. TVA Board Chairman Aubrey "Red" Wagner, who had been appointed to his job by President John Kennedy more than a decade earlier, was unfazed. As a result of decisions made in the buildings overlooking the Square, Tellico Dam was finished in 1979, and its locks closed, forming a new body of water called Tellico Lake. The demonstrations about Tellico Dam and other issues, including TVA's coal-burning furnaces and power rates, didn't let up for a long time; a generation of activists came to know Market Square, especially the north end of it, as a place to protest against TVA.

And during the early 1980s, as the concrete and flimsy faux-modernist adornments of the urban-renewal era were showing their age, that the Square regained some of its old reputation as a place major politicians expected to find crowds to influence. In fact, the otherwise forlorn late Mall era witnessed the most nationally conspicuous moments in Market Square's political history.

At noon on a hot day in September, 1980, the day after an anticlimactic debate which President Carter declined to attend—the Republican presidential nominee debated only third-party contender John Anderson—former California Governor Ronald Reagan and his wife, Nancy, paraded down Gay Street in a black Continental limousine and spoke to a crowd of about 6,000 cheering supporters on Market Square Mall. It might have seemed an odd venue, given that his backdrop was TVA, this major big-government brainchild of a Democratic administration. Reagan had ruffled feathers as far back as 1959, when, still a full-time actor, he had given speeches criticizing TVA and proposing it be sold to private interests. During his run for the Republican nomination in 1976, he'd remarked that he would consider selling TVA off. That warm day in September, hundreds of TVA employees listened to his words with some anxiety. But Reagan assured TVA employees that remarks he'd made four years earlier about privatizing TVA had been taken out of context, and that the agency's "tradition of progress and growth" should continue.

During his speech, he lambasted President Carter, describing his administration in terms of a "misery index." In the crowd were dozens of supporters of the doomed Equal Rights Amendment, waving signs marked ERA NOW; their chanting during Reagan's speech caused some friction, resulting in tussles within the audience. Acknowledging the protesters, Reagan admitted a "great and serious difference" of opinion with them.

Senator Baker, who had opposed Reagan in the primary, introduced the nominee and described Knoxville as "the heartland of Southern Republicanism," a statement plausible even on Market Square. At Peroulas, which half a century earlier had been the informal campaign headquarters of Republican Congressman J. Will Taylor, there were newer framed color photographs of another Republican politician, whose name was Maria Peroulas. A daughter and granddaughter of owners of the restaurant formerly known as the Gold Sun, Peroulas would soon be the popular young state representative from Knoxville.

Baker predicted the "biggest Republican victory of the century." Six weeks after his Market Square visit, Reagan was elected to the presidency by a national landslide.

When President Reagan returned to Knoxville on May 1, 1982, to christen the 1982 World's Fair, he didn't come to Market Square, but Reagan opponents chose it as a site of a counter-demonstration, and drew a couple hundred, a motley assortment of radical feminists, anti-nuke activists, and romantic hippies. Because it was a Saturday, hardly any of the Square's regular customers saw it.

Perhaps impressed with Reagan's turnout four years earlier, and its augury of success, Democratic handlers considering Knoxville in 1984 looked to Market Square. During Walter Mondale's "Where's the beef?" campaign for the Democratic nomination in April, 1984, the former vice president and his wife Joan both visited Market Square, separately, in the same month. Former Second Lady Joan Mondale, nicknamed "Joan of Art," shopped for homemade baskets at a Dogwood Arts display on the Square early in the month, startling some who recognized her, and puzzling others who didn't. At the end of the month, on the evening before the primary, the candidate himself proved there were at least 400 Democrats in Knoxville when his stump speech drew them to Market Square. Several displayed signs for steelworkers and carpenters unions. Mondale criticized both rival Democrat Gary Hart and President Reagan for the unemployment rate, the deficit, rising mortgage rates, and general aloofness—but praised TVA as a "miracle" for the region. Mondale won the Democratic nomination in San Francisco that summer, but of course lost to the popular incumbent in November.

Though Reagan kept his promise to maintain TVA, the Reagan years would bring major changes to Market Square. In the late 1980s, under TVA Chairman "Carvin'" Marvin Runyon, a Reagan appointee, TVA endured several major cutbacks, which eventually left it with hardly more than 1,000 employees, rendering TVA's downtown Knoxville presence only about one-third of what it had been in the 1970s. Later, TVA installed major chain restaurants within the TVA towers, which made it much easier for employees to eat lunch without walking down to the Square. TVA's domination of the Square was over about 20 years after it started. Though TVA's headquarters buildings still loomed godlike to its north, entrepreneurs found it painfully obvious that Market Square businesses, especially restaurants, would no longer be able to thrive purely on the TVA lunchtime business.

Fortunately, other things were stirring. In 1981, construction-company owner Joe Zappa bought the Mall Building, which only the oldest generation of Knoxvillians remembered as the Kern Building, and announced that with the help of preservationist architect Gene Burr, he intended to convert it into a hotel, to be called the Blakley House. Knoxvillians were just getting used to the idea of historical renovation, but a hotel on Market Square Mall might have struck some as bizarre—if not for the imminent World's Fair, then being prepared about four blocks to the west. As a permanent institution, the hotel was probably a decade before its time; Zappa, disappointed with the venture, retired from the downtown-development field. Few residents who could afford to live anywhere else were living downtown then; but in the early 1980s, one old TVA building around the corner from Market Square, at Union and Walnut, opened as a new residential condominium building renamed the Pembroke, which at first seemed to appeal to affluent older part-time residents. Though it had few imitators for years to come, this apartment building one block from Market Square turned out to be the first major residential conversion of an old office building; many would follow, but slowly.

Some of that early flurry of investment was prompted by optimistic expectations of the 1982 World's Fair; the main entrance to the six-month exposition, which drew 11 million visitors, was hardly four blocks from Market Square, and many expected it to be a boon to the aging Mall. However, many downtown entrepreneurs actually noted a decline in business during those six months. "Several local people who often came downtown worried they wouldn't be able to find a place to park," said Randy Mansfield, who became manager of Watson's that year. However, one particular day, the old stalwart did some impressive Fair-related business. Several ballerinas from the visiting Bolshoi Ballet stopped in Watson's and bought 28 fur coats. "That's the most furs we ever sold in one day," said Mansfield. "They thought our prices were better than they could find in Russia."

The subtext of the 1982 World's Fair was the urgency of living differently to save fossil fuels; locals listened politely, but the exhortations to save energy had no discernible effect on their habits. The population of Knoxville kept spilling headlong into the automobile-dependent suburbs, especially to the west. The permanent residential population of Market Square in the 1980s was approximately zero.

～

Despite its early promise of lovely well-lit fountains every evening, the Mall had left its once-famous 24-hour reputation far behind; it had become, almost strictly, a M-F, 9-5 sort of place. For years, it was only obviously busy at lunchtime. If Market Square ever died, as many assume it did, it was always able to draw at least a couple hundred commuters around noon, when there were always at least half a dozen restaurants, including, always, at least one deli-sandwich purveyor and a couple of simple cafeteria-style spots, like the long-lived Soup Kitchen in the old Kern Building, doing good business. Market Square had become a daytime haunt with no institution comparable to Kern's, which a century earlier had sometimes been lively until midnight. The day the Gold Sun began closing after lunch may have seemed the end of an era. The "Mall" was beginning to seem more like a food court for downtown bankers and secretaries.

But Market Square has always been a place of exceptions. The Hang-Up, a counterculture-themed nightclub was a late-night attraction on the east side of the Square by 1983. It would be followed by a jazz club called the Milestone, owned by recording artist Lee Miles Stone, and, briefly, a gay bar. These earnest efforts stirred interest for a few months, then languished.

An unpredictable development just to the south may have gotten people looking at the Square differently. In 1981, a retired TVA photographer named Charles Krutch died at the age of 94. He was the last survivor of a celebrated German family who had arrived in Knoxville at almost exactly the same time that Swan and Mabry were laying out Market Square, and he loved the place. He was the brother of the late author, critic and naturalist Joseph Wood Krutch. But no one had known he was wealthy. As it turned out, he left $1.3 million to the city to establish an urban park. The city chose a block dominated by parking lots and old buildings just south of Market Square, along what had once been Watermelon Row. And though parks had been proposed for downtown for 100 years, Krutch Park was, incredibly, the first park ever established in the central business district, purely as a park, that is. (Part of the old campus of the Tennessee School for the Deaf survived for several years as City Hall Park, but it always seemed more like a big front yard.) Completed in 1985, with lush plantings and a surprising artificial creek motif, Krutch Park seemed to suggest further destinies for Market Square.

By then, an unlikely publishing company originally called 13-30, later known as Whittle Communications, was growing rapidly in the old Arnstein Building. By the mid-'80s, all seven floors were filled with hundreds of magazine editors and art directors, young, talented, and plausibly urbane. A few restaurants on the Square began looking trendy in ways they hadn't in a long time, with polished hardwood floors and bare-brick walls and higher ceilings, as if to appeal to these new downtowners. Chris Whittle himself found himself in charge of a downtown booster organization, and in the plans they proposed, Market Square always seemed central and lively.

Some snooty Whittle kids thought the concrete-toadstool design of the Mall hilarious, and, it finally had to be admitted, it wasn't aging well. The concrete, so gleaming white during the Kennedy administration, aged no better than most modernist concrete construction into a streaky, dirty gray. The "umbrellas" were now, in the popular lexicon, "toadstools." Mayor Kyle Testerman, who was becoming a preservationist developer himself, chose to put a decisive end to the Mall era of Market Square in 1986; the city ripped out the concrete toadstools of the early '60s, and officially removed the word *Mall* from its name. It was 1986, and the word meant something else now, and it had little to do with Market Square.

And old Market Square, though it still attracted some farmers and working people looking for bargains at Watson's or the tiny grocery run by old ladies known as Woody's Market, was slowly turning another page.

CHAPTER 8

Return to Market Square

Two Decades of Surprising New Ideas,
Public and Private, Practical and Far-Fetched

I n the mid-1980s, Market Square Mall seemed a picture of unrealized potential. Urban Renewal styles looked strangely wearier than Victorian architecture, which was back in vogue, nationally. The Square's authentic old brick buildings, which had seemed so embarrassingly out-of-date in the modern 1950s and '60s, peeked from behind their peeling plastic and aluminum modern facades.

Watson's and a couple of small shops gamely kept up the Square's retail tradition, and Market Square Mall was still the locus of the Dogwood Arts Festival, though it had lapsed into a sad remnant of its former vigor, dominated by hucksters selling painted saws and frosted pine cones and evangelists singing over a soundtrack, karaoke style. Market Square was usually ghostly at night, except for a few downtown-wide events, like the annual post-World's-Fair event Saturday Night on the Town. At least one early SNOTT in the post-World's Fair 1980s did feature live music on the Square.

Responding to pleas from the public and advice from various consultants who thought downtown needed a focal point, the administration of Mayor Kyle Testerman directed the demolition of the concrete toadstools and oversaw the replacement of the modernist concrete shelter with a large steel shed building which deliberately echoed some aspects of the old Market House. For a time, the landscaping included a concrete sculpture intended to suggest rubble of the old building. The new shed, designed by local firm Bullock, Smith, a modernist firm known for its work internationally in amusement parks and celebratory buildings, included even a bell tower—in which was rehung the old City Hall bell. In a book about Tennessee architecture, historian Carroll Van West praised the new structure for its coherence with the buildings around it—a clear contrast with the Mall era.

The changes had no dramatic effect on business and traffic in the Square. Several buildings, especially on the east side, emptied, and some landowners seemed content to maintain empty buildings almost as pets. Business at night and on weekends remained slow to nonexistent. And like everything ever built in middle of the Square, the new construction would eventually come to be hated, at least by some.

Market Square survived the diminution of TVA in the 1980s, but suffered a lesser setback late in the decade when the hundreds of editors and art directors who made up the lively young editorial department of fast-growing Whittle Communications moved out of the Arnstein building and into the Andrew Johnson Building on the south end of Gay Street, several blocks away. Whittle recruited nationally, and more than half of Whittle's editorial employees had previously lived in major urban centers elsewhere in the country, and their tastes brought a fresh breeze to some retail businesses across downtown, including the Old City, where trendy nightclubs were opening. Whittle ran its own gourmet cafe in the ground floor of the Arnstein, offering competition to old-line restaurants on the Square. Some businesses on the Square had begun selling strong coffee and fresh bagels.

When Whittle's editorial department departed, they left the magazine company's management at 505 Market Street. But upon the completion of the grand new Whittle Building three blocks to the south in 1991, Whittle emptied the Arnstein entirely, after more than a decade occupying the Square's largest building in an un-usually colorful way. Whittle employees tended to be single, affluent, and outwardly bohemian, often working late hours, and maybe most unusually for Knoxville, driving little. Many, perhaps most, chose to live near the old fashioned and partly abandoned center of town; a few didn't even own cars and tried to depend on downtown for all their needs. They were therefore perhaps the best consumers downtown boosters could have wished for, and they would remain distinctive consumers catered to specifically by some new Market Square businesses into the early 1990s. But the company was not destined to be part of the long-term destiny of downtown Knoxville.

~

Regardless of the Square's economic and aesthetic ups and downs, the strangely political 1980s weren't quite over. In September, 1988, the Square received the third major-party candidate of the decade, and probably the third in its entire history. Introduced by former Senator Howard Baker, the visitor was Republican nominee George Bush's controversial running mate, Dan Quayle. He spoke on the Square, which in the previous eight years had hosted presidential candidates Ronald Reagan and Walter Mondale. About 1,000 attended the lunchtime speech to hear Quayle denounce Mike Dukakis: for whatever it's worth, reporters noted that he introduced the phrase "Alibi Mike" to describe the Democrat. Though that phrase may not have captured the electorate's attention in ways Quayle hoped, the campaign was successful; a few weeks later, Bush and Quayle would be elected. During that speech Quayle also praised Knoxville as "the heartland of Republicanism in the South," echoing Senator Baker's statement on the same spot eight years earlier. As if to prove it, Peroulas displayed a sign declaring "Greeks for Bush." It was a minority sentiment, among American Greeks, as a local reporter noted: most Greeks favored the proudly Greek Dukakis. After the speech, Quayle joined Rep. Maria Peroulas at her family's restaurant for a quick gyro.

The crowd was mostly friendly, but a band of about 25 hecklers blew airhorns and shouted criticisms of Reagan and Bush. Police intervened as partisans began to scuffle. The threat of public violence during Quayle's appearance may have influenced future event planners of both parties; Quayle was the last national candidate to appear on the Square, at least for the next few decades.

∾

Perhaps the most influential retail development of the late 20th century came in like a lamb. Through the 1980s, Market Square maintained about eight restaurants at once. Most of them served pretty good food, and each had its own loyal clientele. None of them were open after lunch, or on weekends.

Mahasti Vafaie, an imaginative young woman originally from Iran, was a former employee of the upscale Italian restaurant Piccolo's around the corner on Union and a trained chef. In the late '80s, she took a fresh look at the Square. Through a deal with an undemanding landlord, Turkish-born speculator Fikret Gencay, Vafaie was able to open, with little capital, a lunch spot at 12 Market Square. Gencay had been much maligned as one of the landowners who were allowing under-code buildings to remain vacant. But precisely because he was undemanding, Vafaie was able to open an innovative restaurant with little cost in a way that might have been impossible if she'd had to depend on conservative investors. Originally called the Flying Tomato, the restaurant needed a new moniker after another by the same name in another state protested, and Vafaie renamed her place Tomato Head.

With a sort of crypto-Mediterranean fare of pizzas and burritos, the Tomato Head was strikingly different from other restaurants, offering dishes that couldn't be found elsewhere in the region. It was an immediate hit with the open-minded Whittle Communications crowd. But unlike other downtown restaurants, it aspired to draw customers beyond the culinarily conservative TVA-banks-courts demographic who had dominated the Square since the '70s. Within the restaurant's first year, many people from beyond the downtown workday, people who obviously hadn't been working in an office all day, were meeting at Tomato Head. Some were students, some were retirees, some were even parents with kids, creatures rarely seen downtown. Some were travel writers who, in writing about Knoxville, mentioned mainly the Tomato Head. After the early success of her lunch business, by 1991 Vafaie had tried Friday-evening hours. After that, she added more weekend hours, and more evening hours—and patio seating on Market Square, which, perhaps surprisingly, had never been a regular feature of Market Square restaurants during the Mall era. The Tomato Head was, in fact, probably the first downtown restaurant to offer outdoor seating as a regular thing. It was a testament, or maybe a risky bet, that downtown was cleaner and safer than it had been perceived to be by previous generations.

The Tomato Head may have played an important role in the future of the Square just by luring people with ideas to Market Square. Soon after it opened, Market Square had a couple of other unusual restaurants, Les Routiers, an upscale French restaurant with evening hours, and Perry's on the Square, another restaurant with a gourmet reputation—plus some other businesses of a bohemian cast that stood sharply apart from the practical businesses that had dominated the Square in recent decades. A used bookstore that specialized in subjects having to do with anarchy and workers' rights, succeeded by another with a feminist/lesbian theme; an alternative nightclub called the Snakesnatch, especially popular with local musicians, closed after an Atlanta-based neo-Nazi group invaded it, mistakenly believing it to be a gay bar, and injured several patrons and employees. Most popular among them was the Mercury Theater. Just a simple hall with a beer bar to the side, and little furniture, it nonetheless became the hippest nightclub in town for a couple of years, attracting crowds to see some of the major transitional performers of the day. At the time, Market Square's advocates were describing it as an edgier alternative to the Old City, which at the time seemed to be catering more to affluent middleaged women.

Even the Tomato Head itself got into the nightclub business for a while, sometimes offering late-night shows by avant-garde acts. While watching kids climb in the small oak trees on the Square, people eating at Tomato Head's patio on a Friday evening in the mid-'90s came to look at old Market Square differently.

The sudden decline and fall of Whittle Communications, which had grown rapidly for 20 years to employ several hundred creative sorts downtown, startled downtown advocates in 1994. As most of Whittle's employees left town, Knoxville worried how the loss would affect businesses like Tomato Head. But just as Whittle handed out severance checks, Market Square received an unexpected gift.

In the 1990s, the nation was developing a high-tech economy, concentrated on the West Coast and in certain other intellectually lively cities. It seemed to play outside the rules of any previous industry. In 1993, Market Square got the sort of boost city planners hope to encourage, but never quite accomplish. An astonishing young company called Cyberflix moved its headquarters into two upper floors of Jim Anderson's old wholesale grocery building at 4-6 Market Square, and for a couple of years were wildly successful. The dynamic, innovative video-game maker aspired to make video games more like realistic movies. Their most famous title "Titanic," a complex and clever immersion-type video game based on the story of the doomed ocean liner, was so precise that divers would use it to familiarize themselves with the real hulk before going down; it sold more than one million copies worldwide. For the Square, the company's significance was that it brought about three dozen bright, affluent young people to Market Square every day. Proud of their trendy loft office space, they threw frequent parties, showing off their offices where clocks kept employees apprised of the time in Tokyo, Los Angeles, Moscow, Berlin.

A quieter presence on the Square was an often-solitary guy in a walk-up office in the four-story building at 30 Market Square. Radio engineer Dwight Magnuson was involved in several public-radio projects in the early 1990s, working out the details of towers and available frequencies, often just a guy working alone in his window overlooking the Square. Though lacking a tower or a microphone, Magnuson's work in that office had a major influence on Knoxville radio, especially public radio, in the late 20th century. By the mid-1990s, independent public station WDVX, broadcasting from Anderson County, would be earning distinction for its unique mix of bluegrass, old-time, folk, and offbeat Americana music. Through its website, the station developed fans worldwide, and its perhaps unique lunchtime live-audience radio show, "The Blue Plate Special," eventually became a phenomenon in itself. WDVX founder Tony Lawson credits his work with Magnuson in 1991 and 1992 as the radio station's earliest origin. Lawson considers 30 Market Square to be the birthplace of WDVX.

Market Square had never been so hip. Then again, it was just one more example of the brand-new reaching its fruition in this very old place.

The first cyber-café many Knoxvillians had ever seen opened in the northwestern quarter of Market Square; a little later, the first non-smoking bar most Knoxvillians had ever seen opened in the Square's southeastern quarter. Neither of them lasted very long, but proved that in the post-Mall era, Market Square still had its old talent for surprising people with the New.

Cyberflix and other stirrings of the new computer era gave the city ideas that maybe the Square could be a high-tech breeding ground; if only these old brick buildings were wired with fiberoptic cable, it was thought, maybe there were a dozen more Cyberflixes out there waiting to happen. For a year or two, the city pushed a project called Digital Crossing. It turned out there was only one Cyberflix, though, and by the end of the decade Cyberflix had flamed out, dissolving into bitter personal disputes, as some of the company's leadership moved to the West Coast. But Market Square was still there, and people were still thinking about it differently than they ever had before. Fiveman Productions, started by a former Cyberflix employee, operated out of a walkup on the Square for another decade or so.

Kristopher Kendrick, the maverick preservationist whose renovation developments had been well known since the '70s, but mostly in other parts of downtown, like the Old City, had never seemed keen on Market Square Mall. But in the mid-'90s he bought the Kern Building, known as the Blakley Hotel, which had apparently been a disappointment. Kendrick reworked it as the St. Oliver, a European-style hotel with no two rooms the same. It became popular with celebrities, both short term, like Luciano Pavarotti, who stayed there once, and Oscar-winning actress Patricia Neal, who made a habit of the place when she was visiting friends back home or attending functions at her rehabilitation center. She once even described the St. Oliver in a magazine article as one of her favorite places in Tennessee. That didn't hurt business. Eventually, the elderly Kendrick himself moved in.

In late 1994, *Metro Pulse*, Knoxville's alternative weekly, still relatively new and growing rapidly, moved from Gay Street onto the third floor of the Arnstein. For the next ten years, its editorial offices overlooked Market Square. It's probably no coincidence that much of the paper's emphasis over the next decade concerned the fate of the Square, which was still, despite the 1986 improvements, characterized by tattered awnings and several boarded-up buildings.

∾

The old Square was clearly coming to a crisis, especially in regard to the perpetuation of Mabry and Swan's original purpose. Only a few farmers were still coming to sell produce on the Square; chiefly one, Mr. Sherrill Perkins, an elderly farmer from the French Broad area who came dutifully to stand under the shed Mondays, Wednesdays, and Fridays, selling a mixture of his own produce and a few exotics he'd pick up at the wholesalers on his way in. He specialized in fruits and vegetables, but occasionally offered unrefrigerated "poke sausage" in its canvas poke, and even tamales, made by his aunt and tied in twine. On Fridays, one or two other modest farmers sometimes loomed in the other side of the shed, but he was usually alone.

As the improvements of 1986 were beginning to tire, the awnings tattered, and the large shedlike building began to annoy developers and prospective residents because it blocked second- and third-story views. With its playful evocation of the old Market House belfry, the steel structure looked, its critics said, like an illustration from a history of postmodernism.

In 1998, the last stalwart of the early part of the century departed Market Square's stage: Old Watson's, now expanded to six adjacent storefronts, closed its original store. The manager claimed that in this new era people weren't coming downtown to shop anymore, and the store's future would be in the suburban Watson's locations. In fact, the entire Watson's chain was in bankruptcy court before the year's end, and closed its suburban stores, too.

Peroulas, the old Gold Sun, followed; it was, at the time it closed, the oldest continually open restaurant site in town, run in the same building since about 1909. The Mall Package Store, one of the oldest liquor stores in town, had been there since 1961. Run by Harry Caracostis, who had been an anti-fascist rebel in Greece during World War II, it closed when the ailing Caracostis retired.

But other new things were stirring on old Market Square. David Dewhirst, who'd previously bought and renovated a couple of other small buildings on the west side of Market Square, bought the Watson's building; eventually he renovated much of it for use, surprisingly, as the home of the Chamber of Commerce.

By the late '90s, for the first time anyone could remember, affluent people were moving into the upper floors of old buildings on the Square, to live. Even the most optimistic Mall proponents of 1961 didn't picture that. The Square's first long-term resident of the modern era was Emily Dewhirst, the intrepid globe-trotting mother of developer David. Mrs. Dewhirst bought 31 Market Square, which still featured part of the interior balcony of a long-gone movie theater. In 1997, she moved into the upper floor, which was equipped with a small elevator, and ran a small boutique on the ground floor.

The fate of Caracostis's old package store turned out to be an emblematic symbol of the new Square. In 1999, fashion merchant Andie Ray bought the same building to open her eccentric clothing store, Vagabondia—named in homage to author Frances Hodgson Burnett's ca. 1870 Knoxville home, and the title of her first novel. She and her husband moved into the renovated upstairs, a space that had been used only for storage for decades. And she painted the facade bright yellow.

Arts organizations got involved in the Square, in modest ways. Theater Central, a small dramatic troupe specializing in fast-paced comedy, had begun years earlier in the Old City, but began featuring shows in the old Watson's space on the Square. The more eclectic Actor's Co-op tried other spaces on the Square. Later, the Tennessee Stage Company would move its annual Shakespeare in the Park series to Market Square.

Art galleries arrived in the Square, perhaps for the first time, in the 1990s. Susan Key, owner of a former Old City art gallery, moved to Market Square in a building partly renovated to include living space for herself and her husband. She would later regret the move, which was perhaps five years too early, but hers was probably the first permanent art gallery in Market Square's history.

Another feature that might not have been anticipated was the sheer popularity of Market Square events, especially the Sundown in the City concerts. Launched in 1998 by AC Entertainment, often with city sponsorship, Sundown drew crowds that astonished downtown's doubters. A performance by a local band, the V-Roys, drew several thousand, perhaps a bigger crowd than Ronald Reagan saw.

And during that period, the Square admitted one of the few uses it had never seen before: formal education. Under the leadership of Rome-Prizewinning architecture professor Mark Schimmenti, UT opened an Urban Design Studio in the old Watson's building. It lasted for only two years, but during that time, architecture students considered urban-design issues with old Market Square as the handiest example, a sort of urban-design laboratory.

The city of Knoxville, under the Victor Ashe administration, launched a project to reconsider Market Square as a redevelopment district. The bureaucracy of the next several years would be tedious to recount, but it involved lots of public meetings—many Knoxvillians learned to define the word *charrette*—and numerous proposals, none of which turned out exactly as advertised.

In 1998, the Victor Ashe administration was keen on building a convention center, and invited the esteemed Urban Land Institute to appraise the feasibility of the project. Ten urban-planning consultants from all over the country spent several days in Knoxville interviewing citizens and surveying the city. The group came back with a fairly skeptical assessment of Knoxville as a major convention-center market, but within it was a surprise: they emphasized the yet-unrealized potential of Market Square.

Their report, illustrated with snapshots of the Market Square shed and the Tomato Head, emphasized the urgency of redeveloping the Square, partly just to add interest to the Convention Center site, four blocks away. "the Market Square redevelopment becomes of the utmost priority—it must produce a mixed-use, 24-hour activity center in the heart of downtown. Implementation of the redevelopment plan should receive the same level of attention as that of the World's Fair site development…."

When Knoxville's first Internet chat group, K2K, launched in 1999, much of the emphasis of the freewheeling discussion concerned the fate of Market Square.

What was already on the Square by the late '90s could sometimes impress random visitors. On a nice day in 1999, just after lunchtime, a short old man with prominent ears took a long, slow walk around the Square by himself, hobbling with a cane. He stopped at several spots, including Tomato Head, and looked around. On his way up the TVA steps, he stopped to talk to a couple of fans. "You should feel lucky," he said. "Most Americans don't have anything like this. They've torn them all down." That night, author Norman Mailer opened his lecture at UT with a description of his walk around Market Square. "I had a very agreeable experience today," he said.

∾

That year, however, the much-admired and well-connected development team of Earl Worsham and Ron Watkins presented the city with an astonishing proposal: a sweeping redevelopment that would include everything from a new upscale office skyscraper, a giant wintergarden, a movie-theater complex, a mall-like retail area passing over Henley Street, and a revolutionary approach to Market Square. The first proposal—and the flaw that may have doomed the whole proposal in the public mind—included a plan to encase Market Square in a weatherproof dome. A later, compromised version omitted the dome but still insisted on whole ownership of the Square and the idea that businesses within it would have to operate within certain covenants concerning opening hours and other business practices. The very idea, which took the ethic of homogenization far beyond anything the Mall era did, appalled many of the Square's champions, who loved the Square most for its individuality and unpredictability. The plan was scrutinized, questioned, and ultimately abused on K2K and in the press, especially *Metro Pulse*. Fortunately for the opponents, the numbers didn't work out right.

As the 21st century opened, in city hall and on the street, Market Square was a problem without a clear solution. Some major property owners were content to leave it in its decaying state and adamant about their rights. Some well-connected developers demanded major government-forced changes to reinvent it as something new with unified control.

In March, 2001, the vacant Watson's Building hosted a public forum, partly prompted by reaction to the Worsham Watkins plan. The following September, stung by public reaction and eventually shunned by Mayor Ashe's administration, which had begun to see it as an expensive boondoggle, Worsham Watkins withdrew its prospects for the Square. One reality that misadventure turned up, to the surprise of some suburbanites, was the depth of public affection for Market Square.

Bill Lyons, former UT professor of political science and chairman of the board of Knoxville's Community Development Corporation, soon to be city director of development, stepped in. Hosting public meetings and working behind the scenes, he got a reputation as a "consensus builder." Throughout Market Square's history of exotic and diverse offerings of countless commodities, consensus had always been in short supply. There followed months of proposals and counterproposals. A succession of high-paid consultants offered urgent advice. One saw tourism, with a special emphasis on UT sports, as key to the Square's future success. Another insisted it could not thrive unless it were opened to automobile traffic, and at the time several retailers agreed. Another thought TVA would have to be removed, in order to restore North Market Street.

Development group Kinsey Probasco, which included former Chattanooga Mayor Jon Kinsey, credited with that city's much-touted turnaround, presented a $41 million redevelopment plan that seemed a compromise between the self-righteous neglect that had been the status quo for much of the Square for a generation or so, and the big-dome, single-developer ideals. The plan included some surprises, including an expansion of adjacent Krutch Park, which had previously been limited to the Market Square half of the block, to Gay Street.

Leading a public charrette in June, 2002, was Stroud Watson. The elderly, white-bearded UT professor of architecture had once lived in Knoxville, but was so pleased with Chattanooga's response to his ideas, which many Chattanoogans believed led to that city's renaissance, that he had moved there. Watson's suggestions emphasized a respect for the old under the rubric of New Urbanism, a doctrine that combined historic preservation with mixed-used development, pushing especially residential construction, along with retail and office space, within existing buildings. The biological adjective "organic," rarely applied to Knoxville development in the past, came to be understood as descriptive of a development philosophy that allowed private business to grow, with some encouragement from government.

That June, Knoxville City Council and Mayor Victor Ashe approved $8 million for the Kinsey Probasco plan. The expenditure angered conservatives who suspected it was another false rebirth for poor old Market Square.

There followed, after a series of city-sponsored public meetings, another, simpler approach to Market Square. Combining an ambitious facelift project with a major practical underground repiping project, with a new movie-theater proposal thrown in for fun, the Chattanooga team of Kinsey Probasco interested the city in a project that would seem the least invasive of all those proposed so far. Property owners would be induced to do something with their buildings, the city would install new facades as needed—but there'd be no overlord instructing proprietors about how to run their businesses. The new design included fountains near the center, acknowledged the Square's new popularity as an outdoor music venue with a stage on the site of old City Hall and, in response to public demand, retained several older trees. One feature showed the limits of the public part of the public process. Though the idea of earth-toned pavers had been overwhelmingly popular in charrettes, it was nixed, behind closed doors, in the city's engineering department. They just couldn't do that, they said, because they sometimes had to dig up utilities.

The plan was coordinated with the city's $8 million redo of Market Square itself. The Square closed—the broad center of it, at least—after the Christmas season in 2002. For about a year, the Square was a massive construction site, as customers could access businesses only by narrow walkways between the old facades and the hardhat-zone fence. Though much of the work below ground level was purely maintenance, an opportunity to fix problems with century-old pipes, it also rendered the new Market Square structure, designed more to shelter performing musicians than farmers—though it could also be used for the latter—and relandscaped the Square to open its sight lines. It may have been the most closely watched construction project in Knoxville history, as the narrow walkways afforded a sort of surgical gallery, and each new development reported and commented upon almost instantly in the online chat groups, which were never more electric than they were that year.

In November, 2002, a novel business had opened near the southeast corner, a bar called Brazo. It was unusual in a few respects; for one, it was brightly lit. But another innovation, unheard of among other bars in Knoxville in 2002, was that it would not allow smoking. Only a few Knoxville restaurants were non-smoking in 2002; no bars were. Brazo was the first. It didn't last, perhaps due to its poor timing, just as the Square itself was being dug up for a year's worth of major work, and the businesses on the sides were accessible only by a narrow walkway, but it was a harbinger of things to come.

When it reopened, public reaction to the concrete floor of the Square was immediate: it was blinding. Even the builders professed to be surprised by the whiteness of the concrete on a sunny day. The city assured complainers that they'd get used to it. Also, after the redo the Square lacked the public toilets that had been a feature of Market Square since the 1800s. But it did, eventually, come with a whole lot of parking, when the city constructed a huge parking garage in the space still known as the Watson's Parking Lot, years after that store had closed.

The city's multi-million-dollar redo of the Square itself was the biggest public project on the square since the establishment of the "mall" more than 40 years earlier, but the private accomplishments which coincided with it were almost as major, and finally more controversial. Attending the ribbon-cutting for the new Square in November, 2003, were Mayor Victor Ashe, former mayor Randy Tyree, Mayor-elect Bill Haslam, and a delegation from Muroran, Japan, one of Knoxville's sister cities.

A bitterly cold day in December, 2003, saw a symbolic return of city government to Market Square, if only for one day. Well-known businessman Bill Haslam was inaugurated mayor of Knoxville on the Square's new outdoor stage, marking the beginning of a notable career in public office. Over the next seven years, Mayor Haslam would often be seen on the Square in the evenings, dining with his family or jogging alone. His public efforts and personal investments in the Market Square area, especially the Regal Riviera Theatre, completed in 2007, would become factors in his successful campaign for governor of Tennessee in 2010.

∾

For many years—since the early 1990s, at least—the city had expressed grave concerns about a string of blighted buildings in the Square's northeastern quarter, and had difficulty inducing some landlords to act. By 2000, a majority of the buildings north of the Tomato Head were vacant, and a long-time landowner seemed unwilling to sell or fix them up. Ultimately several of the buildings, especially those at 18-20, addresses which shared a gaping hole in the roof, deteriorated to levels which city officials privately admitted would have made them targets for condemnation anywhere else. Condemnation would have almost certainly led to demolition, they feared, and that would undermine the viability of a Market Square historic district. The section was the subject of several public and private meetings, some of them attended by the landowner, but nothing was ever done.

Entrepreneurs Scott and Bernadette Trent West, who had made a success of an ecologically themed gift shop called Earth to Old City, liked the Square, and after several months of cajoling the landowner who had fended off all entreaties from the city, bought half a dozen buildings in the troubled quarter. They first moved their gift shop, despite its neighborhood-specific name, to Market Square, where it seemed to fit right in next to Bliss, a new and unusual gift shop opened by another enterprising young couple. The Wests also opened Preservation Pub in the old Mercury Theatre space. It was a much-more elaborate sort of bar than the Mercury had been, and offered every-night live entertainment, much of it from well out of town, some of them bands publicized on public-radio station WDVX, and was almost instantly popular. With it well established, they began a herculean job of disemboweling the rotten interiors of buildings at 18 and 20 Market Square. Shunning tax credits which would have encouraged them to make renovations within historical guidelines, the Wests rebuilt the buidlings from the inside out, using modern steel contruction, incorporating an unusual atrium which became the entrance to their pasta restaurant Oodles, as well as a wine bar touted as Knoxville's first, and above, a three-address-wide residential floor, effectively a small apartment building which they christened WesTrent.

Around 2005 the Wests were also thickly involved in developing an extremely unusual underground nightclub called the World Grotto, associated with a ground-level art gallery and rooms for massage therapy, yoga, and other services; and they began work on perhaps the largest building on the Square, the old Woods & Taylor building at 36 Market Square, the four-story building that fronted on both the Square and Wall Avenue. The four-story brick building's brick facade seemed to be bowing outward dangerously; the Wests shored it up with braces decorated, high on the facade, with caricatures of themselves, of Bernadette's mother, and of Fikret Gencay, the previous owner.

The sheer amount of energy and expense the Wests put into their buildings astonished their neighbors, who wondered where the couple got so much capital. One answer came in July, 2006, when federal agents raided their WesTrent apartment looking for evidence of their involvement in a major marijuana-smuggling scheme. Though the Wests were only peripherally involved in the larger plot, prosecutors proved that about $2.5 million in marijuana wholesaling profits were funneled into Market Square construction projects. Both Wests went to prison, and the government auctioned off their buildings to local developers for about $3.4 million. Feeling for the Wests and the viability of their businesses were such that all the owners who bought the property at auction allowed their businesses to remain as they were; other members of the family, apparently innocent of the scheme, stayed involved as proprietors. (By 2009, the big Woods & Taylor building, the one building in the block still empty, was under redevelopment by preservationist Ken Mills.)

The whole story raised a question, uncomfortable for some, of whether Market Square would have rebounded as it ultimately did without the infusion of illegal money.

The Square tends to attract the extremely unusual, and the next instance of that sort came from a wholly different direction. As the Wests were being prosecuted, the Cornerstone Foundation, a quietly Christian charity, bought the large building at 4-6 Market Square. The building had been the home of Cyberflix in the '90s, and later touted as the site of a comedy club which never materialized. Cornerstone director Laurens Tullock, who as an official in the Ashe administration had worked on Market Square problems and projects for years, led the effort to establish a home base for some Christian leadership programs, and a venue for some worship services, but with the capability to be used for secular purposes. The ground floor when it opened just before Christmas, 2008, hosted a restaurant, cafe and bakery, and large performing space called the Square Room. Acoustically designed with the help of Nashville music-industry consultants, and programmed by AC Entertainment, juggernaut behind the rock festival Bonnaroo, it promised to fill a long-bemoaned gap in size of local venues between the beer hall and the historic theaters of Gay Street.

~

The year 2003 had been the only year since before the Civil War when no farmers sold vegetables on Market Square. A little Christmas greenery sold in December saved that calendar year from being a total loss. But produce returned in 2004, in season, thanks to a vigorous group of young organic-produce advocates, led by 23-year-old recent UT art-school grad, Charlotte Tolley. Modest at first, the market could have been another in a long series of well-meant but naïve bohemian dreams, bringing out the usual counterculture cadre, selling oddities, street-fair style. But within a couple of years, the expanding market of a widening variety of fresh produce and even organic meats had become popular with mainstream Knoxvillians, attracting more than 60 vendors—some of them farmers who drove more than an hour to sell on old Market Square—and thousands of patrons, to the Square during the high season of mid-summer.

Market Square produce once seemed outmoded to generations accustomed to suburban supermarkets, but the local-food movement played a big role in reviving it. From its inception, Market Square had always been intended only for local farmers, but enforcement had been desultory. It may have taken the twenty-first-century locovore movement to make the nineteenth-century ideal a reality. In 2009, a national Internet poll promoting local food markets called Market Square's farmer's market one of the top five in the nation. It was another example of a new phenomenon being introduced to Knoxville via its oldest marketplace.

～

Beyond the obvious and unignorable examples mentioned already, the author here hesitates to offer uneducated assessments of other current retail presences on the Square and their historical significance. Though it is surely, in total, considerable. There are still things you can buy on Market Square that you can't buy anywhere else in town.

Market Square is at this writing busier in the daytime than it has been since the 1970s, and probably livelier after 6:00 p.m. than it has been since the days of Peter Kern's wonderful ice-cream saloon—even if the 24-hour refuge, like the Gold Sun, still eludes us. Market Square in the 21st century may have more visits per year, including all the kids who come to Sundown and other festival-style events there, than it ever did in its history. It has proven itself easy to fill up, as some musical acts and festivals draw enormous crowds. Those that are too popular for the old Square proper spill south, into Krutch Park, just as, in the 1890s, busy market days would spill south along the same block, then known as "Watermelon Row."

～

Another surprise comeback to the Square were movies, at least on occasion. A few downtown entrepreneurs had shown movies outside, on sides of buildings on Gay Street and in the Old City, but in 2004, the Knox County Public Library launched a promotional movie night in the middle of the Square, showing free movies to family audiences on fall weekends, on a big screen on the Square's main stage. The first, aligned to coincide with the annual Greek Festival on one of the rare weekends it was held downtown, was *My Big Fat Greek Wedding*.

That era also saw the first First Friday gallery walk. By the middle of the decade, thousands of people were convening downtown, ostensibly to view new art. In the city's history, art had never been more popular. The largest galleries were on Gay Street, but that first Friday each month, Market Square enjoyed a festival atmosphere.

In 2004, the 150-year-old Square once again demonstrated its promiscuous habit of pairing the very old with the very new. This acre, arguably the oldest part of Knoxville in terms of continuous use, became the first part of Knoxville to get blanket wi-fi access. Laptops at café tables became as emblematic of the Square as gutted pickups and juvenile pickpockets had once been.

Sundown, the spring-and-early-summer concert that had surprised many when it drew more than 1,000 people to Market Square on a weeknight in 1999, hit a new high in April, 2004, when Bela Fleck and the Flecktones played the Square on a Thursday night, bringing an estimated 10,000. Later shows by Steve Winwood, the Neville Brothers, and George Thorogood drew even bigger crowds, drawing hypothetical estimates of as much as 20,000. The numbers were sometimes hyperbolic, but the crowds were proof that many people from around the metropolitan area would come downtown, even on a weeknight, given sufficient motivation. Many seemed to come just to see what 10,000 people looked like, enjoying a crowded party between two rows of nineteenth-century buildings.

The organizers of Sundown looked down on the site of it from the seventh floor of the Arnstein Building. AC Entertainment, then becoming nationally renowned as the outfit behind the juggernaut Bonnaroo, the biggest rock festival in America, planned Sundown, too. Encouraged, they also launched Autumn on the Square; though it didn't prove to be economically viable, it was as popular as Sundown.

≈

The Chamber Partnership, the Chamber of Commerce outgrowth known as the Superchamber, went out on a limb when they moved from their longtime quarters in the 1848 School for the Deaf building to parts of the former Watson's space on Market Square in early 2005.

Though there was reason to regret that so much second-floor space of the Square, much of which might have seemed ideal for residential development, would be committed to what was basically a 9 to 5 business, the move seemed a major vote of confidence in Market Square's future. Even the much-vaunted Mall era saw nothing comparable. It was the first time a major civic institution had been located on the Square since city government left in 1924. Some were still questioning the Square's long-term viability, but the commitment implied by that move seemed intended to convince skeptics that this latest version of Market Square was permanent.

≈

Much of the new life of the Square—the First Night events, the HoLa Latino festival brought to the Square in 2007, the International Biscuit Festival launched in 2010, and the explosive growth of the farmer's market, came under the leadership of John Craig, who became president of the Market Square District Association in 2007. (In the interest of full disclosure, Craig, characteristically, encouraged another promotional effort: the publication of this book.) A Farragut resident and former hospital-supplies distributor who had spent most of his adult life in other cities—his Colombian wife, Patricia Robledo, was one of the organizers of the HoLa festival—Craig might have seemed another of the mostly young twenty-first-century outsiders who re-imagined the Square in a trendy new paradigm.

However, Craig became interested in the Square when he discovered a personal connection to the four-story building for sale at 31 Market Square, the one which still showed a fading advertisement for "phonographs" on the back wall. One of its early tenants was retail maverick J. Frank Walker, his great-grandfather, who ran his main furniture store there for 20 years and likely was responsible for that old "phonographs" sign on the back. Craig bought the building in 2004 and rehabbed it for mixed-use retail, office, and residential uses, beginning a second career as a downtown developer.

Regular live radio, not a regular feature on Market Square since the 1930s, returned in 2009, when station WDVX began hosting its highlighted weekly shows every Friday in the Square Room, often attracting a standing-room only crowd in the hundreds. The same year, the venue began hosting some of the musical events of AC's Big Ears music festival, which drew national attention. Knox ivi, an unusual, perhaps unique internet producer arranged like a TV studio, set up shop at 17 Market Square in 2009, offering live lifestyle, sports, music, and talk shows, most of which could be viewed by the public from a modest cafe. Its flagship hourlong variety show, "Eleven O'Clock Rock," would be transmitted daily. In its first two years, it's safe to say that most of Knoxville's professional musicians had performed in the studio more than once. Though the advertising-based business model for what's essentially an internet television studio remains unproven at this writing, Knox ivi's variety of programming draws tens of thousands of home-computer viewers. The unconventional studio was an unusual new attraction to the old Square, but also drew several full-time technical and show-business professionals to the mix of people who made up a typical day. Through a partnership with WBIR, the studio also made it possible for that powerful regional TV stalwart to establish a semi-permanent presence on the ever-busier plaza, with daily weather and color reporters broadcasting from the site, further raising the Square's profile in the broader East Tennessee area.

≈

The city that some thought was too large for the Square space in 1885 is many times larger now, and the place Mabry and Swan laid out in 1853 as Knoxville's Market Square is still our only Market Square.

The fact that it's once again a more obvious magnet may be reflected by the fact that it may be the one place in town where a visitor is most likely to see anyone from anywhere. In early 2008, iconic musician Elvis Costello materialized on Market Square, shopping for souvenirs for his children; he bought a Knoxville Girl T-shirt at Bliss, and described it when he did his own rendition of the ancient murder ballad of that famous title at the Tennessee Theatre that night. When he was traveling through East Tennessee on a documented nationwide tour in the summer of 2008, maverick street magician David Blaine dropped in unannounced on Market Square as a platform to try his random tricks on an astonished audience at Preservation Pub. In late 2008, avant-garde songwriter David Byrne dined at the new Cafe 4, and was a member of the Square Room's very first audience, for singer-songwriter act My Brightest Diamond.

They joined Julia Ward Howe, Booker T. Washington, Ronald Reagan, Carl Sandburg, Duke Ellington, Norman Mailer, Wallace Stevens, Roy Acuff, Ingrid Bergman, and William Jennings Bryan among the interesting characters one would encounter if only one could dwell forever on Market Square.

At this writing, Market Square is the celebratory center of Knoxville, the host of the greatest number of festivals and public events and municipal parties, as it was in the 1860s and '70s, when the city was struggling to shake off the horrors of a civil war. Market Square is among Knoxville's most popular venues for new music, in spite of, or perhaps because of the fact that it's much older than any auditorium, theater or nightclub in the region. Musicians come to perform on stages, or play for passing crowds, as they did when some of them were creating new forms of American music.

It's once again a home for a few dozen permanent residents, as it was a century ago. And it still hosts the selling, seasonally, of local farmers' fresh produce, and Saturday morning's the biggest day for that, just as it was more than a century ago. And after some years when no one lived on the Square—or, at least, when no one would admit to living on the Square—it's once again a respectable residential area, as it was in the Victorian era. Some people live above their shops.

In many ways, Market Square has come, so to speak, full circle. And even after a century and a half, Market Square is still where we come to be surprised.

Page numbers in **boldface** refer to illustrations.